The Lost White Tribes of Australia

Part One – 1656 The First Settlement of Australia

Part Two – Investigation of lost white tribes in the north-west of Australia and southern Victoria

Copyright © Henry Van Zanden 2012
www.australiadiscovered.com.au

The moral right of Henry Van Zanden to be identified as the author of this work has been asserted in accordance with the Copyright Act 1968.

All rights reserved. No part of this publication may be reproduced or transmitted by any means, electronic, photocopying or otherwise without prior written permission of the author.

First published in Australia 2012 by The Publishing Queen
www.thepublishingqueen.com

Any opinions expressed in this work are exclusively those of the authors and are not necessarily the views held or endorsed by The Publishing Queen.

Van Zanden, Henry H
    The Lost White Tribes of Australia, Part One, 1656 The First Settlement of Australia

ISBN: 978-1-921673-67-2

Consultant Editor: Robert Watson

Preface

1788 is universally regarded as the first white European settlement of Australia. However, situated on almost the same latitude but on the opposite side of Australia, there had already existed another European settlement that had been struggling to survive since the mid-17th century.

Unlike the First Fleet in 1788, these people did not arrive with plans of a settlement with resources, equipment, farm stock and utensils. Instead they crashed onto a reef five kilometres off the Western Australian coast. Men, women and children struggled onto a desolate, desperate and dangerous land too far from help and too far from anywhere.

The Dutch charting of the Australian coast began with Captain Willem Janszoon, who made the first authenticated European discovery and landing upon the coast of Australia in 1606. At least 30 other intentional or accidental discoveries and contacts with the Australian mainland were made by the Dutch over the next 150 years.

The most memorable of these contacts were perhaps the tragic shipwrecks on the Western Australian coast. Shipwrecked on her maiden voyage in 1629, the *Batavia* has become best known for the subsequent mutiny and massacre that took place on the Houtman Abrolhos Islands, west of Geraldton. Two of the mutineers were marooned ashore on the coast of Western Australia becoming our first two European settlers.

Only 27 years later in 1656, the extreme weather and hidden reefs of Western Australia claimed their next victim: the *Vergulde Draeck* (Gilt Dragon). Travelling inland in search of food, water and shelter, these survivors formed Australia's first white settlement.

...he belonged to a small community, all as white as himself, he said about three hundred; that they lived in houses enclosed all together within a great wall to defend them from black men; that their fathers came there about one hundred and seventy years ago, as they said, from a distant land across the great sea; and that their ship broke, and eighty men and ten of their sisters with many things were saved on shore ... 1832 Dale

In 1712 the *Zuytdorp* literally crashed into the cliffs of Western Australia north of Kalbarri. Evidence has been uncovered proving that survivors did make it ashore and camped close by the wreck site. Some historians such as Rupert Gerritsen, believe that the *Zuytdorp* survivors assimilated into the Aboriginal tribes between Kalbarri and Shark Bay.

All three shipwrecks occurred along the mid-west coast of Western Australia. All three deposited survivors on our shores. However, the survival of 75 men and women from the *Vergulde Draeck* has left a distinctive legacy for they formed the first of the Lost White Tribes of Australia.

These new settlers maintained their identity and remained homogenous choosing not to assimilate into the local Aboriginal tribes. Fortified on a hillside, they survived for almost 200 years reaching a population of about 300. This lost white tribe now knew no life other than what was taught word of mouth from generation to generation of a previous existence, in a previous land oceans away.

In 1994, the 'Report of the Select Committee on Ancient Shipwrecks' was presented to the Western Australian Parliament. Usually such reports arouse very little attention but this one stunned parliament with its recommendations.

Report of the Select Committee on Ancient Shipwrecks

"This Select Committee believes that further efforts should be made to bring these theories to some finality. A major reason for this is that generations of Australian schoolchildren have been taught that Australia was settled by the British at Port Jackson in 1788. Evidence put before the Committee and reading material made available to our members strongly suggests that, in fact, a significant European presence could have been in Western Australia at least 76 years earlier. If these theories are proved to be true, they would undoubtedly challenge conventional notions of early British settlement.

Accordingly, this Committee recommends–

Recommendation:
(1) That the Western Australian Government –
(a) mindful of the need to establish once and for all the facts about when and by whom the Australian continent was first settled by Europeans;

(b) aware of the significance of the settlement at Port Jackson in 1788; and

(c) recognising a variety of documents, publications and papers pointing to Dutch settlement in Western Australia early in the 18th century;

(d) agree to the creation and funding of a top–level Inquiry Into Early European Presence in Australia (IIEEPIA) to be drawn from historians, pre-historians, scientific and Aboriginal bodies and other interested groups[1]." [Emphasis made by the Select Committee]

Although excellent archaeological work has been completed on the *Zuytdorp* wreck and its surrounds, the recommendations of the Select Committee have been mostly ignored. It has been left to individuals, interested historians and voluntary organisations such as the Gilt Dragon Research Group and the VOC Historical Society to follow through with the Committee's recommendations.

What became of the three hundred men, women and children? It was a mystery that has baffled historians for decades. After 12 years of exhaustive research, two field trips and interviews, the mystery can be revealed of what happened to not only the shipwrecked survivors but their also descendants.

---

[1] Legislative Assembly Western Australia, *Select Committee on Ancient Shipwrecks* REPORT Presented by: Hon. P.G. Pendal , MLA, 17 August 1994

Foreword

The story of *The Lost White Tribes of Australia* by Henry Van Zanden confirms longstanding rumours, never previously proven true, that a community of Dutch-descended people was found only a day's ride from Perth in the early 19th century.

The "white tribe" was discovered by an official expedition in 1832 more than forty years after Britain began colonising the continent and three years after the Crown seized the western third of the continent from the Netherlands.

The community was living proof that foreigners had occupied the continent long before the British and if its existence became known the UK's claim to sovereignty could be threatened. So it was kept a secret and has remained so to this day.

Mr Van Zanden discloses that the truth was concealed by the invention of a tale that the tribe lived somewhere in Central Australia – a tale that was repeated as recently as 2001 in the book *Stories of Exploration and Survival* by the Bush Tucker Man, Les Hiddens.

The deception became a public exercise with the publication of newspaper stories, the first appearing in the Leeds Mercury in 1834. Mr Van Zanden argues that it was "planted" by the Swan River Colony's Governor James Stirling and that he repeated the practice elsewhere.

What is remarkable about Mr Van Zanden's narrative is that he himself discovered the primary documentary and physical evidence that established the case. He came across a map which showed the location of the settlement while carrying out research in the Mitchell Library in Sydney and tracked down the ruins of the village beside the Moore River north of Perth.

I am confident this book could have a powerful impact on the Australian reading public and in the Netherlands as well and could inspire a television series or a feature movie.

Patrick Connelly
Journalist
Warrnambool Victoria

Thanks

I would like to give thanks to the following people and organisations that have assisted me in writing this book.

Steve Caffery and the Gilt Dragon Research Group Website: www.giltdragon.com.au
Steve has assisted me with his local knowledge and expertise. Some of the photographs used in this manuscript were provided by Steve and the Gilt Dragon Research Group.

Tim Coleman unfortunately has died before the book could be released. Tim allowed me to photograph his own collection of artifacts from the *Vergulde Draeck* and kindly allowed me to stay in an old homestead on the Moore River while I conducted my field research.

Patrick Connelly has been my most constant and closest confidant always encouraging and always supportive of my research.

Sid de Burgh is the owner of the Karakin Lakes property, the site of the Lost White Tribe. Sid allowed me onto his property to search for the site of the original first white settlement.

Johnny de Leeuw and Shell/Woodside Petroleum who donated the use of a Toyota Landcruiser, provided great assistance during my first expedition to Western Australia.

George Dean was invaluable in his local knowledge. He drove me to places such as Wedge Island and Ledge Point, the location where the survivors first landed.

Rupert Gerritsen has been a shining light in this most controversial research. His book, *And their Ghosts May Be Heard*, as well as other research papers, have pioneered the work into the influence of the lost Dutch sailors stranded here in the 17th century.

Kylee Legge, my publisher, has always believed in me and the book. She has assisted me along the way in every respect of publishing.

Many thanks to the Mitchell Library (NSW State Library) for their assistance, professionalism and patience.

John Mallard, a descendant of the first Dutch settlers, gave me an invaluable insight on what the Nanda people always believed: that many of their tribe were descendants of the first white settlers of Australia.

Tom Vanderveldt, as President and later Chairman of the VOC Historical Society, set up all the Western Australian contacts and organised my accommodation in both Perth and the Moore River.

Robert Watson has been invaluable as my editor finding the smallest errors and always offering the best advice.

Dr Robin Watt from New Zealand has proved valuable in allowing me to air my ideas to a critical but supportive colleague.

Dedication

I dedicate this book, firstly to the descendants of the Lost White Tribe, principally the Nanda and Noongar people.

Secondly, to my children: Brooke and Blake; my wife Cathy and my parents, George and Hillechien. With all my love and affection.

Henry Van Zanden

Disclaimer

Readers should keep in mind that the views often expressed regarding Aboriginals are the views that were expressed by settlers and explorers in the 19th century and not those of the author.

The Lost White Tribes of Australia

Cave drawing on Bigge Island of Dutchmen in a boat[2]

by Henry Van Zanden

---

[2] Photo by courtesy of Jean Weber

TABLE OF CONTENTS

Chapter 1 – 1656 The First Settlement of Australia	7
Chapter 2 – Rescue Attempt	21
Chapter 3 – Abraham Leeman and his epic tale of survival	31
Chapter 4 – Leeds Mercury Article 25 January 1834	41
Chapter 5 – Prime Meridian	51
Chapter 6 – The Lost White Tribe	65
Chapter 7 – Karakin Lakes - Site of the Lost White Tribe	83
Chapter 8 – Legend of the Lost White Tribe	103
Chapter 9 – Yagan and Lyon	115
Chapter 10 – Aboriginal Stories of a White Settlement	127
Chapter 11 – Aboriginal Legend of a 'Lost White Tribe' and the Great Flood	135
Chapter 12 – Relocation of the Lost White Tribe	145
Chapter 13 – The Irwin River Valley Settlement	155
Chapter 14 – Champion Bay	159
Chapter 15 – *Dioscorea hastifolia*	169
Chapter 16 – The *Zuytdorp* 1712	179
Chapter 17 – A New Dutch –Aboriginal Language	197
Chapter 18 – Lost White Tribe Descendants	207

Western Australia

Chapter 1
1656
The First Settlement of Australia

Willem van de Velde the Younger, De Windstoot 'A ship caught by a small squall', known as 'The Gust'. Circa 1680. Rijksmuseum, Amsterdam

The *Vergulde Draeck* (Gilt Dragon) – 1656

Commander Pieter Albertsz carefully surveyed each member of his 193 crew as well as the small number of passengers as they clambered aboard the 260 tonne, forty two metre yacht (a Dutch type of fast ship) the *Vergulde Draeck*. Arriving back from Batavia only a few weeks previous to their departure, Albertsz made ready for only its second voyage. The captain was charged with delivering a cargo of treasure to Batavia: 106,000 florins as well as eight chests of coin worth 76,000 guilders.[3]

Their voyage from the North Sea island of Texel in Holland, began on the 4 October, 1655. This time it failed to reach its destination. Late May of 1656, the managers of the Dutch East India Company (VOC) discovered the fate of their treasure ship after seven survivors struggled against all odds to sail a small boat almost 3,000 km to recount their tale of misery.

Above, sketch of the Dutch port, The Anchorage at Texel.

Letter of the Governor General. and Councillors to the Managers of the E.I.C. [East India Company] *December 4, 1656.*

... On the 7th June there arrived here ... from the South-land the cock-boat of the yacht den Vergulde Draeck with 7 men, to our great regret reporting that the said yacht had run aground on the said South-land in 30 2/3 degrees, on April the 28th, that besides the loss of her cargo, of which nothing was saved, 118 men of her crew had perished, and that 69 men who had succeeded in getting ashore, were still left there. For the purpose of rescuing these men, and of attempting to get back by divers or other means any part of the money or the merchandises that might still be recoverable, we dispatched thither on the said errand on the 8th of the said month of June, the flute de Witte Valeq, (sic) together with the yacht de Goede Hoop, which after staying away for some time were by violent storms forced to return without having effected anything, and without having seen any men or any signs of the wreck, although the said Goede Hoop has been on the very spot where the ship was said to have miscarried[4] ...

In the Castle of Batavia, December 4, A.D. 1656.
Your Worships' Obedt. Servts. the Governor-General and Councillors of India
Joan Maetsuyker, Carel Hartzinck, Joan Cunaeus, Nicolaes Verburch, D Steur

---

[3] Max Jeffreys, *Australian Shipwrecks Murder Fire and Storm*

[4] Some of the men of the *Goede Hoop* had gone ashore, but had not returned. The *Witte Valk* had touched at the Southland, but by "bad weather and the hollow sea" had been compelled to return without having effected anything.'
Heeres JE, *The Part Borne by the Dutch in the Discovery of Australia 1602-1765* (1899)

The wreck of the *Vergulde Draeck* (Gilt Dragon)

The *Vergulde Draeck* had taken the now much used Brouwer's route first used by Hendrik Brouwer in 1611. Although longer in distance, it proved to be a much quicker voyage with the roaring forties filling the sails of the Dutch East India ships.

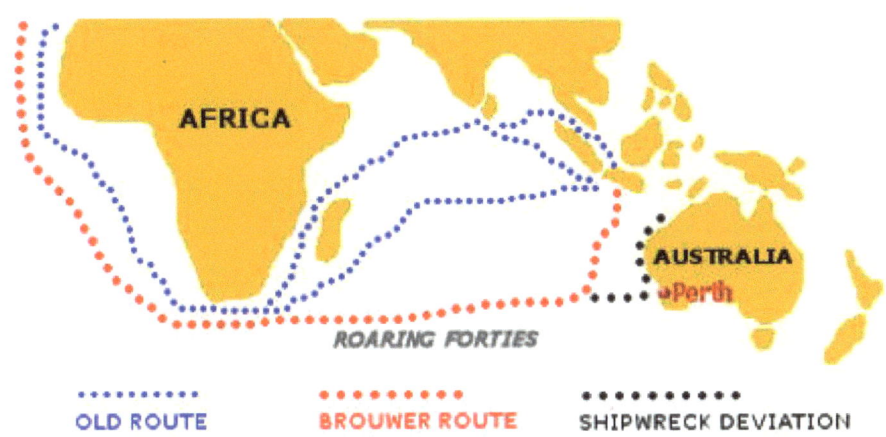

The Brouwer Route[5]

The voyage to Batavia usually took at least six months via the Cape of Good Hope. After she arrived at the Cape, Captain Albertsz took on more provisions and water before resuming his voyage. The day after she left the Cape, another ship that was also on its way to Batavia, anchored alongside her. When this ship arrived at Batavia in March 1656, the captain was most surprised to learn that the *Vergulde Draeck* had not yet reached its destination. Naturally they feared for the worst believing that the ship had sunk. However, on the morning of 7 June, 1656, a long boat containing seven sailors struggling to stay alive, slowly slipped into Batavia Harbour. These poor emaciated men were from the *Vergulde Draeck*. What a tragic story they had to tell! Between sobs of exhaustion, the four sick sailors sang their sorrowful chorus of a tragic shipwreck.

The *Vergulde Draeck* was discovered about 100 km north of Perth. Although there were 193 people aboard, only 75 survived the shipwreck. Significantly the survivors included women and children. Seven sailors volunteered to row to Batavia leaving behind 68 survivors clinging desperately to life on a hostile and desolate shore. Three of the rescuers died from thirst[6] during their epic 40-day rescue mission.

The officer in charge of the seven volunteers, Abraham Leeman, handed over a note from Captain Albertsz. Scrawled onto the parchment, the captain did his best to estimate where the ship had been wrecked indicating a position about 25 km south of Green Head. Unfortunately this was just over a hundred kilometres too far north of the actual wreck site. In his note, however, Albertsz happened to mention that he had been successful in salvaging some of the treasure before the ship had sunk.

On the early morning of 28 April, 1656, the *Vergulde Draeck* was driven onto a reef about 5.6 km from the shore between the present day towns of Seabird and Ledge Point. Scanning the horizon from the cliff tops today, the seas seem clear. You can barely make out the tell-tale signs of white

---

[5] LifeOnPerth.com

[6] Jackson P, Illustration Art Gallery, 1970

water of the reef that lay over 5 km from shore. According to the journal of Jan Van Riebeeck, the impact was so violent because the ship was under full sail with a good wind filling the billowing canvas. The ship immediately burst open upon impact drowning the hapless sailors trapped below decks. Over five and a half kilometres is a long way for the survivors to swim. Most likely only those who made it aboard the two boats would have survived. This would explain why 118 people perished but the 75 survivors who scrambled ashore, were relatively unscathed. With the suddenness and violence of the impact, it's hardly surprising that Albertsz was not entirely sure of his position.

We can imagine the sheer panic that must have gripped the crew. With screams of terror punctuating the cry of creaking timbers, there was little time to rescue all the provisions, treasure and barrels. Crushing for position aboard the long boats, horrified eyes must have stared at the pleading gestures of the men still aboard the wreck lilting precariously upon the reef [7].

Animated voices and shouts would only have been lost in the fury of the pounding waves. Any promises of rescue sank as the wreck suddenly slipped quickly off the reef. Flailing arms grasped the air as giant waves competed with the massive swell to swallow the stricken sailors.[8]

The Schuyt battling with the waves[9]

Anguished cries swept over the long boats. Weeping women wrapped their arms around their loved ones as the heavy, thick swell heaved the boats skywards. Struggling amid the shrieks, the strength-sapped sailors somehow steered their trembling cargo of grief to ground. The larger of the two *schuyts*, burdened with overcrowding, was capsized by an angry surf. Sailors gasping, gulping and grabbing at whatever part of the *schuyt* remained, swam exhausted among the shore breaking waves. As the smaller *schuyt* beached, sailors leapt out crashing through the surf grabbing outstretched arms and

---

[7] A total of 79 safely made their way to shore. One of the *schuyts* was smaller than the other. When a larger ship, *Batavia* sank in 1629, the longboat carried 48, although it was only designed for 40. The smaller *schuyt* must have carried up to 27 passengers. A *schuyt* was a Dutch flat-bottomed sailboat used to ferry people and stores to and from shore. It was towed from the stern of the ship.

[8] McBride, 1970, *Illustrated Art Gallery*

[9] Jackson, P, 1970, *Illustrated Art Gallery*

dragging them coughing to dry land. Gratefully hugging the shore, their eyes slowly scoured their new home: a desolate beach at the end of the earth which is today called Ledge Point.

After scanning the horizon for any potential survivors, Captain Albertsz resisted the temptation in sending exhausted men into the rising whitecaps of eight metre waves and dangerous swells. It was time to focus on the living.

A hostile unforgiving environment embraced the crying children, sobbing mothers and ashen-faced crew. Having no fresh water or food in the immediate surroundings, every geographical outcrop was utilised as there was precious little else available to protect them from the biting winds. The terrified throng, tired and thirsty, trembled with cold fear as they waited for their captain's plan of rescue. A lookout was posted on top of the hill but their eyes scanned inland as often as they strained the seascape. Who was watching them? Who lived on this forbidding shore[10]?

There was little time to waste. Albertsz ordered the understeersman, Abraham Leeman, and six others to prepare the *schuyt*[11], the smaller of the two boats for the long voyage to Batavia.

However, much to the relief of the survivors and with the echoes of the *Batavia* ringing in his ears, Pieter Albertsz elected to stay behind for the purpose of maintaining order and discipline. It was his duty *to maintain order among the crew and guard against quarrels among them which could lead to incidents as God save us, has happened before this*.

The survivors tried *to recover the boat which was buried in the sand. Nothing was saved*, from the wrecked ship, *and only very few provisions were thrown on the beach by the waves*[12]. If we believe the note that Albertsz had given to Leeman, then this wasn't quite true. Some of the treasure had been rescued. However, there is a possibility that Albertsz had deliberately exaggerated the amount of treasure they had salvaged in order to encourage a more sustained rescue attempt.

As much provisions and water was made available as possible for the seven who were to crew the *schuyt* that left nine days later on their rescue mission. Understeersman Abraham Leeman faithfully promised the captain that he would return to rescue them. As they tearfully waved away their only hope, muttering minds speculated on their chances of survival. What if they don't make it? How long will it take for a rescue ship to return? Will they be able to last that long? To calm the frantic utterings of desperate men, Commander Albertsz channelled their energies into an attempt to dig out of the sand the larger boat. More than likely he knew it was a fruitless task but it gave pause to their fear and frustration.

---

[10] The inhospitable shoreline that greeted the survivors. Photo by Henry Van Zanden

[11] On the following page, a Dutch *schuyt*.

[12] Major, Richard Henry, Early Voyages to Terra Australis, *Account of the Wreck of the Ship "De Vergulde Draeck" on the Southland and Expeditions Undertaken*

However, the question that has evaded treasure seekers for centuries was the location of where Albertsz had buried the treasure. Somewhere along the shore or further inland where the survivors made their permanent settlement, a fortune in coin and treasure remains to be discovered.

Painting by Ludolf Bakhuizen, *Merchant shipping anchored near Texel Island*

A Dutch *schuyt* was a flat-bottomed boat with a sail. They varied in size. The *Vergulde Draeck* had two *schuyts*. The larger one was swamped before it could reach the shore. The smaller of the two *schuyts* sailed back to Batavia with seven men where they reported the following: *the sixty-eight persons who remained behind were exerting themselves to get their boat afloat again, which lay deeply embedded in the sand, that they might send it also with some of their number to Batavia*[13].

---

[13] Royal Archives, the Hague

View from the top of a hill at Ledge Point

After searching the surrounding areas for possible artifacts, we discovered a well just south from where they landed. This photo was taken from the top of the hill which would have also been the most logical place for a lookout. The well[14] location also provided some shelter from the winds.

The only other distinguishing geographical feature were the cliffs that showed evidence of wild seas washing up over the high cliff tops.

Large chunks of rock torn away by hungry, clawing seas lay intermingled with broken pieces of stone ripped out of the cliff-face is testimony to the huge seas that occur each year on the Western Australian coast.

The photo on the left is from above the cliff but shows how large sections have fallen away due to the heavy pounding of the seas.

Exploring the immediate area along the coast both north and south would have revealed very little of substance to Captain Albertsz.

Apart from a river or permanent water supply, Albertsz was also hoping to find any stores from the wreck that may have been washed up along the beaches. Perhaps a sailor, stranded upon the wreck, was able to make it to land.

In a more northerly direction we found a possible shelter from severe storms and winds. However, there was hardly enough room to house 68 people. The surrounding countryside was devoid of any food or small animals. Apart from the rock shelter and well site, the whole area is most inhospitable and exposed to the elements. The countryside was punctuated with small bushes that scratched and clawed as we wound our way through the difficult terrain. The northerly coastal route was particularly difficult to traverse. It didn't take long before Albertsz came to the conclusion that there was little hope of survival should they decide to remain in the same location.

---

[14] Photo by Henry Van Zanden

Amongst the survivors, the women were quickest to alert Albertsz to the only other solution not yet tried: travel inland.

... their fathers were compelled by famine, after the loss of their great vessel, to travel towards the rising sun, carrying with them as much of the stores as they could, during which many died; and by the wise advice of their ten sisters they crossed a ridge of land, and meeting with a rivulet on the other side, followed its course and were led to the spot they now inhabit, where they have continued ever since[15].

With their energies sapped and complaints exhausted, it was said at this point that a decision was made to go inland in search of food and water. An initial report stated that *they had got out of the wreck very few victuals and fresh water* and that they were consequently *about to go inland after the departure of the mentioned schuyt (*sailing boat*), where we very much hope they will have found provisions and drinking water.*

Albertsz therefore must have told the seven crew who sailed to Batavia of what his intentions were should they be unable to find food and water. However, the further inland they travelled, the further they were from the coast and a possible rescue.

Vergulde Draeck Wreck site

Small cave at Ledge Point[16]
A natural path[17] on the northerly direction of the beach provided some protection from the weather. Further north, the thick bushes made travel difficult.

---

[15] Leeds Mercury Newspaper, 25 January 1834

[16] Photo by the Gilt Dragon Research Group

[17] Photo by Henry Van Zanden

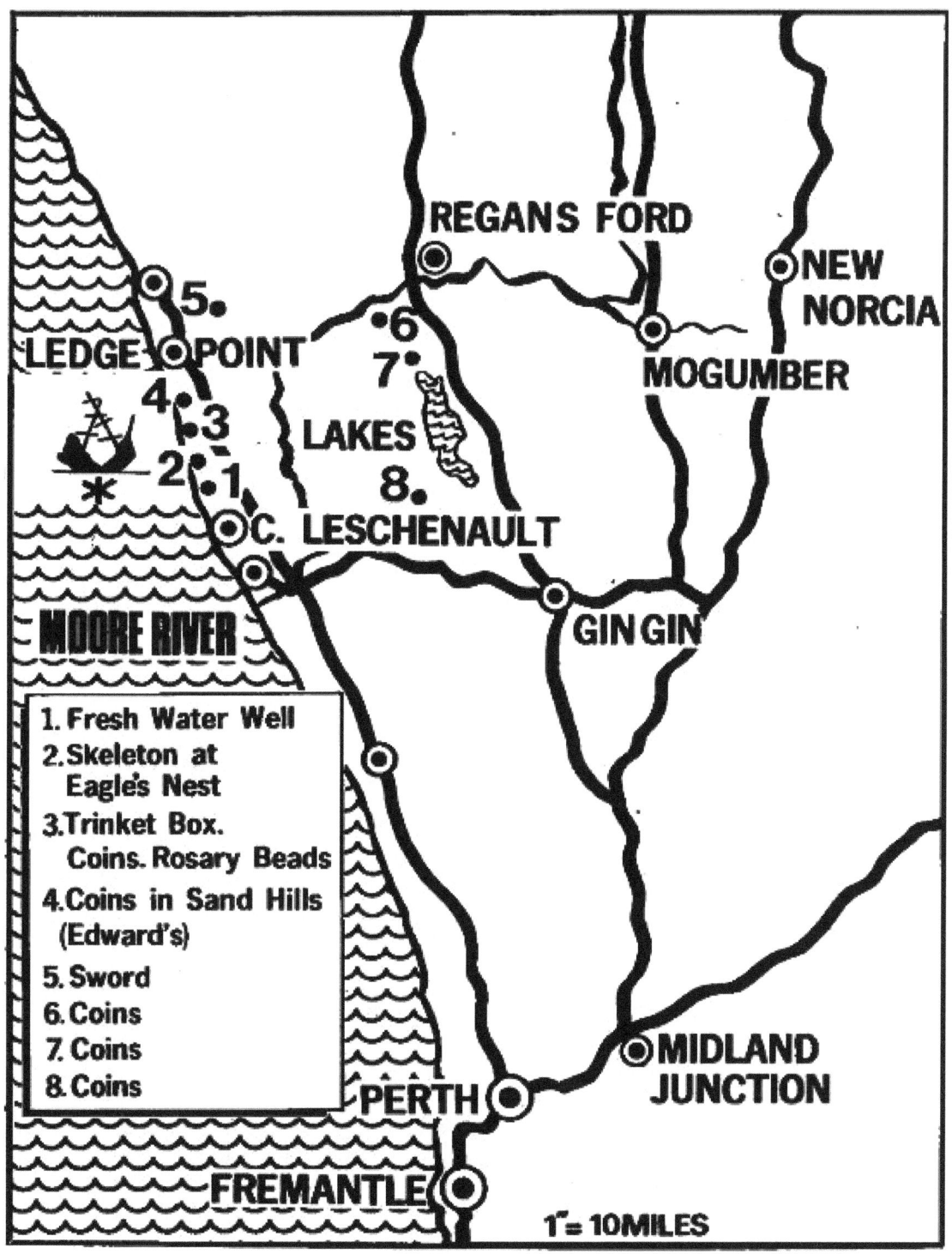

25 mm – 16.1 km

Located both north and south along the coast as well as inland, artifacts lost by survivors have been discovered over a wide area. Map by Frank Pash[18].

The location of the artifacts add further weight to the written evidence claiming that the survivors were forced to travel east eventually settling inland nearby a river.

---

[18] Robinson, A, 1980. *In Australia Treasure is not for the Finder.* Illustrations by Frank Pash. Published by Greenwood, W.A.

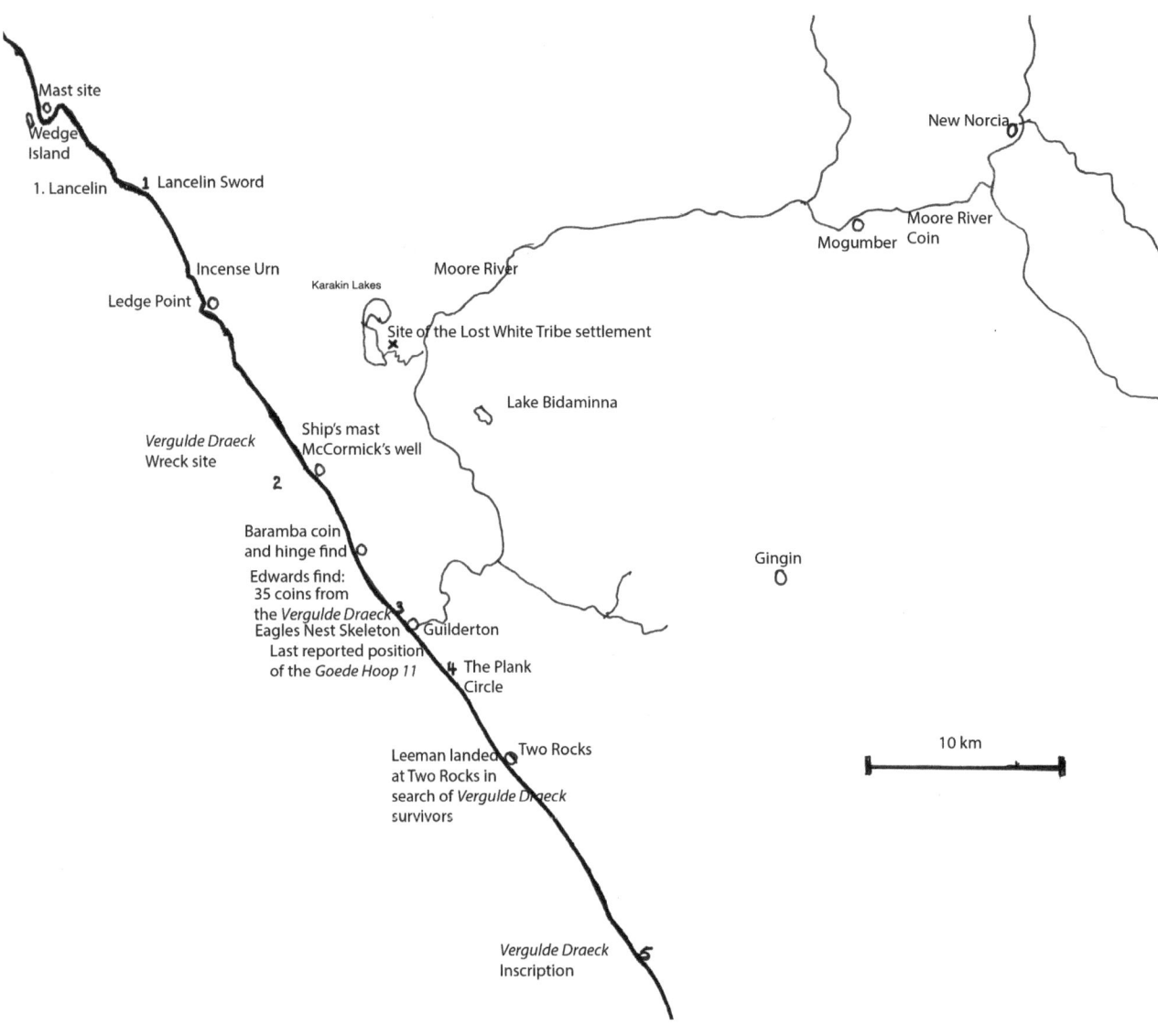

Vergulde Draeck site map Map by Henry Van Zanden

Chapter 2

Rescue attempt

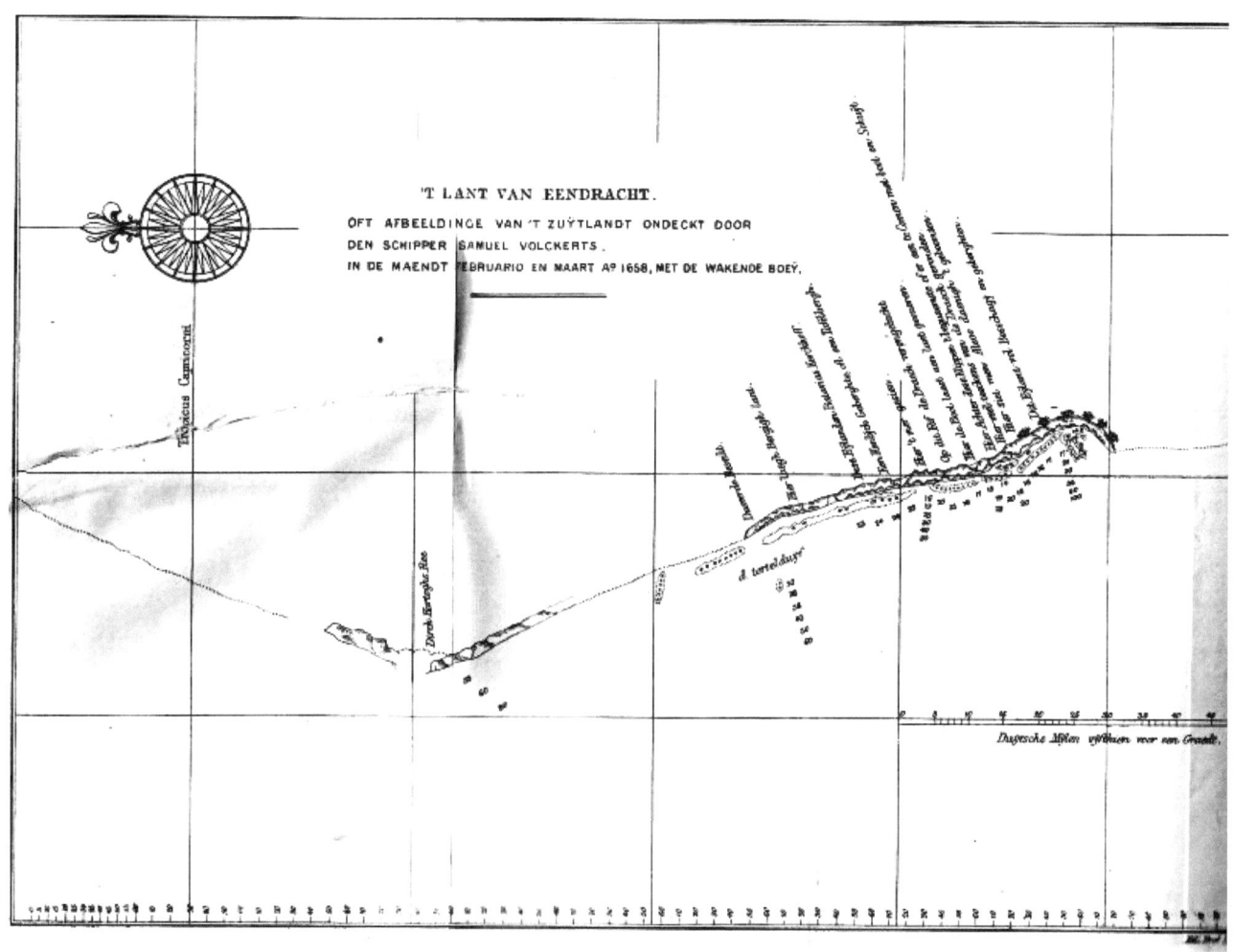

Map made by Captain Samuel Volckertsen, 1658 aboard the ship Waekende Boey

After an epic 3,000 km voyage lasting 40 days and 40 nights, the rescue *schuyt* arrived in Batavia 7 June 1656. Fortunately they were led by the very able Abraham Leeman van Santwitz. Two years earlier, Leeman, an Englishman from the island of Sandwich, may have been fighting his new employers, the Dutch East India Company. He was the perfect choice for command of the *schuyt* as Leeman was the understeersman. This meant that he was both the navigator and 1st Officer.

There are few details of the voyage but the feat was quite extraordinary. Sailing in difficult conditions in a small boat across 3,000 km of ocean was truly a remarkable feat of endurance and seamanship. More than likely the small boat was spotted by a passing East Indiaman as they approached the busy sea lanes of the Sunda Strait before reaching Batavia.

Dutch ship similar to the Goede Hoop

First Rescue attempt – *Witte Valck* and *Goede Hoop*

Weakened by hunger and tortured by thirst, the battered crew almost broken in spirit, were helped ashore. Upon revealing their sad and sorrowful tale, the Governor General Maetsuyker and the Councillors immediately decided to prepare two vessels, *Witte Valck* (White Falcon) and the *Goede Hoop*[1] (Good Hope) for a rescue mission. They included several divers and salvage equipment to recover the lost treasure chests as well as enough food for the survivors.

It wasn't until the middle of July that the two ships finally departed Batavia. Having only had a rough idea where the ship had sunk, the captains were given instructions to sail southwards until they reached about 32° to 33° Southern Latitude. One degree of latitude is an enormous area to cover. Their instructions were to then sail east until they arrived at the coast of the Southland. By charting all the bights, bays and shallows in their northerly return voyage, it was hoped that they would come across either the wreck or the survivors.

Unfortunately things did not go exactly according to plan. A heavy storm separated the ships and the *Witte Valck* returned to Batavia on 14 September. The weather was so bad they they could not safely approach the shore. All they could do was wait anxiously for the *Goede Hoop*.

---

[1] Replica of the *Dromedaris* which was built around the same time as the *Goede Hoop*. Author unknown

Eleven sailors marooned but *Vergulde Draeck* survivors seen

Finally, a month later, the *Goede Hoop* returned but brought no good news of the survivors. Worse still, they had lost eleven men. Three brave sailors had managed a successful landing in the ship's boat but became lost in the dense scrub. Eight men were sent to rescue them but they also disappeared. Those in the rescue craft put themselves at great risk. Strong north westerlies, gales, storms, and constant rough seas made every attempt to land through the high surf a dangerous exercise. A more thorough search discovered their battered boat bashed to pieces on the shoreline. Unwilling to send further men to sacrifice themselves, it was better to assume that they had drowned. The *Goede Hoop* was forced to return to Batavia.

However, the *Witte Valck* claimed to have seen men in their shelters, *knocked down and torn to bits*, and portions of their wreck even though they had not landed. The discovery of the shelters left by the survivors of the *Vergulde Draeck* was significant. Eleven men were put ashore and were lost in the thick scrub close to the location of the shipwreck. If they had survived, they too may have joined the 68 Dutchmen already lost on this part of the coast. Their total, assuming the 68 still remained alive, was now 79.

Despite these setbacks, the Council of the Indies, the supreme body in the Indies, was determined to find these most unfortunate group of men and women. On 28 November, 1656, a decision was made to use every available ship leaving from Cape Town to Batavia as a potential search vessel. Providing the weather was good, all passing ships were instructed to sail along the coast where the *Vergulde Draeck* had been wrecked. In total, five company sponsored expeditions were sent to rescue the survivors. The first to do so was the *Vinck* in January 1657. Although they sailed along the coast for one day, wild westerly winds started to blow hard forcing the vessel into open waters.

By late December 1657, there had still been no sign of the survivors. Authorities were worried that some may have still survived and were still waiting for rescue. However, most thought that they must have surely perished or been murdered by natives. Nonetheless, Councillor Carel Hartzinck decided to send out another expedition in search of the survivors of both the *Vergulde Draeck* and the *Goede Hoop*. An ideal time for such a search was during the months of December, January and February as the approach to the west coast was much safer. Hartzinck argued that even if no survivors were found, the value of surveying the coast with its dangerous shallows and reefs would far outweigh the costs. They looked further than just a rescue mission stressing to their captains to search for any opportunity of trade with the natives or discover what potential the land might hold. In other words they were hoping that there might be something of value on the land that might one day be exploited.

Second Rescue attempt, *Waeckende Boey* and *Emeloort*

The *Waeckende Boey*[2] and the galliot *Emeloordt* left New Years Day 1658 less than 18 months after the *Vergulde Draeck* sank. Both vessels, with their shallow draught, were well suited for the expedition. Perhaps disappointed at previous attempts, the wise Councillors offered a very attractive incentive. Providing they could salvage the treasure from the wreck, part of the money was promised to the crew. This must have encouraged Skipper Samuel Volckersen and his crew of 40 aboard the *Waeckende Boey* as well as Aucke Pietersz Jonck who skippered the *Emeloort* with a crew of 25, as they sailed on 1 January, 1658.

However, there were one or two flaws in their plans. Although given strict instructions to never lose sight of each other, the galliot, *Emeloort,* was agonisingly slow. Well, that's what Volckersen thought after a month of waiting for the *Emeloort* to catch up. Pacing the deck for just one more

---

[2] *Waekende Boey,* a small *fluyt*, pear-shaped cargo ship with a shallow draft, was built in 1656, 178 tonne

week, Volckersen had just about had enough. After the second week, he left the *Emeloort* to take care of itself. Volckersen was not a man to be left waiting.

A Fluyt[3] similar to the Waekende Boey

Despite this, both ships sighted the Southland only one day apart. On 24 February, the *Emeloort*, arrived at 33° 12´ Southern Latitude which meant that they had sighted the coast south of Perth. From here they sailed gradually north accurately charting the coast and sounding the depths as they went. But it wasn't until 8 March that they saw a fire on the shore at about 30° 25´. This was probably about 30 km north of the wreck site. Jonck promptly ordered his men to fire shots. On shore another fire was lit. Surely this must be the survivors!

At once we saw smoke rising ESE and also in the E, which we were sure to be signals. We replied with three guns and showed a big flag from the main topmast[4].

Although they were only about 9 or 10 km from shore, the surf was too big and the captain was concerned with the rocks and shallows. With the weather starting to deteriorate and the seas rising fairly fast, Jonck decided to remain there throughout the night. Once again they observed a fire being lit. However, they had to wait until the following morning for what they believed would be a rescue.

The next morning saw another fire being lit. With great anticipation, the crew once again fired three shots to attract attention. As a result, more fires were lit in reply to the cannon fire. As the excitement swelled amongst the crew, Captain Jonck wrote:

---

[3] Hollar, Wenzel Painting titled, *A Fluyt,* date unknown. Thomas Fisher Rare Book Library, Toronto

[4] Henderson, J.A., *Marooned,* St George Books, Perth, 1982, p. 87. Captain Jonck's log from the *Emeloort*

Rejoicing in our hearts we decided to send our boat there, and nine stout men and the first navigator-officer ... But the moment they touched shore, the smoke or fire was extinguished. Seeing this, our sailors turned around, since it was also getting late, reaching the ship again by nightfall. I suspect that this fire is no honest work, for it was lit at least two miijlen from the other one and extinguished at once. We resolved to send the boat again tomorrow to try our luck again, fired nine cannon-shots and flew a large Prince's flag from the top. At night we fired three cannon-shots and put a light signal in the top.

However, the following morning, there were no fires coming from the shoreline. A boat was sent out but was forced back due to the stiff north-easterly breeze and rough seas. Another attempt was made at noon in response to a large fire that was lit at the same spot on the beach as the previous day. Jonck ordered a signal fire every hour. After two hours, the boat eventually made their way to the shore.

A frustrating night followed with ship's crew spotting four fires as well as musket shots in answer to the ship's signal fire. However, all of the fires had been lit by the boat crew.

The exhausted sailors returned in the early morning of 11 March and reported to the captain of only seeing a group of natives. However, they did see three huts but when the five tall natives beckoned them to come closer, the sailors suspected it was a trap and returned instead to the boat. The natives were also unsure as they followed the men back to the boat but were most reluctant in coming too close. Nevertheless they did report that they had seen cultivated land that was burnt after the harvest. Unfortunately no water or fruit could be found but they did find some fragrant herbs. Inland they described many sand dunes. The immediate inland around Wedge Island and south to Lancelin, does fit the description as it is well known even today for its sand dunes. The position given was a place now called Sandy Knoll Ledge (30° 27´).

Wedge Island[5]

---

[5] *Photo of the author, Henry Van Zanden with Wedge Island in the background.*

Captain's log entry, 11 March, 1658:
We have been near three houses, and five persons of distinction and of very tall build were there who beckoned us ... and sympathetically put their hands under their heads as a signal of sleep. But we, not being simple enough to put ourselves in the hands of such savage people as we had good example (or warning), returned to our boat.

When we were in our boat they came up to the beach. We signalled with our lantern and flag that they should come to us, but they were very timid and we couldn't get them near our boat. They departed from us at dusk and we rested all night in our boat[6].

They also claimed to have explored inland as far as 19 km as well as along the beach. It does seem improbable that they had travelled this distance. However, they did report seeing many fires being lit at night and the reference to 'three houses' is interesting but may also mean three Aboriginal shelters. On his chart, Jonck named the land 6 km south of the the *Vergulde Draeck* wreck site as 'The *Draeck's* Headland.' However, he had drawn on his chart the description, 'The Three inhabitants' houses' a further 19–20 km north.

Vergulde Draeck survivors attempts to signal ships

Logically, some plans must have been made to enable a rescue from passing ships. It is also logical that the beaches both north and south from the wreck site would have been explored. Firstly, they would have hoped to settle in close proximity to the seashore. Secondly, any wreckage flung ashore would need to be regathered and utilised.

Unfortunately, no suitable site could be found close to the sea that could sustain them for a long period of time. If, therefore, they had to settle much further inland, then smaller parties may have been sent to the shoreline to signal passing ships. Evidence of this possibility can be seen in the finds made by two kangaroo shooters, JW Regan and the brothers Jack and Dan Skipworth.

1890 – 12 metre mast found buried in a sandhill

'One mile north of Wedge Island' the two kangaroo shooters found a 12m mast buried in a sandhill. A 50 litre rusty pot, a copper shovel, two horn spoons and two half moon shaped hatchet heads were also found. Could this have been the campsite of the *Vergulde Draeck* survivors who had attempted to signal the rescue ships?

The discovery was confirmed by J H Turner who rediscovered the 12 m mast. He noted that the diameter was 40 cm and had a 6 m heavy chain attached to it. Down one side was an iron rod and five iron bands were also around the mast[7]. This is precisely the reason why George Dean and I ventured across kilometres of shifting sand dunes to Wedge Island. There was just a faint hope that we could rediscover the mast ourselves or perhaps speak to the locals who had seen it uncovered in the past.

The possibility the signal fires were from the Vergulde Draeck survivors

The mast of the *Vergulde Draeck* had been washed up onto the beach north of Wedge Island. Logically a stranded sailor would set up fires to signal ships and stand the mast upright in a sand dune so that it could be easily recognisable from out to sea or from an approaching boat.

---

[6] Log of the *Emeloordt*, in J Henderson, *Marooned*, pp88-89

[7] Letter from JH Turner to the Chief Archivist, Public Library, Rupert Gerritsen, *And Their Ghosts May Be Heard*, p52

When the *Emeloort* was sighted, a signal fire was lit. Cannon shots were fired! As was the custom, the second signal fire was lit to acknowledge the cannon fire. Surely now a rescue boat would be put to sea. But unbelievably the ships had turned away. They didn't know that the *Emeloort* was merely retreating to a safe anchorage for the night and was prepared to send a boat in the morning.

Back to the survivors – frustrated, tired, anxious but still hoping for rescue. Climbing the highest dune, they scanned the horizon to see a faint flicker of a lantern filtering through the sea haze. The ship was still there. But what happened next? The following day the *Emeloort* once again fired the cannons but signal fires were out.

Large sand dunes south of Wedge Island[8]

A boat went ashore and discovered *three houses, and five persons of distinction and of very tall build were there who beckoned us ... and sympathetically put their hands under their heads as a signal of sleep*[9].

We know that the rescuers were too frightened to approach. Perhaps the Aboriginals were trying to communicate to the sailors that the survivors were asleep. Why else would they have beckoned them and then give the signal for sleep? Most likely there were only two men who had been sent to search and signal passing ships. Exhausted from their vigil, the tired survivors, simply overslept. This is exactly what was to later happen to Leeman and his men when they became stranded. When the morning arrived, there was no fire, no signal. Leeman and his men, tired and exhausted, overslept.

---

[8] Photo of sand dunes by Henry Van Zanden

[9] Log of the *Emeloort*, in J Henderson, *Marooned*, pp88-89

The Aboriginals may have been watching the whole episode from the fire signalling, the survivors falling asleep to the boat coming ashore. However, it doesn't explain why contact wasn't made later in the day. Perhaps they were prevented from doing so by the Aboriginals. Although there is one other possibility – they were dead, injured or too exhausted. The signal given for sleep may have meant one of the above.

1972 – The Lancelin Sword

Further evidence that some of the survivors had explored the shoreline north of Ledge Point came with the discovery of a sword. Just 20 km north of the *Vergulde Draeck* wreck site, an eight year old boy, Grant Borwick found a 'heavily rusted sword in the bush near Lancelin'. The 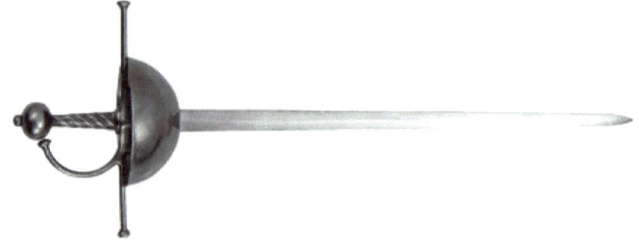 sword with its 'long tapering blade' was of 'a rapier design'[10] having 'a steel cup for the protection of the hand'. Such swords were a common model 'in Britain and the Low Countries in the 17th century'. Employing a metal detector, a further piece of the sword and 'some charred sections of the hilt which resembled leather'[11] were also found.

Unfortunately after a couple of weeks of sailing along the coast, bad weather intervened forcing Jonck to return to Batavia. On their way, fortune would have it that they would meet up with the *Waekende Boey* just off the west point of Java. This time Volckersen elected to stay with the *Emeloort* and they arrived in Batavia together.

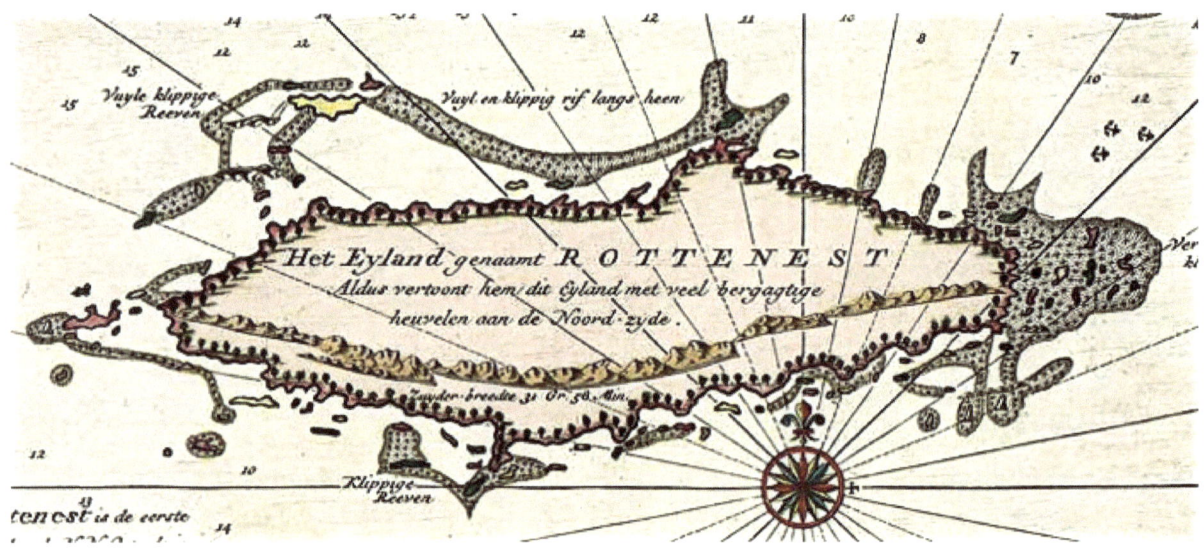

Samuel Volckersen's chart [12] 1658

Volckersen had approached the Southland further north than Jonck at 31° 40′ South at an island that is now called Rottnest Island which is not far from the entrance to the Swan River and Perth. After

---

[10] Rapier sword with steel cup. Photo from discount cutlery

[11] Log of the *Emeloort*, in J Henderson, *Marooned*, p57 He quotes M Robertson, *Report by Dr. Milne Robertson upon Certain peculiar Habits and Customs of the Aborigines of Western Australia*, p7

[12] Map of Rottnest Island made by Samuel Volckersen. Courtesy of the Western Australian Museum

charting the island, Volckersen continued north coming ashore at several places. At about 31° 20´ South, the steersman who went ashore in the boat, claimed that he had seen wreckage of the *Vergulde Draeck* but could not see any sign of people. They walked up and down the shoreline gathering pieces of wood, bits of broken chests as well as a small barrel. 31° is just north of the wreck site where Lancelin is today. There is no doubt that the wreckage they had found belonged to the *Vergulde Draeck*.

What is most interesting of all is the strange discovery of a circle of planks put upright in the sand surrounding a heavy beam. This was not wreckage flung together by the wind and seas, but a deliberate attempt by the survivors to let any would be rescuers know that they were still alive!

A truer picture of what really happened could only come after a thorough debriefing. Most of the VOC documents have either been lost or still to be studied. However, historians are fortunate to have the benefits of the research and writing of Wouter Schouten, a Dutch writer who documented the rescue attempt made by the *Waekende Boey*. Although he wrote this in 1676, he had the advantage of having access to any existing documents held in Batavia.

Schouten was a Dutch surgeon who served in the Dutch East Indies. After he returned to the Netherlands, he published three books including a best seller, *Remarkable Voyage made by Wouter Schouten to the East Indies*,(1676)

Schouten reveals in much clearer terms that the *Waekende Boey* found the location of the wreck as well as the remnants of the *Vergulde Draeck*'s camp site. He includes the controversial act by Volckersen of sailing away after ordering his officer, Abraham Leeman and twelve others ashore while a storm was approaching.

The Waekende Boey duly arrived at the location where Den Draeck was wrecked and the place from where its boat with some of the survivors of the ordeal had brought the news to Batavia, who were now helping to find that location. Once they found the location of the wrecked ship, they anchored at a suitable anchorage, and sent the boat as soon as they could for their countrymen who had made it to land from the ship Den Draeck.

They eagerly lowered the boat from the ship, which examined the wreck which had been battered by the waves and flooded, and following that to the spot where the folk left on land had been living in a commodious tent when their boat had left, with the intention of waiting there until a vessel from Batavia could come to collect them. **When they landed they found the tent-poles broken but did not find any of their countrymen in the vicinity**. [Author's emphasis] *They were quite surprised by this and looked for canvas, nails, knives and so forth, but couldn't find any sign of carpentry or part of any watercraft, let alone any letters or messages – not a sign – so nobody could figure out where all these people had gone. When they sailed back to the ship and reported this unexpected news, everyone else also found it strange. However, after some deliberation it was decided to continue searching the surrounding area, with men making quite a few landings and carefully searching this uninhabited land. But again this was fruitless. They made loud sounds with their muskets, shouting and by other means, even using a small cannon. All this proved to be useless and it seemed impossible to find anyone in the area, and so I never was able to learn what became of these Netherlanders.*

They then searched the wreck of the Draeck. But this produced no result either, as the ship's holds and cabins were all inundated by powerful waves, so that the constant pounding of the ocean thwarted their efforts. They did not have any other option than to prepare to return in the Waekende Boey to Batavia. As they were basically at risk of being hit by a storm and strong winds, and if a gale struck them they would surely be wrecked, they prepared to leave. The boat, having been sent ashore again to get fresh water, the crew, after landing near a small stream and beaching the boat, wandered off inland, instead of hurrying along. Then a heavy storm came which continued unabated, blowing so strongly (or so the Skipper later claimed) that they were forced to sail away, in the belief that the boat, in attempting to return, had been wrecked – they had been away so long, against orders, so that there was no longer any doubt, especially as the raging storm forced her to make, with great difficulty, away from the lee shore to reach for open sea. The ship headed straight for Batavia where this plausible speculation would ultimately be challenged by the real truth. When the winds and sea abated and they were able to cross a narrow channel and make seaward, the boat and its crew sought to find their missing ship. They fell silent, and with heavy sighs, tears came to their eyes. Softly at first, their expressions of sorrow and pity grew louder. After some discussion they decided to return to the shore, forced to do so if only to escape from the wild waves lashing their little boat. On coming ashore they regarded each other with great sadness. They didn't have anything to eat or drink and there was nothing of the sort in the area.

This lonely, inhospitable and sad place provided nothing but rocky hills, wild valleys and sandy plains. The bare beaches were strewn with cliffs and rocks and the sea continuously moaned. They could find no sustenance for themselves of any sort. And so these Netherlanders, standing there,

thirteen in all, weak, hungry, cold and wet, in despair and without any hope, it seemed they would all starve to death. How could they survive? Nothing could be obtained from the wreck as it was under water so that all they could feel were dark pangs of hunger, ready to end their miserable life. Cries, sighs, screams and curses were the only thing they could resort to. But others showed courage and began to look for food. They found between the rocks along the shore some edible sort of fish. Because they had to rely on this meagre source of food, raw at the time (they were unable to make fire), they began to lose their strength as they starved and their health declined. They finally decided, rather than stay there and die, to trust God's mercy and take to the sea, to find out what the Almighty had in store for them there[13].

Schouten, Wouter [14] 1676

Translation by Reynders and Gerritsen

---

[13] Major, RH 1859, *Early Voyage to Terra Australis, Now Called Australia*

[14] Wouters Schouten, From his book '*Aanmerclijke Voyagie Gedaan door Wouter Schouten Naar Oost-Indien*, Amsterdam: Jacob Meurs and Johannes van Someren, 1676
[*Remarkable Voyage made by Wouter Schouten to the East Indies*,(1676)]

Chapter 3
Abraham Leeman
and his epic tale of survival

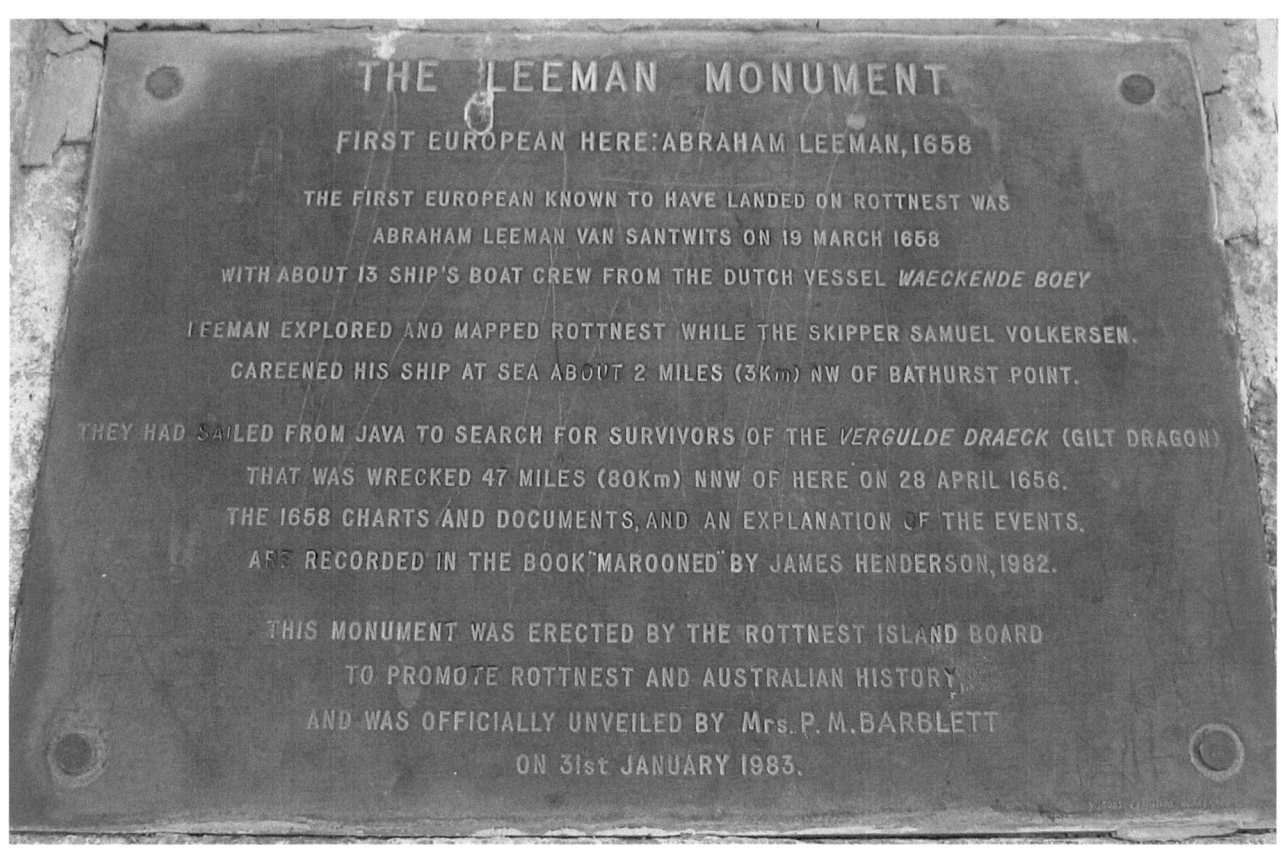

The Leeman Monument on Rottnest Island. Wikimedia Creative Commons

The search party from *Waeckende Boey* that discovered the circle of planks, was led by upper-steersman (navigator and first officer) Abraham Leeman van Santwitz, an Englishman from the town of Sandwich. They went ashore on 28 February, 1658 somewhere near Yanchep.

They had gone ashore in several places to investigate the numerous fires and on 25 February, wreckage had been found strewn along the coastline. However, no one could be found. A cannon was fired at regular intervals to attract any survivors who surely must have been able to see the ship from any good vantage point. However, they didn't give up. For days they walked along the shoreline searching for more evidence and hoping to find the survivors only to find more broken timber, buckets, a small barrel and smashed up bits of wooden chests but no silver.

It was on 26 February that an arrangement of timbers or planks that had been put in a circle with their ends upwards was found. The reading that they gave was 31° 20' S but Rupert Gerritsen believes that it was probably 31° 28'S or 4 km north of Two Rocks[1]. Latitude readings in the 17th century were generally inaccurate. There was plenty of rain during the winter months in this area and I found numerous rock formations where water could be collected such as the one pictured found near the wreck site[2]. However, the coastline is quite rugged and exposed to the elements.

The Plank Circle was found about half way between the mouth of the Moore River and the *Vergulde Draeck* wreck site or a further 26 km south. It is difficult to determine whether or not it was a defensive structure or a marker.

A number of pieces of planking had been put into a circle with their ends upwards[3].

However, it is a strong possibility that the Plank Circle was erected by the 11 survivors of the *Goede Hoop* as we know that they had approached the wreck site from the south.

A second wooden structure was found by Leeman on 21 March, 1658 but this one was very close to the actual wreck site.

A deal plank 8 to 9 feet long [2.5 to 2.7 m] *and a foot wide put upright in the earth and round 12 to 13 struts of similar planks, also struck in the sand.* They *pulled out the timbers and dug four to five feet deep* [about 1.5 m] *into the soil, thrusting our cutlasses as deep as we could into the sand but found nothing*[4].

What they had hoped to find was a message indicating where they had gone. The survivors obviously wanted any would be rescuers to know that they were still alive. Unfortunately the message that they surely must have left had withered away during the intervening two years. It may

---

[1] Gerritsen bases his belief on the consistent errors made by navigators at that time in estimating latitude

[2] Photo taken by Henry Van Zanden at Ledge Point (near wreck site)

[3] Gerritsen, R *And their Ghosts May be Heard*, p42

[4] Gerritsen, R *And Their Ghosts May be Heard*, p218

have been placed inside some kind of container or a bottle but this would be the most logical item an Aboriginal would have picked up should they have stumbled upon the structure.

Signal fires sighted on the coast

Leeman returned to the ship because a storm was approaching. Volckersen sailed out to sea but the small boat he was towing capsized and sank. This loss turned out to be crucial for Volckersen only had one boat left to make any exploratory search of the mainland. They had to be careful. On 28 February, fires were seen on the coast but the seas were rough. Nevertheless an attempt was made to land the one remaining boat. Frustratingly close to shore, they were forced to return due to the very high surf. They could not afford to lose the boat and risk being stranded along with those they had hoped to rescue. If the fires were lit by stranded sailors, their hearts must have sunk to even greater depths of despair when they watched their rescuers floundering in the huge surf.

If they thought that they need only wait for the following day for a second rescue attempt, they would be even more disappointed as severe weather forced the *Waeckende Buoy* southwards back towards Rottnest Island, away from the fires, and further away from rescue.

On 19 March, Volkersen ordered Leeman to go ashore at Rottnest Island to collect firewood. What seemed an impossible task due to the numerous reefs that surrounded the island was achieved. Not only did he return with firewood, he found ship wreckage consisting of *a dead-eye, a knighthead and a block*[5].

Extraordinarily, despite having only one boat, Volkersen ordered Leeman out again on 22 March despite a threatening storm. Leeman protested but to no avail. Leeman and an unlucky 13 reluctantly rowed towards shore. They were well on their way when suddenly, the wind strengthened. Skipper Samuel Volkersen realised too late the danger in which he had placed his men. He ordered the firing of a cannon shot and lit a lantern to warn Leeman to return to the ship. It was too late for the weather worsened. Leeman and his men rowed furiously through the lines of reefs about 5 km from the shoreline only to see Volkersen pull up anchor and sail away to safer waters. If we believe the skipper, the waters were too dangerous and he risked the whole ship being dashed upon the shore.

In his defence a storm did erupt forcing the ship to stand out to sea where she remained while the storm raged for a further five days. However, Leeman and his 13 crewmen were blown onto an island many kilometres north of the *Waeckende Boey*. Not only could they not make their way back to the ship, it was impossible to come any closer to the shore due to the high surf. All they could do was tack back and forth along the coast until they could find a place to land. After an exhausting day being tossed at will by an unforgiving surf, they were driven further north until their helpless craft was literally thrown ashore just before dark. This was most likely Fisherman Island which is about 17 km south of the town of Leeman.

For two very anxious days amid the howls of the storm, Leeman and his men repaired the damaged boat. Although the storm was to last five days, Leeman could not risk waiting to be left behind. With the storm lessening in intensity, they carefully made their way southwards back to their last sighting of the *Waeckende Boey*. Imagine their angst when they could not sight the ship. Their tired tormented eyes turned to Leeman for an answer. He must have answered, "Sail to the nearest island. We can light signal fires from there and perhaps find food, water and shelter." They most likely

---

[5] Sigmond JP, Zuiderbaan, LH, *Dutch Discoveries of Australia*, p93

Glossary: A dead-eye – a type of block; Knighthead – a big pulley block

landed between Green Island[6] and Rottnest Island. Green Island was a a tiny outcrop only 100 km offshore from Rottnest.

Two or three hours after midday I saw two high hills in the sea and some broken land quite a long distance from the mainland and directly ahead[7].

One of theses hills must have been Green Island. With their boat sailing at frightening speed with the wind lifting the sails, the boat sped headlong into the frothy fringe of the two islands. The high swells washed into the boat forcing the men to furiously bale out the water racing over the boat. They could not heave to or change direction as the swell would have rolled the boat onto its side. However, they were now so close to the rocky ledge on Green Island that the swell also threatened to smash the boat to pieces. Fortunately, Leeman was able to steer towards the bay where they caught a huge wave that threw them about forty metres over the rocks. When the boat landed, it crashed onto a rocky coral spilling some of the sailors into the surf. Leeman immediately called out to all of the sailors to keep hold of the boat to stop it being broken into pieces in the violent surf. Exhausted, the men manhandled the boat through the reefs and coral to a sandy shore on Rottnest Island.

Unfortunately the boat was damaged and the food soaked with seawater but at least they were saved. The fat seals looked on not realising that they would become fresh meat to these hungry sailors. Two seals and a few sea birds were captured and later roasted on a welcome fire.

---

[6] Photo of Green Island courtesy of Green Island by Rodney Swartz, 19 October 2004

[7] Henderson, JA *Marooned*, 1982 Published by St George Books Perth, pp117, 118

The next few days Leeman occupied his men in repairing the boat as best they could, capturing more seabirds and searching for water. Water, however, was difficult to find. Only in the rock hollows were they able to retrieve three or four litres of murky water.

After six days the weather improved enough for the *Waekende Boey* to return to the coast where they had left Leeman and his men. All seemed well when they saw the *Waekende Boey* approach on the horizon. Piles of dry bushes that they had already prepared, were immediately lit. It was 28 March at sunset when the lookout sighted a fire. A cannon-shot broke the sound of the westerly wind. They had been spotted! There was no time to celebrate. Another signal fire was lit to acknowledge the cannon-shot. The boat was at the ready to fight its way back to the *Waekende Boey,* but it had to wait patiently until the endless thunder of crashing, smashing waves would subside long enough for them to risk a hazardous attempt to reunite with their ship. It was also too dark. However, they may have braved the rough dark seas if the boat's rudder had not been badly damaged. Night time stole their chance. A sleepless night, punctuated with a few prayers, forced them to endure an even longer wait. Awake and exhausted long into the night, they fell asleep well into the next morning. Volckersen did not fire off another cannon to wake up a weary crew left stranded without food or shelter for nearly a week. The sun shone brightly across the great expanse but there was no *Waekende Boey.* Their hopes had sailed away!

Volckersen claimed the fires must have been those of Aboriginals as they could not see any signs of a fire in the morning. He couldn't explain on the previous day why there was an immediate signal of a second fire after they had fired their cannon.

Meanwhile, Leeman and his men still expected Volckersen to return. After all they did signal the *Waekende Buoy* with their two fires. They waited with patience for a few days and impatience for another week. Eleven days passed but no ship. Volckersen had left them stranded, marooned, abandoned. Feeling betrayed by their skipper, they looked forlornly and feebly to Leeman for an answer. The crew must have cursed and then cried. They were stranded – marooned on a desolate island. Their salvation had simply sailed stealthily away in the wind.

Volckersen claimed that the day after they lost sight of the boat, there appeared to be no sign of the 14 men but it's not surprising for his ship was now much further north. Why didn't Volckersen return? The official version or Volckersen's version is that they had to leave when the wind rose again and it looked likely there could be more bad weather. The skipper, Samuel Volckersen, surmised that the group they had found on the beach must have been aborigines or that his own men were now lost. The *Waekende Boey* made its final farewell 8 km from Dirk Hartog Island on 31 March. On 10 April, the *Waekende Boey* reached Java where they rejoined the *Emeloort* just four days later. Volckersen must have been a relieved man when he sailed into the harbour with the *Emeloort* given that his instructions were to not lose sight of each other. However, he did have a little trouble explaining the loss of 14 men. The good Councillors were not impressed.

But back to Leeman. Mustering all of his persuasive skills, Leeman made them realise that they had to make their own way back to Batavia. An impossible task, it would seem, but they had little choice. They spent the next few days preparing themselves for the impossible voyage rebuilding the boat to make it more seaworthy. The sides were raised with seal skins and a new makeshift rudder was built from the wreckage of the *Vergulde Draeck*. Seal meat was cut up and possibly stored inside seal skins. A plant that Leeman called 'sea-parsley' was added as their only vegetable. The few water casks they did have were filled with fresh water and on 8 April they began their epic voyage. Seal skins may have also been used for the purpose of carrying extra water.

Inevitably, they ran out of water but Leeman, always showing resourcefulness, had hoisted a blanket each night. In the morning, the 14 thirsty crew sucked the dew out of the blanket. However, there is only so much moisture you can suck out of a blanket. Drinking your own urine was the next best thing while others resorted to drinking seawater to quench a desperate thirst. Leeman, a religious man, must have prayed for good winds and rain. Fortunately the weather provided some supplement to their meagre water supply without being too severe as to capsize their new vessel. The winds also proved favourable allowing them to sail to Java in just over four weeks. Despite this, three men died of thirst before they had sighted land on 28 April at the south coast of Java. It seemed that their prayers had been answered!

Unfortunately it was impossible to land the boat yet his men were willing to risk all in order to taste the water ashore. Leeman relented and allowed five of his men to swim ashore with a small cask attached to a long line instructing them to fill the cask so that they could pull it into the boat[8]. Incredibly, these five men sated themselves so full of water that they totally forgot or chose to forget the very thirsty men still waiting for their first drink of beautiful, fresh, clean, pure water. Remembering every curse in the Dutch language, these men watched helplessly from their boat trying to attract their attention in the way only a seasoned sailor could. What were these cruel men thinking! Possibly they were worried that Leeman would leave them stranded ashore and therefore tried to entice Leeman to join them. Maybe they felt too weak and exhausted to swim and conspired to persuade Leeman to come ashore. In fact they taunted the tortured men who glared back angrily with their salt scorched eyes, their shiny red sunburn now angrily glistening a brighter red. Their parched throats pleaded a red raw retort. 'Attach the cask with cool, fresh water!' Between sips and gulps, the men cheekily told them to come and get the water themselves. Frustrated and struggling to restrain the remainder of his crew, Leeman sent out two more men with the same instructions.

Unfortunately, before they could attach a full cask to the line, the weather sent one last cruel blow. Leeman was forced to pull away from shore and wait until the next day before attempting a landing. But the next day proved disasterous with the huge waves smashing the boat to pieces on the beach.

---

[8] Example of a seal skin boat in Alaska. Photo by Stephen-Karen Conn. Description: Bearded seal skin boat seams where seal skins are sewn with water proof stitching. Barrow, Alaska.

The four men barely escaped being drowned as the boat capsized. Angry, thirsty and frustrated but too exhausted to vent their pent up feelings, they dragged themselves ashore. However, they could not reach the seven men already ashore due to the impenetrable coastline. Their stupidity was to cost them their lives as they were never heard of again.

After replenishing their thirst and regathering their strength, they simply headed west hoping to eventually reach a Dutch settlement. Severely weakened after two months of fighting their way through a choking jungle, the four worn out four survivors could barely go on. Fortunately they were rescued by a friendly tribe who nursed them back to health before taking them to Japara.

Leeman arrived at Java on 28 April, 1658 but it wasn't until 23 September that the weak and exhausted men entered Batavia[9]. It took Leeman and his men 5 months to cross the island and reach Batavia.

The Castle of Batavia – 1656

Leeman needed a little time to recover and write up his official report before presenting his epic tale of survival to the amazed Councillors. His journal proved to be a very touching story revealing a good man who simply placed his trust in God and determination to live to extricate himself and others from what seemed an impossible situation.

The question of the fate of the *Vergulde Draeck* survivors still remained a mystery. However, the Councillors at the Castle of Batavia, now knew that the treasure could not be recovered. The justification for sending further rescue ships evaporated. Nevertheless there always remained a lingering hope that the survivors had somehow remained alive.

---

[9] Beeckman, Andries, *The Castle of Batavia*, circa 1656

Willem de Vlamingh – 1696

As late as 1696 three Dutch ships left Holland to search for the survivors of two ships: the *Ridderschap van Holland* which went missing in 1694, and the *Vergulde Draeck* wrecked forty years earlier.

Believing the quokkas to be giant rats, Vlamingh gave the name Rotte nest (rat nest) to the island located just 18 km off the West Australian coast near Fremantle. No sign of missing Dutch sailors was found despite a thorough search of the coastline.

Although they had no success in their search for survivors, they mapped, entered and named the Swan River. He is believed to be the first European to sail up the Swan River. Vlamingh continued north mapping and scanning the coastline in search of any signs of life.

Willem de Vlamingh's ships, with black swans, at the entrance to the Swan River, Western Australia, coloured engraving, derived from an earlier drawing (now lost) from the de Vlamingh expeditions of 1696–97.

Incredibly Vlamingh did find the original plate of Dirk Hartog erected on Shark Island in 1616. Hartog was the first European to sight Western Australia. At the age of only 21, Hartog had his own ship and made several profitable voyages to the Baltic and the Mediterranean. He was 26 when he was ordered to sail the route in 1616 and slightly miscalculated where to turn north. As a result, he saw a group of low islands and further to the east, he could see the extreme western tip of mainland Australia. Naturally he named the island, Dirk Hartog Island and is famous for leaving behind a pewter plated attached to a pole to mark his discovery with the following inscription:

1616 the 25th October has arrived here the ship "Eendracht" of Amsterdam, the uppermerchant Gillis Miebais of Liege skipper Dirck Hartichs of Amsterdam. The 27th ditto we set sail for Bantum, the under merchant Jan Stins, the upper steersman Pieter Dockes van Bil;. Anno 1616[10].

Pewter is made mainly of tin and lead and was used widely by sailors for plates and mugs because it was easy to keep clean and unbreakable. It was also not too hard a metal for Hartog to scratch a message on its surface. Captain Hartog stayed two days on the 70 kilometre island before setting off to Java which he reached in December. He named the land that he discovered, *Eendrachtsland*. Hartog returned to Amsterdam in 1617 where he continued his voyages as a merchant to the Baltic.

The inscribed pewter plate stared out at the empty Indian Ocean for over eighty years until 1697 when Willem de Vlamingh discovered the plate. Vlamingh decided to take the plate back to Holland and replace it with his own suitably inscribed plate at exactly the same spot but nailed to a new pole. Vlamingh inscribed what Hartog had written on his plate and then added the following:

1697, the 4th February has arrived here the ship the Geelvinck of Amsterdam; the commander and skipper Willem De Vlamingh of Vlielandt; assistant Joannes Bremer of Copenhagen; upper-steersman Michil Bloem of the diocese of Bremen the Hooker; the Nyptangh, skipper Gerrit Colaart of Amsterdam, assistant Theodoris Hairmans of the same, uppersteerman Gerrit Geritsen of Bremen the Galliot; the Weeseltie, skipper Cornelis De Vlamingh of Vlielandt, steersman Coert Gerritsen of Bremen; and from here set sail with our fleet to explore the Southland with destination Batavia.

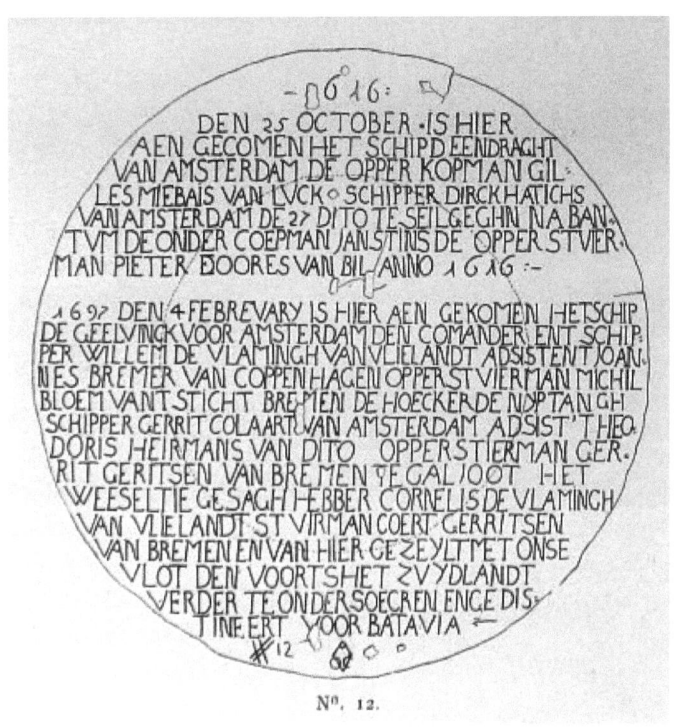

N°. 12.

Dirk Hartog's plate is now in the Rijksmuseum in Amsterdam but Vlamingh's plate[10] was incredibly found by a French explorer, Captain Hamelin, in 1801. It's amazing that he even found it because it had fallen from its pole. Hamelin decided to renail the plate back onto the pole and it was still there when another French expedition under Louis de Freycinet visited Dirk Hartog Island. It was taken back to Paris and given to the *Academie des Inscriptions et Belles Lettres*. Over the years the plate was probably put away in a storeroom and was forgotten until it was rediscovered in 1940 by the secretary of the Academie, Fr Renie. The Valmingh plate was presented to the Australian government and is now in the Western Australian Maritime Museum in Fremantle.

---

[10] Heeres, JE, *The Part Borne by the Dutch in the Discovery of Australia 1606-1765,* Copy of the Vlamingh plate, 1697 [A Project Gutenberg of Australia ebook produced by Colin Choat]

De Vlamingh sailed away from Shark Bay[11] condemning the *Vergulde Draeck* survivors to the isolation and harshness of an unforgiving land. Their memories were only resurrected when a surprising article appeared in England's second largest newspaper outside London: The Leeds Mercury. It was a story of a lost white tribe stranded in Australia since the 17th century.

The title of the article was:

Discovery of a White Colony on the Northern Shore of New Holland.

'T Landt van de Eendracht[12] *[Western Australia] and Dirk Hartog Island*

---

[11] Shark Bay map, courtesy of *OpenStreetMap project data*

[12] Gerritsz, Hessel, *Map of Eendracht Land, discovered by Dirk Hartog in 1616*, (1627) National Library of Australia

Chapter 4

The Leeds Mercury.

Article

25 January

1834

Story of the Lost White Tribe

After researching and writing the book, *1606 Discovery of Australia*, I had always believed that it was highly probable that shipwrecked sailors had survived this distant shore. Between 1606 and 1756, over 30 Dutch ships had made contact with Australia. Many of these contacts were accidental or ships crashing onto the coast of Australia.

There had already existed a great deal of evidence to support the idea that shipwrecked sailors had survived on the mainland. However, it has generally been assumed that these desperate sailors either died or had simply melted into the indigenous population thus losing their identity. The remarkable sight of blue-eyed, blond-haired Aboriginals with 'European features' discovered by the early explorers in Western Australia, have usually been attributed to two men: Jan Pelgroem and Wouter Loos who were marooned on the Western Australian coast in 1629 as punishment for their role in the *Batavia* mutiny. Told to 'make friends' with the Aboriginal tribes, they must have had an Aboriginal harem if we are to attribute all of the sightings to only two men.

Leeds Mercury article 1834 and the Palm Valley Settlement in Central Australia

What brought my attention to the concept of the 'Lost White Tribe' was the publication of the Leeds Mercury article in 1834. Nationwide attention to this newspaper article was brought into sharp focus with the ABC television series, *The Bushtucker Man* featuring Les Hiddens. Also fascinated by the Leeds Mercury article, Hiddens meticulously followed the coordinates in the article leading him to Central Australia – a place unlikely to have a colony of 300 Dutchmen. Nevertheless he persisted in his search and assumed that the latitude given was purposely wrong. A more plausible location was discovered in Central Australia at a place called Palm Valley south of Alice Springs.

The story was based around a secret English expedition led by Lieutenant Nixon who discovered 300 Dutch settlers in a desert oasis that Hiddens believed was Palm Valley. According to the article, the settlers were the descendants of mid-17th century Dutch shipwreck survivors.

The *Vergulde Draeck* (1656), the *Concordia*[1] (1708) and the *Zuytdorp* (1712) were the only shipwrecks that came close to the suggested timeframe. Out of these three, Hiddens thought that the *Concordia* was the ship that provided the eighty men and ten women who trekked from northern Australia to over 1500 km inland to establish a settlement in Central Australia.

Living in houses, they built a great wall for protection against attacking Aborigines. They survived on fish that they caught on a wide river. Plantations of maize and yams and the occasional kangaroo or other wildlife supplemented their diet. However, they often experienced food shortages.

Despite their isolation, they still maintained a semblance of Dutch culture wearing trousers and jackets made from animal skins, speaking a form of old Dutch and observing some Christian traditions.

Historian Karen Cook examined in detail the theory put forward by Hiddens but especially concentrating on one English explorer: Robert Dale. She also discusses the possible motives for keeping the settlement a secret.

Based on research reported to the Society for the History of Discoveries in 2000, it is possible that Stirling had sent Robert Dale on a secret expedition to the centre of Australia during March-May 1832. The expedition party may have landed at Fowler's Bay on the south coast, marched due north to an area near Alice Springs and then returned to the coast. If so, the expedition took place in territory that then belonged to New South Wales. Stirling might have wanted to keep secret the

---

[1] The *Concordia* was actually listed by the Dutch as being lost near Mauritius

trespass onto the territory of a rival colony. Nevertheless, an anonymous account of such an expedition appeared in the Leeds Mercury newspaper in England in January 1834. It published an anonymous report of the discovery of several hundred Dutch-speaking descendants of shipwreck survivors, who had walked to central Australia from the west coast in the early 18th century. The account went on to say that the expedition, described as originating in Singapore and landing on the northern shore of Australia (possibly to hide its true origin), had been supported by the local government and a scientific society but was being kept secret for unexplained reasons.

If Stirling[2] had reported the discovery of a Dutch colony to his superiors in the Colonial Office, their reason for continued secrecy would likely have been the strained relations between the Dutch and English nations, especially in the East Indies. The English were already worried that the French might land on an unsettled stretch of coast and try to claim part of Australia. The discovery of a Dutch colony with a possible prior claim to Australia would have alarmed his superiors in the Colonial Office. If that was one of the reasons why Stirling returned to England, though, no evidence in the official written record has yet been found[3].

Although there is still no specific evidence that points to Stirling as the author of the article, there is a great deal of circumstantial evidence that at the very least, makes Stirling the prime suspect. He had already had form in publishing anonymous newspaper articles for his own purposes. This was revealed by Berryman[4] who lists a number of occurrences where he believed that Stirling was the author of such letters to the press.

It's interesting to note the sequence of publishing events. The article first appears in the northern newspaper, the Leeds Mercury after Stirling's appeal for assistance for the struggling colony was turned down by the London authorities. Next it appears in Scotland. Stirling was also a Scot.

The Leeds Mercury article appeared 16 days before Stirling was to begin his return voyage to Western Australia. It mysteriously appears in Cape Town, just after Stirling had passed through it on his way home. Finally it appears at the Swan River Colony but only after Stirling has returned where a summary of the journal was published in the Perth Gazette and Western Australian Journal on 20 September, 1834.

Although there were many convincing elements to Hiddens' theory, I was more inclined to believe that any Dutch colony, if it existed, was close to the Western Australian coast. Almost every Dutch shipwreck had occurred along this coast. The only possibility of a Dutch shipwreck in South

---

[2] Portrait of Governor Sir James Stirling, 1832. Courtesy of the Battye Library 409B

[3] Cook, Karen Severud, *The Secret agenda of Western Australian explorer, Robert Dale (1809 - 1853)*, 1999

[4] Berryman, Ian, *Swan River Letters Vol.1* Swan River Press, 2002

Australia was the missing *Ridderschap van Holland* (Knighthood of Holland) which had a crew of around 300 as well as two passengers.

In 1694 the ship sailed for Batavia but did not reach its destination and was never heard from again. Some historians believe that the ship may have been wrecked off the west coast of Australia. There is some evidence from both south and north of Perth that this may have been the case. There is little doubt that she encountered a violent storm. Fearing being smashed upon the cliffs of the Western Australian coast, the captain may have decided to sail below the mainland and across the Great Australian Bight.

Finding a landing along this coast is almost impossible with sheer cliffs marking the coastline until South Australia. Fowlers Bay was one of the few locations that a ship could make a safe landing. Therefore it remains a possibility that Hiddens was right. That is, that Palm Valley was the site of an early Dutch colony.

Until the discovery of a shipwreck is made in Fowlers Bay, there is not enough evidence to confirm Hiddens' theory. However, even if evidence does come forth confirming the existence of Dutch settlers at Palm Valley, I disagree with the connection Hiddens has made with the Leeds Mercury article and the *Discovery of a White Colony*.

The Leeds Mercury article, if confirmed, rewrites Australia's history making our first European settlers arriving not in 1788 but in 1656. The sensational article is enclosed in full below without alteration or editing. It includes spelling errors. However, the words in bold type are the author's.

JANUARY 25, 1834

ORIGINAL ESSAY.

DISCOVERY OF A WHITE COLONY ON THE NORTHERN SHORE OF NEW HOLLAND.

A Correspondent living near Halifax has favoured us with the following interesting communication:

TO THE EDITORS OF THE LEEDS MERCURY.

GENTLEMEN,– A friend of mine lately arrived from Singapore, via India overland, having been one of a party who landed at Raffles Bay, on the north coast of New Holland, on the 10th of April, 1832, and made a two months' excursion into the interior, has permitted me to copy the following extract out of his private journal, which I think contains some particulars of a highly interesting nature, and not generally known.

The exploring party was promoted by a scientific Society at Singapore, aided and patronized by the Local Government, and its object was both commercial and geographical; but it was got up with the greatest secrecy, and remained secret to all except the parties concerned. (For what good purpose it is impossible to conceive :–)

Extract from an unpublished manuscript Journal of an exploring party in Northern Australia, by Lieutenant Nixon.

"May 15th, 1832.--On reaching the summit of the hill, no words can express the astonishment, delight, and wonder I felt at the magical change of scenery, after having travelled for so many days over nothing but barren hills and rocks, and sands and parching plains, without seeing a single tribe of aborigines excepting those on the sea coast, and having to dig for water every day.

"Looking to the southwards, I saw below me, at the distance of about three or four miles, a low and level country, laid out as it were in plantations, with straight rows of trees, through which a broad sheet of smooth water extended in nearly a direct line from east to west, as far as the eye could reach to the westward, but apparently sweeping to the southward at its eastern extremity like a river; and near its banks, at one particular spot on the south side, there appeared to be a group of habitations, embosomed in a grove of tall trees like palms. The water I guessed to be about half a mile wide, and although the stream was clearly open for two thirds of the distance from the southern bank, the remainder of it was studded by thousands of little islands stretching along its northern shores: and what fixed me to the spot with indescribable sensations of rapture and admiration was the number of small boats or canoes with one or two persons in each, gliding along the narrow chanels (sic) between the little islands in every direction, some of which appeared to be fishing or drawing nets. None of them had a sail, but one that was floating down the body of the stream without wind, which seemed to denote that a current ran from east to west. It seemed as if enchantment had brought me into a civilized country, and I could scarcely resolve to leave the spot I stood upon, had it not been for the overpowering rays of a mid day sun, affecting my bowels, as it frequently had done, during all the journey.

"On reaching the bottom of the hill in my return to our party at the tents, I was just turning round a low rock, when **I came suddenly upon a human being whose face was so fair and dress so white**, that I was for a moment staggered with terror, and thought that I was looking upon an apparition. I had naturally expected to meet an Indian as black or brown as the rest of the natives, and not a white man in these unexplored regions. Still quaking with doubts about the integrity of my eyes, I proceeded on, and saw the apparition advancing upon me with the most perfect indifference: in another minute he was quite near, and I now perceived that he had not yet seen me, for he was walking slowly and pensively with his eyes fixed on the ground, and he appeared to be a young man of a handsome and interesting countenance. We were got within four paces of each other when he heaved a deep and tremulous sigh, raised his eyes, and in an instant uttered a loud exclamation and fell insensible on the ground. My fears had now given place to sympathy, and I hastened to assist the unknown, who, I felt convinced, had been struck with the idea of seeing a supernatural being. It was a considerable time before he recovered and was assured of my mortality; and from a few expressions in old Dutch, which he uttered, I was luckily enabled to hold some conversation with him; for I had been at school in Holland in my youth and not quite forgotten the language. Badly as he spoke Dutch, yet I gathered from him a few particulars of a most extraordinary nature; namely, that **he belonged to a small community, all as white as himself, he said about three hundred; that they lived in houses enclosed all together within a great wall to defend them from black men; that their fathers came there about one hundred and seventy years ago, as they said, from a distant land across the great sea; and that their ship broke, and eighty men and ten of their sisters (female passengers?) with many things were saved on shore.** I prevailed on him to accompany me to my party, who I knew would be glad to be introduced to his friends before we set out on our return to our ship at **Port Raffles,**[5] from which place we were now distant nearly five hundred miles, and our time was limited to a fixed period so as to enable the ship to carry us back to Singapore before the change of the monsoon. The young man's dress consisted of a round jacket and large breeches, both made of skins, divested of the hair and bleached as white as linen; and on his head he wore a tall white skin cap with a brim covered over with white down or the small feathers of the white cocatoo. The latitude of this mountain was eighteen degrees thirty minutes fourteen seconds south; and longitude one hundred and thirty-two degrees twenty-five minutes thirty seconds east. It was christened Mount Singapore, after the name and in honour of the settlement to which the expedition belonged."

A subsequent part of the journal states further, "that on our party visiting the **white village**, the joy of the simple inhabitants was quite extravagant. The descendant of an officer is looked up to as chief, and with him (whose name is Van Baerle), the party remained eight days. Their traditional history is, that their fathers were compelled by famine, after the loss of their great vessel, to travel towards the rising sun, carrying with them as much of the stores as they could, during which many died; and by the wise advice of their ten sisters they crossed a ridge of land, and meeting with a rivulet on the other side, followed its course and were led to the spot they now inhabit, where they have continued ever since. They have no animals of the domestic kind, either cows, sheep, pigs or any thing else; their plantations consist only of maize and yams, and these with fresh and dried fish constitute their principal food, which is changed occasionally for Kangaroo and other game; but it appears that they frequently experience a scarcity and shortness of provisions, most probably owing to ignorance and mismanagement; and had little or nothing to offer us now except skins. They are nominal Christians: their marriages are performed without any

---

[5] At the beginning of the article, Raffles Bay is mentioned as the starting point. However, there is an unconscious slip up probably made by Stirling, in now calling it Port Raffles. Stirling had helped set up Port Raffles in 1827.

ceremony: all the elders sit in council to manage their affairs; all the young, from ten up to a certain age, are considered a standing militia, and are armed with long pikes; they have no books or paper, nor any schools; they retain a certain observance of the sabbath by refraining from their daily labours, and perform a short superstitious ceremony on that day all together; and **they may be considered almost a new race of beings.**" [1]

Comparing Leeds Mercury Article with *Vergulde Draeck*

The *Vergulde Draeck* sank in 1656. The Leeds Mercury article states that, *their fathers came there about one hundred and seventy years ago, as they said, from a distant land across the great sea; and that their ship broke ...* The timeframe fits in far better than any other shipwreck along the Western Australian coast. The *Vergulde Draeck* sank 176 years before 1832, that's *about one hundred and seventy years ago*. The Netherlands is *from a distant land across the great sea* and *Vergulde Draeck* also broke after striking the reef.

The calculation that *eighty men and ten of their sisters (female passengers?)* [Dale's assumption] *with many things were saved on shore* was also very close to the 79 *Vergulde Draeck* survivors. The Leeds Mercury total adds up to 90 survivors. In 1657, two rescue ships arrived in search of the survivors. The extra eleven could be accounted for by the 11 men from the *Goede Hoop* who were sent ashore to search for the survivors. Unfortunately the rescue boat was smashed in the heavy surf. Unwilling to risk any more men, the *Goede Hoop* sailed away leaving the eleven sailors marooned. The second rescue ship sighted shelters left by the survivors as well as men in their shelters. The 11 from the *Goede Hoop* plus the original 79 *Vergulde Draeck* make exactly 90, the same number given in the Leeds Mercury article.

Eventually the survivors could wait no longer along the beach without sufficient food or water. A report stated that *they had got out of the wreck very few victuals and fresh water* and that they were consequently *about to go inland after the departure of the mentioned schuyt (sailing boat), where we very much hope they will have found provisions and drinking water*. According to the Leeds Mercury, *their fathers were compelled by famine, after the loss of their great vessel, to travel towards the rising sun ... and by the wise advice of their sisters they crossed a ridge of land, and meeting with a rivulet on the other side, followed its course and were led to a spot they now inhabit, where they have continued ever since.*

Travelling towards the rising sun meant that they travelled in an easterly direction and the only river that they could have met was the Moore River. Coins from the *Vergulde Draeck* wreck have subsequently been found in various locations along the Moore River[2].

The Leeds Mercury article refers to the Dutch survivors as growing *plantations consisting of maize and yams*. In this part of south western Australia, we know that there was a deliberate planting of yams which grew no where else in Australia. This yam is known as the *Dioscorea hastifolia* and is related to yams in South Africa. It was also popular in the Dutch East Indies in the seventeenth century. These types of yams were often taken on board the Dutch ships as a food supply during long sea voyages. In 1836, George Fletcher Moore, the man who discovered the Moore River, described a bulbous root called Conne by the natives which was almost the size of a large potato.

---

[1] Leeds Mercury, 1834, *Discovery of a white colony on the northern shore of New Holland*, 25 January.

[2] Moore River on following page, photo by Henry Van Zanden

In the same year, Moore had come across a native and his "cardo" (wife). She is described as a young woman of a very pleasing countenance, and something of **European features**, and long, wavy, almost **flaxen-coloured** hair[8]. [flaxen – pale yellowish to yellowish brown colour] [Author's emphasis].

The Moore River

Raffles Bay

The Leeds Mercury article claimed the Expedition had set off from Raffles Bay.

A friend of mine lately arrived from Singapore, via India overland, having been one of a party who landed at Raffles Bay, on the north coast of New Holland, on the 10th of April, 1832, and made a two months' excursion into the interior.

Port Raffles, from which place we were now distant nearly five hundred miles ... [804 km]

Raffles Bay suddenly becomes Port Raffles, a place that Stirling had helped to set up in 1827. The 39th Regiment mentioned in the journal also happened to be there as well.

The first attempt at colonization was in 1825, when an expedition from Sydney, consisting of a detachment of the 39th Regiment ... landed in Albany[9].

Although Ensign Marmaduke George Nixon, was not at Port Raffles, he had served with the 39th Regiment.

Located on the Cobourg Peninsula in the Northern Territory, it was named by the explorer Phillip King in 1818 after Sir Thomas Raffles, the founder of Singapore. However, disease, attacks by Aboriginals and the negative reports London received from Commandant Smythe, its first commander, caused the settlement to be closed down in 1829. Therefore the expedition could not

---

[8] *Extracts from the letters and journals of George Fletcher Moore*

[9] MacDevitt, EO. *Handbook of Western Australia: Being a Short Account of its History, Resources, Scope for Settlement, and Land Laws*. p5.Published Perth [W.A.]: Sands & McDougall, 1897

have departed from Port Raffles. Port Raffles was a name used to hide the real starting point of the expedition: Albany.

Albany

The Swan River Colony didn't have a reliable port in their early years and so had to rely on the very distant port of Albany which was the colony's only deepwater port. The construction of Fremantle Harbour was not completed until 1893. Albany was founded in 1826 and like Raffles Bay was set up as a military outpost to check possible French ambitions but was initially named Frederickstown after King George III's son, Prince Frederick, Duke of York and Albany. After 1831, Frederickstown was transferred to the control of the Swan River Colony and renamed Albany by Governor James Stirling at the beginning of 1832. Stirling assumed the political authority of Albany in 1832.

Albany[10] was settled three years before the Swan River Colony. Therefore there could only be one port in Western Australia in 1832 from which an expedition could possibly depart and that was Albany.

Coincidentally Albany is about five hundred miles [804 km] from the Karakin Lakes if they followed the path that every explorer took from Perth. That is, after travelling first from Albany to Perth, they travelled in a ENE direction to York before turning in a NNW direction. The geography fits well with the story of the Lost White Tribe and the *Vergulde Draeck* survivors. Albany and not Port Raffles was the point of departure of the expedition. However, the longitude and latitude coordinates did not fit well with Western Australia as the location.

Map of the south-western corner of Western Australia

---

[10] Historical Map of the Australian Colonies in the 19th Century. University of Texas at Austin. From the Cambridge Modern History Atlas, 1912.

JANUARY 25, 1834.

ORIGINAL ESSAY.

DISCOVERY OF A WHITE COLONY ON THE NORTHERN SHORE OF NEW HOLLAND.

A Correspondent living near Halifax has favoured us with the following interesting communication:—

TO THE EDITORS OF THE LEEDS MERCURY.

GENTLEMEN,—A friend of mine, lately arrived from Singapore, via India overland, having been one of a party who landed at Raffles Bay, on the north coast of New Holland, on the 10th of April, 1832, and made a two months' excursion into the interior, has permitted me to copy the following extract out of his private journal, which I think contains some particulars of a highly interesting nature, and not generally known.

The exploring party was promoted by a scientific Society at Singapore, aided and patronized by the Local Government, and its object was both commercial and geographical; but it was got up with the greatest secrecy, and remained secret to all except the parties concerned. (For what good purpose it is impossible to conceive :—)

Extract from an unpublished manuscript Journal of an exploring party in Northern Australia, by Lieutenant Nixon.

"May 15th, 1832.—On reaching the summit of the hill, no words can express the astonishment, delight, and wonder I felt at the magical change of scenery, after having travelled for so many days over nothing but barren hills and rocks, and sands and parching plains, without seeing a single tribe of aborigines excepting those on the sea coast, and having to dig for water every day.

"Looking to the southwards, I saw below me, at the distance of about three or four miles, a low and level country, laid out as it were in plantations, with straight rows of trees, through which a broad sheet of smooth water extended in nearly a direct line from east to west, as far as the eye could reach to the westward, but apparently sweeping to the southward at its eastern extremity like a river; and near its banks, at one particular spot on the south side, there appeared to be a group of habitations, embosomed in a grove of tall trees like palms. The water I guessed to be about half a mile wide, and although the stream was clearly open for two thirds of the distance from the southern bank, the remainder of it was studded by thousands of little islands stretching along its northern shores; and what fixed me to the spot with indescribable sensations of rapture and admiration was the number of small boats or canoes with one or two persons in each, gliding along the narrow channels between the little islands in every direction, some of which appeared to be fishing or drawing nets. None of them had a sail, but one that was floating down the body of the stream without wind, which seemed to denote that a current ran from east to west. It seemed as if enchantment had brought me into a civilized country, and I could scarcely resolve to leave the spot I stood upon, had it not been for the overpowering rays of a mid day sun, affecting my bowels, as it frequently had done, during all the journey.

"On reaching the bottom of the hill in my return to our party at the tents, I was just turning round a low rock, when I came suddenly upon a human being whose face was so fair and dress so white, that I was for a moment staggered with terror, and thought that I was looking upon an apparition. I had naturally expected to meet an Indian as black or brown as the rest of the natives, and not a white man in these unexplored regions. Still quaking with doubts about the integrity of my eyes, I proceeded on, and saw the apparition advancing upon me with the most perfect indifference: in another minute he was quite near, and I now perceived that he had not yet seen me, for he was walking slowly and pensively with his eyes fixed on the ground, and he appeared to be a young man of a handsome and interesting countenance. We were got within four paces of each other when he heaved a deep and tremulous sigh, raised his eyes, and in an instant uttered a loud exclamation and fell insensible on the ground. My fears had now given place to sympathy, and I hastened to assist the unknown, who, I felt convinced, had been struck with the idea of seeing a supernatural being. It was a considerable time before he recovered and was assured of my mortality; and from a few expressions in old Dutch, which he uttered, I was luckily enabled to hold some conversation with him; for I had been at school in Holland in my youth and not quite forgotten the language. Badly as he spoke Dutch, yet I gathered from him a few particulars of a most extraordinary nature; namely, that he belonged to a small community, all as white as himself, he said about three hundred; that they lived in houses enclosed all together within a great wall to defend them from black men; that their fathers came there about one hundred and seventy years ago, as they said, from a distant land across the great sea; and that their ship broke, and eighty men and ten of their sisters (female passengers?) with many things were saved on shore. I prevailed on him to accompany me to my party, who I knew would be glad to be introduced to his friends before we set out on our return to our ship at Port Raffles, from which place we were now distant nearly five hundred miles, and our time was limited to a fixed period so as to enable the ship to carry us back to Singapore before the change of the monsoon. The young man's dress consisted of a round jacket and large breeches, both made of skins, divested of the hair and bleached as white as linen; and on his head he wore a tall white skin cap with a brim covered over with white down or the small feathers of the white cockatoo. The latitude of this mountain was eighteen degrees thirty minutes fourteen seconds south; and longitude one hundred and thirty-two degrees twenty-five minutes thirty seconds east. It was christened Mount Singapore, after the name and in honour of the settlement to which the expedition belonged."

A subsequent part of the journal states further, that on our party visiting the white village, the joy of the simple inhabitants was quite extravagant. The descendant of an officer is looked up to as chief, and with him (whose name is Van Baerle,) the party remained eight days. Their traditional history is, that their fathers were compelled by famine, after the loss of their great vessel, to travel towards the rising sun, carrying with them as much of the stores as they could, during which many died; and by the wise advice of their ten sisters they crossed a ridge of land, and meeting with a rivulet on the other side, followed its course and were led to the spot they now inhabit, where they have continued ever since. They have no animals of the domestic kind, either cows, sheep, pigs or any thing else; their plantations consist only of maize and yams, and these with fresh and dried fish constitute their principal food, which is changed occasionally for Kangaroo and other game; but it appears that they frequently experience scarcity and shortness of provisions, most probably owing to ignorance and mismanagement; and had little or nothing to offer us now except skins. They are nominal Christians; their marriages are performed without any ceremony; all the elders sit in council to manage their affairs; all the young, from ten up to a certain age, are considered a standing militia, and are armed with long pikes; they have no books or paper, nor any schools; they retain a certain observance of the sabbath by refraining from their daily labours, and perform a short superstitious ceremony on that day all together; and they may be considered almost a new race of beings."

EXTRAORDINARY PROCEEDING IN CANADA—The House of Assembly of Upper Canada have expelled Mr. W. Mackenzie, returned as Representative for the county of York a fourth time, for no other reason than that he is the proprietor of a newspaper, in which at different times have appeared comments & strictures that unpalatable to them. This seems a strange proceeding. Mr. Mackenzie, who is thus expelled, without any other cause than that the Assembly do not like to have a newspaper proprietor among them, is the Representative of a wealthy, large, and populous county. Were the Canadian Assembly satisfied with the people, no motion for his expulsion could be listened to for a moment; but the party interested in the continuance of all abuses obtain majorities in the poor and thinly peopled districts, which are subject to an improper [...]. It is by availing themselves of the inequalities in [...]

The Leeds Mercury Article, January 25, 1834

Chapter 5
Prime Meridian

Teide Volcano on the island of Tenerife in the Canary Islands. Image taken aboard the space shuttle Endeavour, 11 October, 1994 on a joint mission of the German, Italian and United States space agencies. It is part of NASA's Mission to Planet Earth. bruce.chapman@jpl.nasa.gov

Prime Meridian

The Prime Meridian – zero degrees – was not always through Greenwich, England. The prime meridian used by the Dutch, was different to the prime meridian used by the English. To further complicate matters, it even varied from map to map. Some navigators used Tenerife in the Canary Islands whereas others used Corvo Island, Flores or San Miguel in the Azores. Other captains used Boa Vista in the Cape Verde Islands, Fuerteventura in the Canary Islands or Cape Verde as their Prime Meridian.

Europa[1] *The Prime Meridian can be seen on the left of the map.*

As early as the second century AD Ptolemy considered the definition of the zero meridian to be the most western-position of the known world. Thus it comes as no surprise that the prime meridian was later located at El Hiero, the smallest and furthest south and west of the Canary Islands. In fact its nickname is 'Isla del Meridiano' or the 'Meridian Island'. The western end of El Hiero was for a long time considered by Europeans to be the end of the known world. Therefore it became the Prime Meridian for many European countries for quite some time.

However, El Hiero was replaced by the island of Tenerife which was to become the most popular prime meridian due to its mountain peak rising to 3,718 m. Seamen believed that this mountain was the highest in the world. Using This is quite significant because a different prime meridian would

---

[1] *Europa*, Harmen Janszoon en Marten, 1610 From Henry Davis Consulting hdavis@ix.netcom.com

shift the location of the Dutch colony in Australia further to the west. Tenerife, was 16° 34´ west of Greenwich. On the Western Australian map, this would shift the longitude from 132° 25´ 30¨ E, to 115° 40´ 30¨ E. In the 1838 map[2] of the upper reaches of exploration of the Colony, the Karakin Lakes (spelt L. Garagan on the map) are about 115° 40´ E longitude. Not only does the west coast of Australia come into view, but also the Karakin Lakes!

On the Swan River Colony map, the longitude fits exactly. The longitude meridian on the map below is 116°. However, on other maps from the 1830s, the longitude varies by up to 15´.

The latitude as written in the Leeds Mercury article still presents a puzzle. *The latitude of this mountain was eighteen degrees thirty minutes fourteen secs south*[3]. Unfortunately this latitude would place the settlement in the middle of the ocean.

---

[2] 1838 map of the northern most section of the Swan River Colony. Map by Arrowsmith

[3] Leeds Mercury article.

Governor Stirling and the 'Lost Dutch Tribe'

In 2001, the VOC Historical Society and Shell Petroleum had sponsored an expedition to investigate the possibility that the Lost Tribe was located somewhere along the Murchison River[1], possibly Lake Wolleen. My fellow explorer, Johnny de Leeuw and I chartered a plane from Kalbarri, followed the course of the river and landed at Lake Wolleen. However, there was little there to resemble the description of the settlement given in the Leeds Mercury.

Arriving back in Sydney, I lost no time in renewing my research in the rare book section of the Mitchell Library. In particular, I searched for clues in the explorers' journals especially those compiled by Joseph Cross. I felt that the answer must lie somewhere in these journals. Cross had accompanied Governor Stirling back to England not long after the Lost Dutch Tribe had been discovered. He had with him all the journals of explorers in Western Australia which must have also included the journal of the Lost Dutch Tribe.

Having previously been unable to gain any concessions from the British Government for the colony, Stirling arrived back to the Swan River Colony in triumph. Not only had he gained significant concessions, but he arrived back with a knighthood.

Was it Stirling who leaked the journal to the Leeds Mercury newspaper?

The Leeds Mercury article stated that the expedition was promoted and sponsored by an Agricultural Society. It was probably no coincidence that Stirling was the chief promoter of the 'Agricultural and Horticultural Society of Western Australia'. Therefore it was more than worthwhile to have a studied look into the minutes of the society and compare it to the article.

The exploring party was promoted by a scientific Society at Singapore, aided and patronised by the Local government and its object was both commercial and geographical; but it was got up with the greatest secrecy, and remained secret to all except parties concerned. (for what good purpose it is impossible to conceive)[2].

The patron was none other than James Stirling, Lieutenant-Governor of the Swan River Colony of an ever dwindling colony of very disappointed adventurers.

Continued attacks on the colony's food supplies, such as cattle, sheep, pigs, wheat and flour, sent food prices rocketing. Under the leadership of the Aboriginal chief Yagan, the future of the entire colony was under threat. The attacks, assaults and murders of white settlers only increased their anxiety. By 1832, the colony was in dire straits and desperately short of food.

John Morgan, the Colonial Storekeeper wrote to the Under Secretary informing him that, *The colony is at this moment in my opinion in a state of perilous in the extreme ... At the moment there*

---

[1] Map of Murchison River from Wikipedia

[2] Leeds Mercury

is not more than five tons of flour in the Colony ... should no other vessels arrive during the next fourteen days, the people will generally be in a state of absolute starvation[6].

With the colony's future in question, Stirling sent out explorers to find the rich and profitable promised land not only to lift the hopes of the existing colonists, but also to provide more incentive for the British Government to invest more money and manpower in a colony that they expected to fail. Seventeen expeditions were undertaken between July 1829 and July 1832 around the south western corner of Western Australia. One of these explorers was Ensign Robert Dale who took part in at least seven of these expeditions.

These expeditions were outlined in a book written by Joseph Cross[7]. This publication was taken back to England by Stirling hurriedly leaving Western Australia in September, 1832 with Dale's journal – all 200 pages –- perhaps to use as a bargaining tool for more government support for the struggling Western Australian colony.

Stirling couldn't just leave the colony without permission. He had to provide a very good reason for abandoning his post. Stirling's first attempt occurred in March, 1832 when he attempted to persuade the Executive Council that he should return to England. Not all agreed as Captain Irwin had already been given permission to return to England. Many of the Councillors thought that Stirling should remain and instead, allow Irwin to press the Colony's case for assistance. Too many opposed his departure that he reluctantly agreed to stay.

However, just a few months later at an Executive Council meeting on 29 June, the same people who were most opposed to Stirling's departure in March, *had now become the most strongest advisors of the measure*[8]. There seemed to be no logical explanation to explain the change of mind. Stirling had organised food to be brought in from Van Diemen's Land,[9] thus relieving the food shortage. If anything, the situation had now improved. What event changed their minds?

On 10 April Dale had set out on his journey to discover the Lost White Tribe. It is described as a two month's excursion. Therefore this colony of Dutchmen was discovered in May. When Dale arrived back to Perth in late June, Stirling organised an Executive Council meeting. Here he exposed the story of the Lost Dutch Tribe enunciating the implications this had for all of the Swan River settlers. It's hardly surprising that those who were previously most opposed to Stirling leaving the colony were now the strongest proponents.

The local Fremantle newspaper thought that there was more to his departure than seeking immediate food relief from England. The paper wrote, *With real sorrow we announce that his Excellency the Governor has intimated by Public Notice his intention to proceed to*

---

[6] Drew-Statham, Pamela, *James Stirling, Admiral and Founding Governor of Western Australia*. p212

[7] Cross, Joseph, *Journals of Several Expeditions made in Western Australia during the years 1829, 1830, 1831, and 1832, under the sanction of the Governor, Sir James Stirling*

[8] Arthur Papers ML A2209 f35, *Collie Letters and Morgan Letters re the lady, and Stirling to Governor*. Arthur, 10 August 1832 that leave had been approved.

[9] Van Diemen's Land named by its discoverer, Abel Tasman in 1642 later renamed Tasmania.

England immediately. There is a vast deal more to this arrangement, we apprehend, than meets the public eye.

According to Mary Durack, the British Government was very unhappy with Stirling.

It was revealed that Stirling was given a very cool welcome by the Government. They were unhappy that he had left his post without permission. He was also criticised for his lack of system in the allocation of land grants[10].

Initially Stirling had little success until the mysterious appearance of extracts of Nixon's journal appeared in not only the Leeds Mercury (January 1834), but also *The Scotsman*, a Liverpool paper and even in Cape Town and Perth itself. Two Dutch papers, *Nederlandisch Magazijn* (1837) and although 17 years later, *Tijdschrift voor Nederlandsch Indie* (1851), also picked up the story. The story in the Dutch newspaper was possibly run in response to Britain's decision to begin the transportation of convicts to Western Australia in 1851.

However, there were other factors involved in the Government wishing to keep the story of a lost Dutch Settlement in Western Australia a secret. British politics was at the heart and core of its secrecy.

At the time of Stirling arriving in England, the middle and working classes were in power from 1830 to 1834. Known as the Whigs, their period in office was extremely turbulent. During these four years, England suffered from an economic recession with a budget deficit of £2.5 million. The banking system and business suffered a loss of confidence and a trade deficit existed.

Sir Robert Peel (1788 – 1850)[11]

Their political opponents were called the Tories also know as the Conservatives. The Government's main opponent within the Tory party was Robert Peel, one of the most important men in Britain during the nineteenth century dominating parliament between 1830 and 1850.

At the time of Stirling's arrival, the British Government decided to take advantage of a rebellion in the Netherlands where the Catholic south wished to proclaim independence from the Protestant north. By confiscating Dutch ships and cargo, the Government hoped to reduce some of its £2.5 million deficit. It was nothing short of Government-sponsored piracy.

ORDER IN COUNCIL
At the Court at St. James's, the 6th day of November, 1832,
Present, The King's Most Excellent Majesty, in Council.
It is this day ordered by His Majesty, by and with the advice of his Privy Council, that no ships or vessels belonging to any of His Majesty's subjects be permitted to enter and clear

---

[10] Durack, Mary, *To Be Heirs Forever,* Printed by Constable & Co Ltd, 1976

[11] Portrait of Sir Robert Peel, Wikimedia Commons

out for any of the ports within the dominions of the King of the Netherlands until further orders.

And His Majesty is further pleased to order that a general embargo or stop be made of all ships and vessels whatsoever, belonging to the subjects of the King of the Netherlands, now within, or which shall hereafter come into, any of the ports, harbours, or roads within any part of His Majesty's dominions, together with all persons and effects on board such ships or vessels, and that the commanders of His Majesty's ships of war do detain and bring into port, all merchant ships and vessels bearing the flag of the Netherlands; but that the utmost care be taken for the preservation of all and every part of the cargoes on board any of the said ships or vessels, so that no damage or embezzlement whatever be sustained, and the commanders of His Majesty's ships of war are hereby instructed to detain and bring into port every such ship and vessel accordingly.

Peel's Opposition to the Piracy of Dutch Ships

Peel was a staunch opponent of the declaration and fiercely attacked the embargo in parliament criticising the ***forcible seizure on the open seas, by his Majesty's ships of war, of all merchant vessels bearing the flag of the Netherlands—and the sequestration of their cargo***. [Author's emphasis] *This Order in Council assigns no reason whatever for so violent a proceeding; it merely states, that it is by order of his Majesty, with the advice of his Privy Council, that restrictions are imposed on our commerce with Holland, and vessels belonging to a nation at peace with this country are to be forcibly detained ...*

I maintain they cannot—that there is no proof, no presumption even, that this embargo, as it is called, was imposed, or is now continued, either as a measure of necessary precaution to protect our own vessels from seizure in Holland, or as the means of redress for injuries sustained by British subjects, or as a measure of hostility preparatory to actual war. If it can be defended on none of these grounds, the Order in Council which authorizes the embargo is an exercise of discretionary power unwarranted by the law and constitution of this country, and at direct variance with the public law of nations ...

Why is it that for thirteen weeks British commerce has been suspended, and the armed vessels of his Majesty have been ordered to seize on the trading vessels of a friendly power?

We revert for our precedents to ages of barbarism, when injuries and measures of retaliation were directed—not against the State—but against the innocent subjects of that State. At this period, when we discountenance plunder by armies on land, are we, in England, to encourage it by sea upon defenceless traders? I say that these acts and decrees are the acts and decrees of barbarism, and not of civilization. You seize upon vessels proceeding from a Dutch colony to Holland, the captains of which have never heard of your dispute with their country, and received no notice whatever of the hazard which they run! You do not authorize the detention of vessels of war. No; you reverse the practice which this country has followed in former instances, by making war, not upon armed vessels, but defenceless merchant ships; and you not only take possession of those in our own ports, but seize upon others on the open sea ...

It may be, and probably is, that the real motive for this Order in Council is the hope that the severities which it authorizes will indispose the people of Holland towards their own Government and thus coerce that Government into submission to our will.[12]

---

[12] British Hansard, *Embargo on the Dutch Trade Vol 15 cc770-831*, 15 February, 1833

No governing political party wants to provide the opposition with ammunition that they can use to both attack and embarrass them. The story of a lost Dutch Settlement in Western Australia placed a serious question over the legality of England's annexation of New Holland in 1829.

Stirling's Knighthood

It was in April, 1833 that Stirling became Sir James Stirling. Possibly the Government tried to placate Stirling by making him a knight. If they had hoped that he would now quietly go back to Perth, they were mistaken. Stirling continued to lobby the cash-strapped government for greater support.

The Secretary of State, Lord Goderich[13] (afterwards Earl of Ripon) writing in 1833 with a veiled reference to Stirling, said:
The present settlement at Swan River owes its origin, as you may perhaps be aware, to certain false rumours which had reached the Government of the intention of a foreign power to establish a colony on the west coast of Australia. The design was for some time given up entirely on the ground of public economy, and would not have been resumed but for the offer of a party of gentlemen to embark in an undertaking of this nature at their own risk, upon receiving extensive grants of land and on a certain degree of protection and assistance for a limited period being secured to them by this Government[14].

Stirling knew how to use the press to further his ambitions. In 1828, Stirling had just been turned down by the British Government to begin his colony in New Holland (Western Australia). It was actually an annexation of New Holland from the Netherlands.

*On the 2nd May, 1829, Captain Fremantle hoisted the British flag on the south head of the Swan River, and **took possession of "all that part of New Holland** which is not included within the territory of New South Wales, ..."* [Author's emphasis]

*For a fuller account of the discovery and **annexation** of Western Australia ...* [15]

For a whole year Stirling lobbied the Colonial Office helped by some deliberate leaks to the British newspapers so that his scheme would become the talking point throughout the country. Stirling was able to sway public opinion into believing that the French were about to take over New Holland. Public pressure became overwhelming and the government bowed to public opinion. However, it would not bear any of the expenses.

His Majesty's Government do not intend to incur any expense in conveying settlers to the New Colony on the Swan River; and they will not feel bound to defray the expense of supplying them

---

[13] Portrait of Lord Goderich by an unknown author but who died in 1830. National Portrait Gallery, London

[14] Rusden, GW, *History of Australia volume 1* p326, Chapman and Hall, Limited, 1883

[15] Commonwealth Bureau of Census and Statistics Melbourne. Official Year Book of the Commonwealth of Australia, No. 17.– 1924. p5

with provisions or other necessaries after their arrival there, nor to assist their removal to England or elsewhere should they be desirous of quitting the colony[16].

The British Government bowed to public pressure but had made it clear that once Britain established the settlement, they were on their own. The British Government was reluctant to upset their most important ally in Europe. To emphasise this special relationship, the Prime Minister, Lord Liverpool, stated the following in 1823: *there existed on our part a more special obligation to defend the Netherlands than any other kingdom or state in Europe[17].*

New Holland was formally annexed by Sir Charles Fremantle in 2 May, 1829. Unfortunately, the existence of 300 Dutch settlers could have spoilt the party.

Discovery of the Map of the Lost White Tribe

Thinking that there had to be something in this journal to link the newspaper article, Stirling and the discovery of a white colony, I poured through the journals searching for a clue linking Dale to the Lost Dutch Tribe.

The Missing Link

1832 was the missing link. There was no recorded expedition by Dale or anyone else in April/May 1832. Stirling had taken the original manuscripts of Joseph Cross back to England to be published. Could he have deliberately omitted the April/May journal describing Dale's amazing discovery? His last reported expedition was in January and was made from King George's Sound. However, there was one very obvious omission: 200 pages of Dale's journal. The entire book, *Journals of Several Expeditions made in Western Australia during the years 1829, 1830, 1831* edited by Joseph Cross was barely over 200 pages. Most of Dale's 200 page journal was missing.

A sentence, a word, a footnote – there had to be something that might reveal the location of the Lost White Tribe. As I sat carefully leafing through the original edition by Joseph Cross in the Mitchell Library, I wondered if there could have been a slip up somewhere that made an oblique reference to Dale's last expedition. Although I found some interesting descriptions of aboriginal cave drawings alluding to the rays of the sun, there was nothing. Nothing, that is, until I found neatly inserted into an envelope at the back of the book, a very flimsy but also a very large map. Unfolding before my eyes was the proof I was looking for: Dale's elusive expedition.

Immediately my eyes fixated upon the top half of the map for I had already decided that the only logical place for a lost white colony was north of Perth, somewhere between the Moore River and possibly as far as the Murchison River. After already investigating the Murchison River theory in 2001, I came to the conclusion that the best bet would have been the survivors of the *Vergulde Draeck*, wrecked in 1656. Thus it was hardly surprising that my eyes glanced immediately to the north-western part of the map: the Moore River. Suddenly my tiredness became excitement, no elation! In the depths of the quietness of the Mitchell Library I wanted to leap and punch the air. Instead I satisfied myself with a victory walk around the large table and a two armed stretch to reinvigorate my senses. The finding of the map was the moment that changed Australia's history. Here was the location of the Lost White Tribe! This meant that more than ever, I had to check, recheck and rethink all of my findings. I needed to check for any references to this journey.

---

[16] Hancock, Denis, *The Westerners: the making of Western Australia,* published by Bay Books, 1979

[17] van Sas, NCF, *Unspoken Allies: Anglo-Dutch Relations since 1780,* p33 Amsterdam University Press, Amsterdam, 2001

After reading the journals of the explorers once again, I found that there had been no reference to the expedition by Dale as outlined on the map. Stirling had made his slip up.

There was still one giant piece of the puzzle to work out. Where were those lakes today? Unfortunately, the map is not as accurate as a modern map and was a little misleading as to the exact position of the lakes. The coast line is almost straight on the 1832 map, but on a modern map the tip of the map lies at about 115° longitude. Thus the map was at least half a degree out. This also meant that the lakes would be at 115° and a half.

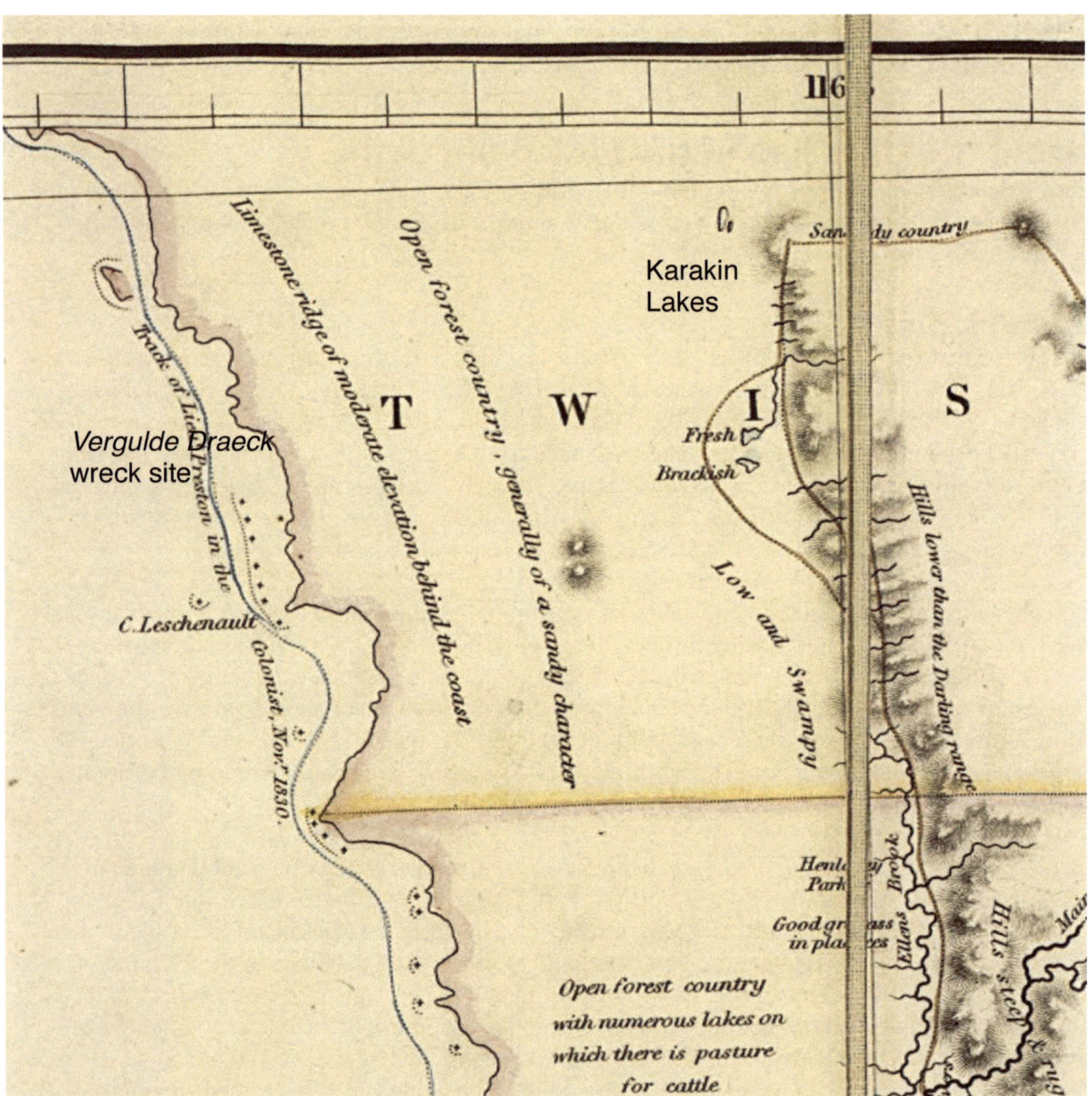

Arrowsmith, J, *Swan River Settlement*

The longitude is particularly important because, as previously discussed, the longitude given in the Leeds Mercury article, 132° 25´, was based on the zero meridian going through Greenwich. Changing it to the Tenerife Prime meridian and the real longitude becomes somewhere about the 116° mark.

The features of the map[18], such as *sandy country* correspond to the description given in the Leeds Mercury. It also reveals the direction which Dale must have come from.

After having traveled for so many days over nothing but barren hills and rocks, and **sands** *and parching plains…. Looking* **southwards** *I saw below me at the distance of three or four miles,* [5 or 6 km] *a low and level country … through which a broad sheet of smooth water extended in nearly a direct line from east to west …* [Author's emphasis]

Dale had discovered a 'Lost White Tribe' consisting of about 300 people who lived in houses *enclosed all together within a great wall*. He discovered from their leader, Van Baerle, that their ancestors had been shipwrecked '*about 170 years ago.*' (1662)[19] Eighty men and ten women made it ashore and, after suffering from hunger, they were forced to travel inland '*towards the rising sun.*' (east) After crossing a ridge and discovering a 'rivulet,' they followed its course until they

[18] The three maps are from Arrowsmith, J. *Swan River Settlement,* 1832 Digital Collections of Maps Western Australia, National Library of Australia

[19] The *Vergulde Draeck* was wrecked in 1656, an error of only six years.

arrived at the Karakin Lakes. That they would decide to build their settlement at the site of the largest permanent water in close proximity to the wreck site, is hardly surprising[20].

The fertile land that existed on the banks of the river allowed the survivors to grow *maize and yams*. The wide expanse of water not only provide fish but acted as a magnet to the native animals in search of water and green grass to graze upon. *Fresh and dried fish constitute their principal food, which is changed occasionally for kangaroo and other game*.

The scant details of the journal at least provided a starting point to the two big questions: what happened to the *Vergulde Draeck* survivors and what happened to the settlement after 1832?

Swan River Colony Map 1833 showing the extent of its Exploration

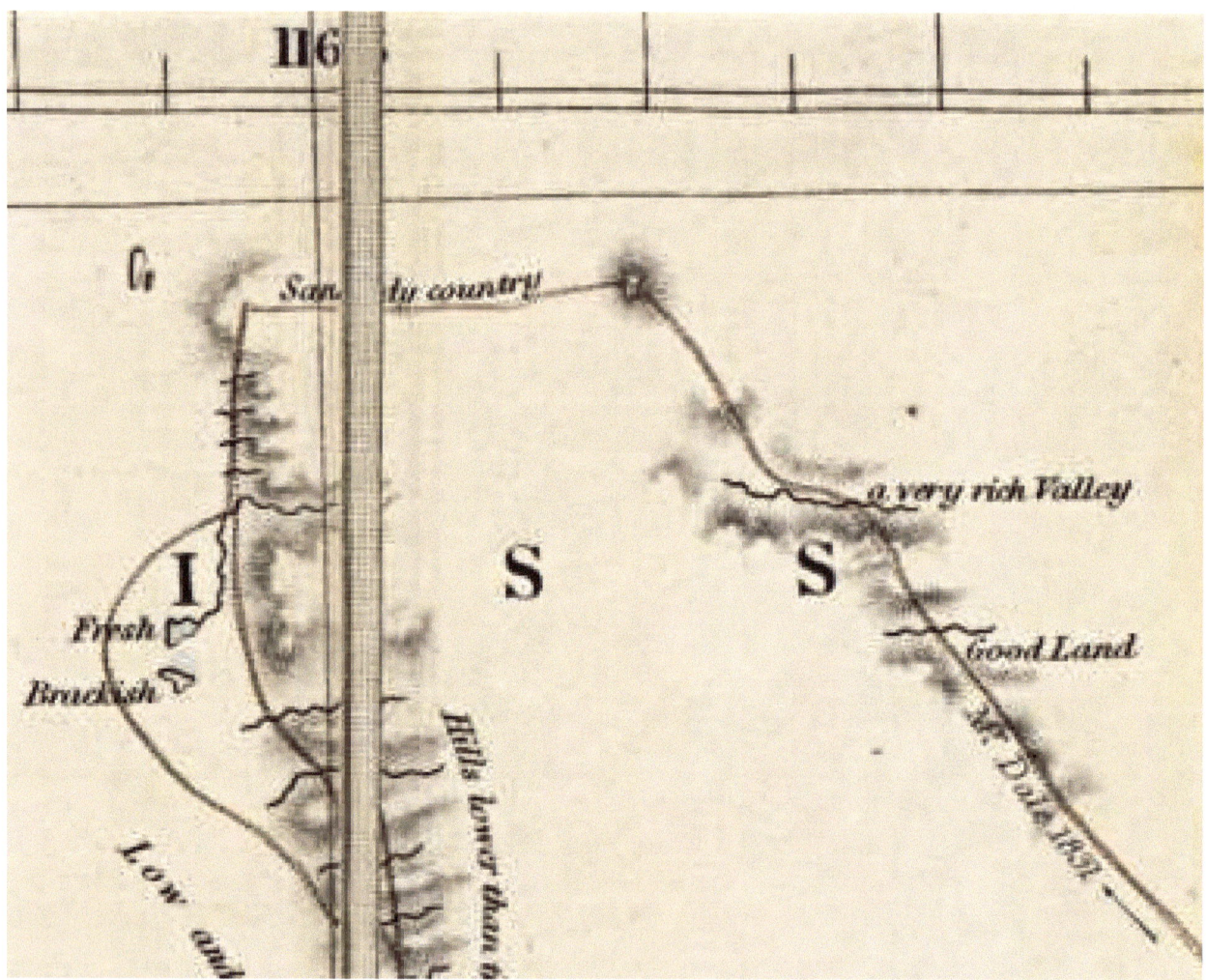

Almost all the early northern explorations travelled first in an easterly direction to York. From there they ventured in a north westerly route.

On the right hand side of this magnified version of the map, it can be clearly seen that Dale was travelling from York in a north westerly direction. He appears to have circled in a wide area around the Karakin Lakes noting that the northern most lake was fresh while another lake further to the south was brackish. This was the map of the Lost White Tribe.

---

[20] Close up of the 1832 map published in 1833 by J Arrowsmith

JOURNALS

OF

SEVERAL EXPEDITIONS

MADE IN

WESTERN AUSTRALIA

DURING THE YEARS

1829, 1830, 1831, and 1832;

UNDER THE SANCTION OF THE GOVERNOR

SIR JAMES STIRLING,

CONTAINING THE LATEST AUTHENTIC INFORMATION

RELATIVE TO THAT COUNTRY,

ACCOMPANIED BY A MAP.

LONDON:

PUBLISHED BY J.CROSS, 18, HOLBORN

AND SOLD BY ALL BOOKSELLERS.

1833

TO

HIS EXCELLENCY

SIR JAMES STIRLING,

𝕮𝖆𝖕𝖙𝖆𝖎𝖓 𝕽𝖔𝖞𝖆𝖑 𝕹𝖆𝖛𝖞,

THE FOLLOWING JOURNALS

OF

EXPEDITIONS PERFORMED IN HIS SUPERINTENDENCY AND

BY HIS DIRECTION,

ARE RESPECTFULLY INSCRIBED,

BY HIS VERY OBEDIENT

HUMBLE SERVANT,

JOSEPH CROSS.

Chapter 6
The Lost White Tribe

Beardman Jug[1] *from the wreck of the Vergulde Draeck* from the Tim Coleman collection

---

[1] Photo by Henry Van Zanden

The 'devil and the deep blue sea'

68 people including 10 women were literally caught between the devil and the deep blue sea. If they remained at the wreck site close to the sea, they would surely die of either starvation or thirst. If they travelled inland and found food, water and shelter, their chances of being rescued deteriorated. There is evidence that lonely lookouts were posted for at least two years searching the blue horizon for a rescue ship or any ship that might save them from their living hell.

Eleven others were also lost from search parties put ashore by the rescue ships *Waeckende Boey* and *Goede Hoop* bringing the possible total to 79 which is very close to the *eighty men and ten women* claimed in the Leeds Mercury article.

Author, Rupert Gerritsen came up with the following conclusion. 'If any of these people did somehow survive, especially in the longer term, they would soon have been obliged to meet and treat with regional Aboriginal groups in order to co-exist amicably at first, to sustain their survival, then later perhaps to intermarry. If that is so, it may be said that these men represent the earliest Europeans to settle on the Australian continent, albeit unwittingly, along with the two mutineers who were marooned on the mainland by Francisco Pelsaert after the *Batavia* incidents of 1629[2].'

Was their survival likely? Much is contained in Gerritsen's book to suggest that some at least did survive. He suggests that by a remote chance, (aided by the Aboriginal 'bush telegraph'), they may have even joined up with the two *Batavia* mutineers who had been abandoned on the coast less than 200 km to the north. Gerritsen also suggests that there may have been another independent group of *Vergulde Draeck* survivors who drifted ashore elsewhere on debris or makeshift rafts. Using a great deal of physical evidence to support his view, Gerritsen's argument is compelling.

In tracing what happened to the survivors before they arrived at the Karikan Lakes settlement, I based my conclusions on the archaeological and written evidence.

1963 – The *Vergulde Draeck* Wreck Site

Although there had been discoveries of coins and other artifacts on land, the wreck site remained a mystery until 1963. A teenager, Graeme Henderson, discovered a very odd artifact on the seabed while diving with his father, James, about 5 km off the coast and 12 km south of Ledge Point: an elephant tusk. What was an elephant's tusk doing at the bottom of the ocean? Of course they realised that they had stumbled onto something very big. There had to be a shipwreck nearby. Excited by the possibilities, they continued to make dive after dive until they recovered not only artifacts ranging from a simple house brick[3] to some very ancient coins from the wreck of the *Vergulde Draeck*.

---

[2] Rupert Gerritsen, *And Their Ghosts May be Heard*, p33

[3] Photo of elephant tusk, ballast bricks and cannon ball by Henry Van Zanden. All the items courtesy of the Tim Coleman private *Vergulde Draeck* collection.

From top left: ballast bricks, a cannon ball, a necklace made up from coins *Vergulde Draeck* coins, and a beardman jug. All items courtesy of the Tim Coleman collection.

Marooned on a strange shore
Captain Pieter Albertsz chose seven strong sailors to depart in the surviving boat for the torturous voyage thousands of kilometres to Batavia. If they were to be rescued, the success of the seven was crucial. However, Albertsz chose to stay behind to take charge of the remaining 68.

Where the survivors landed and the seven sailors departed from in their schuyt[4]

Meanwhile, a battle of survival against the odds began. Albertsz had to find shelter, water and food upon a desolate shore that provided none of the essentials readily at hand. There were no rivers, lakes, forests or acceptable shelter.

Realising that it would be some time before a rescue ship would come, Albertsz sent scouts to the north, south and inland to find a more suitable place for habitation. Evidence that they travelled north can be found from the following archaeological finds. However, a question mark remains over what year the articles were lost. Parties may have been sent to the coast for more than two years.

Exploring North from the Wreck Site
1846 – Incense Urn
North of Gingin, an incense urn was found by an Aboriginal shepherd in 1846 at the newly founded mission of New Norcia. According to the Aborigines it was found about 30 km south of Lancelin at a place called Mission Well. The well was supposed to have been lined with ship's timbers.

1890 – The Mast Site
Approximately 15 km north of Lancelin near Wedge Island, three kangaroo shooters, Regan and brothers Skipworth, found a mast buried in a sandhill around 1890. It was about 12m with a heavy chain attached to it and five iron bands around it. They also found a rusty pot, two horn spoons, a copper shovel and two hatchet heads. Drinking water was found by digging 75cm into the sand. This may have been the camp site of a few *Vergudle Draeck* survivors stationed on the coast as a lookout for passing ships.

---

[4] Photo of the shore line at Ledge Point by Henry Van Zanden

A 360º view of a variety of Beardmen Jugs taken from the Vergulde Draeck wreckage

The Lancelin Sword
Twenty kilometres north of the wreck site, a 17th century sword was found. It was of a design used by sailors and the most likely source was from a scout from the *Vergulde Draeck*. Therefore we know that the scouts explored at least 20 km from the wreck site.

Exploring south of the Wreck Site
The scouts that were sent south were at least able to find a significant water source less than 20 km from the wreck site, the Moore River.[5]

1931 – Moore River Coins

It was the discovery of the Moore River Coins[6] in 1931 that led to the eventual discovery of the wreck of the *Vergulde Draeck*. In the sandhills north of the mouth of the Moore River, two brothers, Alan and Fred Edwards, were doing what boys do whenever they find sand – play in it. Most young boys dream of finding 'treasure' but the Edwards brothers really found the 'reale' thing: Spanish *reales* or pieces of eight. There were 16 Ducatons and half Ducatons from the Spanish Netherlands their dates ranging from 1637 to 1655. But where was the treasures chest? Fred fossicked around until he found 'a hinge and side piece of an old chest[7].'

In total, the young boy found about 40 silver coins. Most of the coins were Japanese which reflected the ongoing trade the VOC had with Japan. 24 Mameita-Gins coins with dates as early as 1601 were recovered. The exact location of the find was 31° 19' S.

---

[5] Photo of the mouth of the Moore River by Henry Van Zanden

[6] Photo by Henry Van Zanden of a coin from the *Vergulde Draeck* from the Tim Coleman collection

[7] *West Australian*, 8 May, 1963 p2; J Henderson, *Marooned*, pp170-172.

Today near the site of where the coins[8] were found stands the Guilderton Lighthouse. It was such an exciting find that they changed the name of the town from Gabbadah to Guilderton in 1951. The discovery of the Moore River coins sparked off some search parties to find the hidden treasure. However, the elusive treasure chests still remain to be discovered.

Edwards 1931 Coin Find

1-5 (5) Spanish Netherlands
  Ducatons 1637, 1635, 16xx, xxxx, xxxx

6 (1) Spanish Netherlands
  ½ Ducaton 1636

7 (1) Japanese silver
  Keicho Chogin ingot

8-27 (20) Japanese silver
  Keicho-Mameita-gin

27 coins in photo by Jeremy Green

36 coins found in dunes   7 Spanish Netherland Ducatons, 1635, 1635, 1637, 1638, 1640, 1648, 1653
4½ Ducatons, 1636, 1636, 1637, 1647
1 Albert and Isabella Ducaton, 1618
1 Japanese Chogin ingot, 23 Japanese Mameita-gin

There are reports that 42 coins were found - James A. Henderson 'Marooned'

---

[8] Photos courtesy of the Gilt Dragon Research Group

Eagles Nest Skeleton

800 m from the Moore River coins, a skeleton was found among the rocks. A cave was later discovered that showed evidence of being improved by the human hand[9]. Small rocks had been neatly stacked to keep the wind out. Pieces of green bottles were also found that were identical to green bottles found on the wreck of the *Vergulde Draeck*. The kangaroo shooter, Regan, who found the mast, also revealed that Aboriginals had told him of a cave that existed somewhere in the vicinity of the Moore River which contained skeletons of white men.

Skeletons of white men would seem to indicate that these scouts did not return. Possibly they were exhausted, injured or both and were unable to return. The green bottles would have been used to store water. The only other explanation is that they were sent to the coast after the Karakin settlement to act as a lookout for possible rescue ships. This scout may have travelled as far a 30 km north of Perth where he engraved into a rock, *Vergulede Draeck 1656*.

Both north and south proved fruitless and so the only option that remained was to trek inland and hope that they would find a place that could provide them with food, water and shelter. Leaving their rough shelters behind and most likely a message or marker of some sort, the survivors *were compelled by famine ... to travel towards the rising sun, carrying with them as much of the stores as they could, during which many died; and by the wise advice of their ten sisters they crossed a ridge of land, and meeting with a rivulet on the other side, followed its course and were led to the spot they now inhabit, where they have continued ever since.*

[9] Photo of a cave at Eagles Nest where the survivors possibly sheltered. Courtesy of the Gilt Dragon Research Group

Evidence of their easterly inland trek can be seen from two major discoveries of coins along the Moore River and a clump of coins near a chain of lakes towards Gingin.

The Moore River Coin

On the banks of the Moore River, an old coin was discovered dated 1637. However, it was found 65 km upstream at a place called Mogumber. If this coin was from the *Vergulde Draeck* then it indicated the possibility that either the survivors travelled as far as 65 km inland, or the coins were carried there by Aboriginals. Coins from the *Vergulde Draeck* were also found opposite the wreck site.

Clump of coins discovered

A clump of coins was discovered near a lake towards Gingin. Unconfirmed reports claimed that they were found around a chain of inland lakes 'towards Gingin' that ran north-south.[10] A clump of coins[11] near a chain of in-land lakes! The Karakin Lakes run north-south and are not far from Gingin.

The inland archaeological finds make even more sense when we read what was reported to the Governor-General after the seven sailors sent by Albertsz from the *Vergulde Draeck* miraculously sailing 2,500 km to Batavia. The exhausted men recounted their tragic story but also revealed the safe landing of 68 men and women who still remained hoping for rescue.

---

[10] Gerritsen,R. *And Their Ghosts May Be Heard* p6 West Australian Newspaper, 8 September, 1990

[11] Coins from the *Vergulde Draeck*, courtesy of the Gilt Dragon Research Group

However, they informed the Governor-General that due to the sparse conditions, **they were about to go inland** ... where we very much hope they will have found provisions and drinking water[12]. [Author's emphasis]

For 176 years the Lost White Tribe grew into a white indigenous settlement. Keeping to themselves, they built stone wall fortifications for protection against any possible attack by a neighbouring Aboriginal tribe on the southern side of the river. They had learnt to survive by fishing, hunting kangaroo and small animals. Planting of yams provided them with a vegetable staple while the river, springs and the lake solved their biggest obstacle of all: shortage of water.

Tales of an indigenous white tribe filtered through to the Swan River Settlement and one who pursued the stories more than most was George Fletcher Moore. However, he became more interested in the stories not so much because of the white people sightings, but because of the prospect of finding an inland sea.

George Fletcher Moore

George Fletcher Moore was Western Australia's first Advocate General. He was also an explorer, farmer and a prolific writer. Moore had one advantage over other settlers in his observations of what was a new and very strange land. He had excellent relations with the Aboriginals and could converse satisfactorily with the local tribes. It was through his conversations with his Aboriginal companions that led him to believe that there existed a very large inland sea or lake north of Perth. In his book, *Evidences of an Inland Sea*, published in Dublin in 1837, Moore recounted the conversation he had with a native called Tomgin who went north in voluntary exile after slaying a man. He had gone a considerable distance.

When he returned (1835), Moore asked what strange things had he seen. Tomgin spoke of seeing *a man called Mannar who said he had gone a long way to the north east till he had gone to Moleyean; that it was very far away 'moons would be dead.' (Meaning more than a month) before you would arrive at it; that you walked over a great space where there were no trees; that the ground scorched your feet and the sun burned your head; that you came to very high hills; that standing upon them, you would look down upon the sun rising out of the water beyond them. – that the* **inhabitants were of large stature***; and that the* **women had fair hair,** *and long as white women's hair; that all the people's eyes were "sick ;" that they contracted the eyelids and shook their heads as they looked at you*[13]. [Author's emphasis]

If you are looking down at the sun rising out of the water, it would be either a description of the east coast of an island or the sun rise over a large lake. Tomgin had frequently spoke of Moleyean and pointed to the north east. On further investigation, Moore found from a Mr Armstrong who helped to interview Tomgin, that *the natives seem all to be aware that they are living on an island, and Tomgin appears to be speaking of the other side of the island*. It was not possible for Tomgin to get to the other side of Australia in one month but looking across a very large lake, there may be parts that would seem like an island. During a very large flood, the Karakin Lakes must have appeared as though they were an inland sea.

---

[12] Letter from the Governor-General and his Council to the Chamber of Amsterdam, 4 December, 1656. ARKA-VOC 1214 fol. 84r in Gerritsen, *They will offer all friendship: The evidence for cohabitation between indigenous Australians and marooned Dutch mariners and VOC passengers.*

[13] Fletcher Moore, George, *Evidences of an Inland Sea collected from natives of the Swan River settlement*, 1837

Moore had two months earlier made an excursion that followed a river course to a spot about 160 km from Perth in a NNE line. Moore asked a native where the waters of the east of the river went. The native replied, *The waters there go to the east, and out at Moleyean*. The Karakin Lakes are about 160 km in a NNE line from Perth and the waters of the east or the Moore River, flowed into the Karakin Lakes. Moleyean was the Aboriginal term for Karakin Lakes.

Comparison between the native Tomgin's account, the Leeds Mercury Newspaper and Dale's map of 1832

Tomgin was a native who had gone some considerable distance to the north in voluntary exile because he had killed a man. We know that he returned in 1835. The Leeds mercury article was printed in 1834.

He had first told me that he had seen a man called "Mannar" who said he had gone a long way to the north east till he had gone to Moleyean.

Mannar sounds remarkably like man which is similar in both Dutch and English. The plural of man in Dutch is 'mannen'. However, '*Mannar*' is also a Dutch surname.

…. before you could arrive at it … you walked over a great space where there were no trees; that the ground scorched your feet, and the sun burned your head; that you came to a very high hills; that, standing upon them, you would look down upon the sun rising out of the water beyond them. Now compare this with the Leeds Mercury.

May 15th, 1832, – On reaching the summit of the hill, no words can express the astonishment, delight and wonder I felt at the magical change of scenery, after having travelled for so many days over nothing but barren hills and rocks, and sands and parching plains … Looking to the southwards I saw below me at the distance of about three or four miles, … a broad sheet of smooth water extended in nearly a direct line from east to west …

In Dale's map, he describes the countryside (116° 15´ E, latitude 31° S), as *sandy country*. He then turns south east where he places a river running east to west at about 116° 25´ longitude and about 31° 20´ latitude, as a *Rich valley*. Still further south–east Dale writes on his map, *good land*.

Tomgin
.. that the inhabitants were of large stature; and that **the women had fair hair**, *and long as white women's hair; that all the people's eyes were 'sick;' that they contracted their eyelids and shook their heads as they looked at you.* [Author's emphasis]

Leeds Mercury

… I came suddenly upon a human being whose face was so fair and dress so white.

Tomgin had found the Lost White Tribe. Thus we now have numerous pieces of evidence from a variety of sources that all confirm the existence of the Lost White Tribe. However, Tomgin was not the only Aboriginal to claim that he had seen a tribe of white people.

'There were other white men'

A Benedictine monk reported the following after two Aboriginals came to the New Norcia Mission in the 1840s: *They told me through one of the mission natives that near the coast, four days journey north of New Norcia there were other white men. After looking into this matter I came to the conclusion that these could well be the descendants of the mutineers Captain Pelsaert left behind.*

1836 – Perth Gazette

It was reported in the Perth Gazette as early as 1836 that natives had spoken of a tribe who had landed upon the northern coast armed with knives.

The northern tribes have told the Swan tribe that some time in the life-time of the present generation, some black people who had no guns but were armed with knives landed on the northern coast among them.

Also in 1836, it was reported that Moore had come across a female native who differed remarkably from other native women. *On this day we saw a native and his 'cardo'(wife) a young woman of a very pleasing countenance and something of* **European features** *and long wavy, almost* **flaxen-coloured hair**. (Mt Anne – 150 km east of Perth.) [Author's emphasis]

However, it was the rumour of a shipwreck *30 days journey* to the north that captured the imagination of the whole settlement.

It was Moore who discovered the Moore River which is about 30 km south of the wreck site. During his expedition, he came across a bulbous root called Conne by the natives which was almost the size of a large potato. The Leeds Mercury article refers to the Dutch survivors as growing plantations, *consisting of maize and yams*. In this part of south western Australia, we know that there was a deliberate planting of yams which grew no where else in Australia. This yam is known as the *Dioscorea hastifolia*. Although native to Australia, the native yam is also related to the yams in South Africa which were popular in the Dutch East Indies in the 17th century. These types of yams were often taken on board the Dutch ships as a food supply during long sea voyages[14].

Dioscorea hastifolia or better known as yams

---

[14]*Dioscorea hastifolia* Photo by Gladys Clancy in Webshots

The *Vergulde Draeck* Inscription

Discovered in 1956, the *Vergulde Draeck* rock inscription was found by a Wanneroo dairy farmer, Harry Duffy. Two years later the slab was broken up and removed.

There was a great deal of conjecture as to whether or not the inscription was authentic. Complicating matters further, the site of the inscription was also the site of a new ocean marina. What was surprising was how close it was to Perth. Located on a large rock on the coast between Mullaloo and Burns Beach, it was only 30 km north of Perth.

At first it was declared a hoax by two University of WA lecturers, Dr J E Glover and Dr B Glenister who concluded that the engraving had been done by someone ten years ago. Unfortunately less than two years later, someone had smashed the rock inscription, breaking it up and taking it away.

It was more recently re-examined by two other experts who disagreed with each other's findings. Dr Wendy Van Duivenoorde declared that the inscription was unlikely to be real basing her findings on 'its geological examination and study of the script itself.' Although her expertise is in timber, she has studied Postal Stones from 1601–1657 relating to ships heading to and from Batavia.

Her opinion is opposed by Dr Robert Bednarik who is a world-renowned expert in Petroglyphs dating methodology with his area of speciality in dating rock carvings. He has enormous experience all over the world in dating rock carvings.

At stake was the preservation of the remains of the rock carving. If it was declared to be a fake, then the site could be developed meaning the engraving could be destroyed forever. Dr Bednarik was enraged that Australia's oldest European rock inscription could be so callously disregarded with little thought to its preservation or tourism potential. I contacted Dr Bednarik who confirmed his belief that the inscription was genuine. His anger was also genuine. His letter is enclosed below.

Dear Sir or Madam,

Having just received a copy of a brochure entitled Ocean Reef Marina: Concept Plan, I wish to provide some highly relevant information and prevent a planning error from occurring.

According to the map you provide, it seems to me that within the zone affected by this development is the site of Australia's earliest known European inscription. Purporting to be an inscription by survivors of a Dutch shipwreck, this was found in the 1950s, reported in a Perth newspaper and then examined by two geology students and pronounced a fake. After being ignored for half a century, a group of researchers tried to relocate the inscribed rock, and after initially failing did find, almost buried in the sand, one piece of the rock, with part of the inscription. The rock slab had been smashed with a sledgehammer, apparently still in the 1950s. I conducted a microscopic examination of the remaining letters, using a method of estimating the antiquity of petroglyphs (rock art), and determined that the letters were indeed made several centuries ago, and could not possibly be a fake.

It is apparent that the remaining fragments of the rock slab, which was over two metres long, are still buried in the sand. In view of the vandalism that occurred probably in the 1950s, we decided that the best protection of the site and its contents is to keep silent. Your development, however, will re-shape the coast and thus destroy both the site and its contents. Fortunately there is a simple solution that will not only solve our problem, but also considerably enhance your development.

This site is of major historical significance to Australia. I have examined about a dozen very early European rock inscriptions (see e.g. enclosed article) and there is no doubt that this is the earliest in the country. I propose that the site be fully explored, the remaining pieces of the slab be recovered if possible, and be permanently exhibited on site, in a small museum / exhibit emphasising the importance of early Dutch contact. Not only would this solve our problem of protecting the relic(s), it would enhance the marina development and add a new dimension to it. For instance, you could name specific features of it after Dutch individuals of the time.

On that basis I request that the site be excavated under my supervision by Perth archaeologists, and that whatever is found be housed in an exhibition building next to the original site. Can I suggest that you request three of my collaborators who are Perth residents to meet the person responsible for planning this project, to arrange an inspection of the site, and to determine what course of action you wish to take. I emphasise that my position of Convener / CEO of the International Federation of Rock Art Organisations forbids me from financially benefiting from my work, i.e. I am not interested in gaining from this exercise financially. My purpose is purely to preserve this relic.

Yours sincerely,

Robert G. Bednarik

CEO, IFRAO

The Gilt Dragon Research Group

A dedicated group of Gilt Dragon enthusiasts developed their own website outlining their quest for the location of further archaeological finds but most of all, the location of the survivors of the *Vergulde Draeck*. Included in their research was a portfolio of photos from all the archaeological sites including the *Vergulde Draeck* Inscription site. The coloured card is 10 cm long.

The Gilt Dragon Research Group[15] were able to locate the inscription despite it being covered in sand. Its location is still kept secret and it is surprising that it has not been displayed in a museum. Eventually the harsh surf and abrasive sand will erode the engraving or it may be further vandalised, stolen or destroyed.

Although it is listed as a protected site, Dr Bednarik has every right to be furious at the scientific and historic disregard for Australia's oldest European inscription. His own scientific findings based upon extensive and meticulous examination, has concluded that the engravings appear to be genuine and were made around 1656. After receiving the following letter by Dr McCarthy, he was particularly scathing in his criticism of the Department of Marine Archaeology, WA Museum in Fremantle Western Australia.

All...you are in receipt of the note below hence this cc to you in explanation.
It is sad that Mr Bednarik has refused to assist the museum in the inspection of the Vergulde Draeck rock inscription and that he has departed with such rancour and ill feeling towards this department and me as its representative. We regularly utilise external expertise in our work, indeed one could observe that it is standard practice. To that end it was our desire to conduct the inspection with him and to have Mr Bednarik as part of the subsequent deliberations and analyses. He is highly regarded by us and his reputation and capacities are undoubted.
While I appreciate the reasons underlying why he has linked this instance with the Burrup and while I share his concerns for it and have personally agitated against the damage caused to that irreplaceable, unique and essential Indigenous and global icon, the two come under different legislative and management regimes. One (Indigenous inscriptions) is managed outside this Museum's structures, the other (inscriptions possible from historic ships and or explorers) within it.

I will ask Dr Van Duivenvoorde to make the necessary inquiries with the developers and the City of Wanneroo with a view to locating and examining the remains.

Thank you all for bearing with us.

Dr M.McCarthy
Curator of Maritime Archaeology
Acting Head.
Department of Maritime Archaeology
WA Museum
Fremantle
Western Australia

Dr Bednarik made the following reply:

Dear Dr McCarthy,

If there have been delays in this discussion they are attributable to avoidance of the key question: does your agency have the expertise to estimate the antiquity of rock substrate modifications? Had you admitted that it doesn't, I would not have hoped to find in your agency the ability of testing already available scientific data, and our discussion would have been shorter.

---

[15] The Gilt Dragon Research Group, www.giltdragon.com.au Steve Coffey

Permit me to list the facts: the Ocean Reef inscription was publicly reported over half a century ago, yet your agency has no knowledge of it. Similarly, it has no knowledge of most other early rock inscriptions in WA, be they fake or authentic, and shows no inclination of taking a sustained interest. Moreover, it appears to have no expertise in dealing with such phenomena in a scientific manner. Nevertheless, you claim that it has responsibility of such material. If it lacks both knowledge and expertise, why is it given this responsibility? Several rock inscriptions in WA have been deliberately destroyed, at least in some cases by 'official agencies'. Moreover, WA legislation for protecting immovable cultural heritage is pitiful: 99.7% of all applications made for the destruction of such monuments have been approved since 1972, and applications for protection have only been approved by the federal government, and strenuously opposed by the WA Labor government.

These are unpalatable facts, Dr McCarthy, and as the CEO of the International Federation of Rock Art Organisations, dealing with rock art protection worldwide, in every continent, and working directly with UNESCO, I can assure you that WA is historically the world's foremost state vandal of immovable cultural heritage. Believe me, this is not a lightly made or frivolous claim. Your government has sanctioned the destruction of 95,000 petroglyphs at Dampier alone; this is unheard of in the rest of the world, and dwarfs the Taliban's achievements. The Ocean Reef inscription was defaced and smashed in the 1950s.

I therefore find that your agency is unable to assist the existing project dealing with all known rock inscriptions. You lack the ability of authenticating such features, without which you cannot realistically decide what is and is not relevant to the maritime history of WA. In your own view, the authenticity of the inscription is not established, hence it is not a maritime relic - yet you are unable to authenticate it. You have nothing to offer our project.

My apologies for wasting your time.
Good bye.
Robert G. Bednarik[16]

Although I had asked Dr Bednarik to make further comment, he has declined. His fury is more than understandable as his decision not to make any further comment.

The question of when the engravings were made still represents a problem. Dr Bednarik believes that they were made around the time of the date, 1656. It's unlikely that it occurred immediately after the shipwreck. No mention was made of the southern exploration by the men who sailed their *schuyt* to Batavia to report the shipwreck. Instead they remarked only that the survivors were forced to travel inland due to the lack of food and water on the coastline.

The expedition to the south most likely occurred after they had become settled at the Karikan Lakes. After building a small boat, a crew of one or two men could have easily sailed[17] or rowed with the current to the mouth of the Moore River. From there it was still a 60 km journey to the inscription site. There is a possibility that the skeleton at Eagle's Nest was the author of the rock inscription.

---

[16] www.treasurenet.com

[17] The survivors may have been able to recover the sail from the capsized *Schuyt*.

The Vergulde Draeck Inscription. Photo courtesy of the Gilt Dragon Research Group

Chapter 7
Karakin Lakes, site of the Lost White Tribe

Site of the Lost White Tribe Settlement nearby Karakin Lakes. Image from Google

Using the evidence from the Leeds Mercury article and after checking other possible sites, the Karakin Lakes seemed like the only logical place where the Dutch survivors of the *Vergulde Draeck* could possibly have settled. There was a large lake, river, and I was to later discover two sites where there existed a great deal of stone. It was due east from the wreck or 'towards the rising sun.'

Their fathers were compelled by famine, after the loss of their great vessel, to travel towards the rising sun ... and by the wise advice of their sisters they crossed a ridge of land, and meeting with a rivulet on the other side, followed its course and were led to a spot they now inhabit, where they have continued ever since. Leeds Mercury.

However, the Karakin Lakes cover quite a large area. It would still be a difficult task to pinpoint the exact location. To further complicate matters, the lake had been pumped dry over the many years through the sinking of bores.

After I was sure that these lakes were the right location, I informed Tom Vanderveldt, President of the VOC Historical Society in Perth. It just so happened that he knew the owner of the property on Karakin Lakes, Sid de Burgh. (Pictured right on his property)

Tom, an amateur but passionate historian, made a few trips to Karakin Lakes but came away with the conclusion that no Dutch settlement had existed there. However, Tom had only explored Quinn's Castle as he was led to believe that this was the only area that had a large amount of rocks. He believed that the settlement was much further north due to the large number of explorer's reports and artifacts that had been found. I was sure that the Lost Settlement was somewhere in the Karakin Lakes area . Unfortunately we parted our ways. I hitched a ride back to Perth and hired a 4-wheel drive. Tom ventured north.

A number of factors convinced me that the Karakin Lakes was the right location. It was the right timeframe for the *Vergulde Draeck*. *... their fathers came there about one hundred and seventy years ago*. This would bring the approximate date to 1662 which is not far removed from 1656, the date of the shipwreck.

Records show that there were women amongst the survivors. *... eighty men and ten of their sisters ... were saved on shore*. There were also 79 *Vergulde Draeck* survivors. However with a further 11 men marooned from the rescue ships that arrived in 1657, the total number of survivors becomes ninety which is the same number recorded in the Leeds Mercury article.

Using the old method of measuring longitude, the Karikan Lakes is very close to the longitude in the Leeds Mercury article.

The settlement was Dutch so it can only have been a Dutch shipwreck.

The story of their shipwreck fits perfectly with the *Vergulde Draeck* story. *Their traditional history is, that their fathers were compelled by famine, after the loss of their great vessel, to travel towards the rising sun, carrying with them as much of the stores as they could, during which many died; and by the wise advice of their ten sisters they crossed a ridge of land, and meeting with a rivulet on the other side, followed its course and were led to the spot they now inhabit, where they have continued ever since.*

Travelling in the direction of the rising sun meant that they travelled east toward the Karakin Lakes. The article also states that they met with a river which they followed to their present location. There is only one river that they could have come across: the Moore River. Therefore the settlement had to be close to the Moore River and nearby a very large lake.

With the assistance of George Dean and his local knowledge, we searched every other possible site close to the Moore River but we could not find any other site comparable to the Karikan Lakes.

I had asked the owner, Sid de Burgh, whether there was any large concentration of stone near the lakes. He directed me a rocky outcrop called Quinn's Castle. It seemed a logical place to settle as it had all the natural features of a fort. From the top of the outcrop, I could see in every direction. However, it is easy to forget that the lake was once full of water making Quinn's Castle impossible to access other than by boat or canoe. It had to be somewhere else.

View from the rocky outcrop of Quinn's Castle[1] emphasises the wide expanse that was once covered in water.

---

[1] Photo by Henry Van Zanden

The mistake I had made was to follow the existing tracks in my car. It became an aimless search along meandering trails that seemed to go nowhere. I was going nowhere. Time was running out. A change of direction was needed urgently[2]. After re-reading the article and studying the map just one more time to see what I had missed, it occurred to me that the location of the Lost Tribe was on the eastern side of the lake.

A panoramic view of the Karakin Lakes from Quinn's castle. In 1832 the vast open spaces were once covered in water forming a giant lake almost resembling an inland sea. All photographs by Henry Van Zanden

*... a broad sheet of smooth water extended in nearly a direct line from **east** to west.* [Author's emphasis] Dale had descended the mountain on the eastern side of the lake. I had been searching the wrong area! I resolved to leave the car behind, put on a backpack and follow the footsteps of Dale from the north as best I could. Map in one hand and the Leeds Mercury in the other, I began my trek. To be absolutely thorough, I decided to check every hilltop so that there would be no doubt when I finally found the right location.

After a few kilometres of walking, I finally came to the location I had been searching for: the northern approaches to the lake and only three possible hilltops to examine. I was almost in shock when I realised that I could see the hill top that Dale had traversed almost immediately. It was the only one that had a large area of sand covering the top. However, I remembered my pledge to search every hilltop to make sure I had reached the correct one.

Impatiently, I scoured the only other hilltops that could possibly have been Dale's route. Satisfied that I could rule them out, I turned to the hill with the sandy top. As I approached, I decided to once more to check the Leeds Mercury article and decide what 'had' to be there once I reached the top. The approaches to the hill had to experience a *magical change of scenery*. I had to be able to see a distance of three of four miles [5 or 6 km] of *low level country... straight rows of trees ... a broad sheet of water extend(ing) ... east to west, as far as the eye could reach to the westward* but *sweeping to the southward side at its eastern extremity like a river.*

With great anticipation, each step brought me closer to the top of the hill. Each step brought into view – a distant view of trees and low level country. As I reached the sandy summit, my

expectations were realised. The only thing missing was the water. Only a dry lake[3] exists now where there was once a broad sheet of water. In the distance I could see rows of trees.

Northern approaches to the eastern bank of the Karakin Lakes.

This had to be it! Somewhere a Lost Settlement was waiting to be discovered.

It's worthwhile studying the picture from the top of the hill and compare it to the Leeds Mercury article. But imagine the dry expanse filled with water!

... Looking to the southwards I saw below me at a distance of about three or four miles, a low level country, laid as it were in plantations, with straight rows of trees, through which a broad sheet of water extended in nearly a direct line from east to west, as far as the eye could reach to the westward, but apparently sweeping to the southward at its eastern extremity like a river; and near its banks, at one particular spot on the south side there appeared to be a group of habitations embosomed in a grove of tall trees like palms.

Comment: In the photo above and on the following page, looking southwards, we can indeed see at a distance of three or four miles of level country. We can still see straight rows of trees as well as the dry boundary of a lake that extends east to west. The fullest extent of the lake is to the east (or pictured left on the photo), and the furtherest extent of the lake is to the west. In fact should you look to the west, one would not be able to see the end of the lake. The entire width of the lake was probably about 8 km. The 'habitations' were of particular interest to me as I clambered excitedly down the hillside.

---

[3] Photo by Henry Van Zanden of the north-eastern approach to the Karakin Lakes

The water I guessed to be about half a mile wide, and although the stream was clearly open for two thirds of the distance from the southern bank, the remainder of it was studded by thousands of little islands stretching along its northern shores: and what fixed me to the spot with indescribable sensations of rapture and admiration was the number of small boats or canoes with one or two persons in each gliding along the narrow channels [sic] between the islands in every direction, some of which appeared to be fishing or drawing nets. None of them had a sail, but one was floating down the body of the stream without wind, which seemed to denote a current ran from east to west. It seemed as if enchantment had brought me to a civilised country, and I could scarcely resolve to leave the spot I stood upon, had it not been for the overpowering rays of a mid day sun affecting my bowels, as it had frequently done, during all the journey.

To the west or right of the photo, the lake extends many kilometres.

On reaching the bottom of the hill[4] in my return to our party at the tents, I was just turning round a low rock, when I came suddenly upon a human being whose face was so fair and dress so white, that I was for a moment staggered with terror, and thought I was looking at an apparition. I had naturally expected to meet an Indian as black or as brown as the rest of the natives, and not a white man in these unexplored regions. Still quaking with doubts about the integrity of my eyes I proceeded on, and saw the apparition advancing upon me with the most perfect indifference: in another minute he was quite near, and I now perceived that he had not yet seen me, for he was walking slowly and pensively with his eyes fixed to the ground and he appeared to be a young man

---

[4] Photo just above where Dale must have stood '*On reaching the bottom of the hill.*' Of course the plain was covered in water. Photo by Henry Van Zanden

of handsome and interesting countenance. We have got within four paces of each other when he heaved a deep and tremulous sigh, raised his eyes, and in an instant uttered a loud exclamation and fell insensible to the ground. My fears had now given place to sympathy, and I hastened to assist the unknown, who I felt convinced, had been struck with the idea of seeing a supernatural being. It was a considerable time before he recovered and was assured of my mortality; and from a few expressions in old Dutch, which he uttered I was luckily enabled to hold some conversation with him; for I had been at school in Holland in my youth and had not quite forgotten the language. Badly as he spoke Dutch, yet I gathered from him a few particulars of a most extraordinary nature: namely, that he belonged to a small community, all as white as himself, he said about three hundred; **that they lived in houses enclosed all together within a great wall**[5] **to defend them from black men; that their fathers came there about one hundred and seventy years ago,** *as they said,* **from a distant land from across**

The hill was littered with stone seemingly in a haphazard fashion. However, closer examination revealed long rows of stone. It was difficult to assess whether the rows of stone were man-made or a natural formation.

[5] Apart from Quinn's Castle, this was the only location that had enough rock to build walls and houses. Photos by Henry Van Zanden

the great sea; and that their ship broke, and eighty men and ten of their sisters (female passengers?) *with many things were saved on shore.* [Author's emphasis] *I prevailed on him to accompany me to my party, who I knew would be glad to be introduced to his friends before we set out on our return to our ship at Port Raffles, from which place we were now distant nearly five hundred miles, and our time was linked to a fixed period so as to enable the ship to carry us back to Singapore before the change of the monsoon. The young man's dress consisted of a round jacket and large breeches, both made of skins, divested of the hair and bleached as white as linen; and on his head he wore a tall white skin cap with a brim covered over with white down or the small feathers of the white cockatoo. [sic] The latitude of this mountain was eighteen degrees thirty minutes fourteen secs south; and the longitude one hundred and thirty two degrees twenty five minutes thirty seconds east. It was christened Mount Singapore, after the name and in honour of the settlement to which the settlement belonged.*

A conglomeration of a mixture of small stones that seem to be cemented into the larger stone. Further research is required but there may have been an attempt to combine river clay with smaller stones.

A subsequent part of the journal states further:

That on our party visiting the white village, the joy of the simple inhabitants was quite extravagant. The descendent of an officer is looked up to as a chief, and with him (whose name is Van Baerle) the party remained eight days. Their traditional history is, that their fathers were compelled by famine, after the loss of their great vessel, to travel towards the rising sun, carrying with them as much of the stores as they could during which many died; and by the wise advice of their ten sisters they crossed a ridge of land, and meeting with a rivulet[6] on the other side, followed its course and were led to the spot they now inhabit, where they have continued ever since. They have no animals of the domestic kind, either cows, sheep, pigs or anything else; Their plantations consist only of maize and yams, and these with fresh and dried fish constitute their principal food which is changed occasionally for kangaroo and other game; but it appears that they frequently experience a scarcity and shortage of provisions, most probably owing to ignorance and mismanagement; and had little or nothing to offer us now except skins. They are nominal Christians; their marriages are performed without any ceremony; and all the elders sit in council to manage their affairs; all the

---

[6] The 'rivulet on the other side'. The stream is quite close to the rock wall and houses. Over the page shows the river and the rocky area just above the stream. Photos by Henry Van Zanden

young, from ten up to certain age are considered a standing militia, and are armed with long pikes; they have no books or paper, nor any schools; they retain a certain observance of the Sabbath by refraining from their daily labours, and perform a short superstitious ceremony on that all together; and they may be considered almost a new race of human beings.

Further to the south, the stream stops flowing. Although it is a dry bed, there is evidence that there had been a swift flowing stream in flood. The banks are low allowing an easy overflow into the level farm land to the east and southeast. The stream skirts the perimeter of the south-eastern side of the lake.

The Leeds Mercury article describes the stream in the following way:

...the stream was clearly open for two thirds of the distance from the southern bank.

Lines of stone resembling the foundations of walls were common. The bottom right resembles a lookout post at the corner of two defensive walls. Further examination would be necessary to confirm how much human interference there has been these rock formations.

Over 150 years of occupation has made any analyses extremely difficult. However, apart from the Quinn's Castle site, this was the only location with an abundance of stone. There also appeared to be natural springs in some of the rock formations as in the one below.

Parts of a crumbling wall that provided the settlement protection from attack. Further examination is required to test the stone for any evidence of stone masonry.

This scene is interesting because it could represent the foundations of the rock wall. Further investigation is necessary to ascertain how far it extends.

Below the wall and towards the stream, a spacious flat ground appeared that also provided much needed shade from the hot sun. In fact it was noticeably cooler here than the hillside.

Facing the tree-lined banks of the stream, there appeared to be the remnants of another wall.

Amongst the flotsam and jetsam of stone[7], vacant squares of dirt appeared. Could this have been the rooms of the stone huts built behind the rock walls?

---

[7] All photos by Henry Van Zanden

Vacant square 'rooms' surrounded by stone.

The photos show the the top of the sandy hill where Dale gazed down at the lake and the proximity of the river to the settlement. Satellite images courtesy of Google.

Satellite photos

The most significant find from the satellite photos[8] is a line of about 5 or 6 large stone formations which can be seen in more detail on the following page. The line runs roughly parallel to the stream.

Nearby, surrounding the trees, the scarring of the ground seems to reveal a trench that is shaped almost like a square tipped onto its corner. At the tip of the corner is the line of stones. However, what looks like a trench could also be the natural result of rain run off from the hill above.

The *Vergulde Draeck* Treasure

There still exists a feeling by many that the *Vergulde Draeck* treasure is still out there somewhere. Any suspicious looking formations that may have been made by shipwrecked sailors have usually been dug up, moved or even blown up. The Ring of Stones and the *Vegulde Draeck* rock inscription are two such examples which will be dealt with in later chapters.

Bidaminna Lake

The biggest problem with the site was human interference over the last 160 years. A great deal could have been moved, used for building or cleared for farming. I therefore tried to find possible other sites nearby that were less disturbed. One such site was the Bidaminna Lake, a place that I had also considered as the site of the Lost White Tribe which is only about 7 km away. Although I had found nothing, I recently received information regarding a gentleman, Wally Fry, who had spent much of his youth living in a house on the eastern side of the lake.

Wally had spoken about three stone cairns that were on the south eastern side of the lake. At about a metre high and 15m apart, they formed the shape of a triangle. According to Wally's father, the cairns had something to do with a Dutch wreck. However, as Wally was only 10 years old, he could not recall the reasoning behind this. Unfortunately his father and his friends decided to dig up the stone cairns with earth moving equipment hoping that they may find some hidden treasure. Nothing was found so they moved the stone cairns to create sheep dips.

According to the stories and legends told by the Aboriginals, a black tribe lived south of the lakes and lived on the southern side of a large river whereas a white tribe lived on the opposite side. Initially the two tribes lived happily together until there was a change of heart prompting the white tribe to remain separate from the southern black tribe. The stone cairns may have been built when both tribes were on amicable terms or they may have been a defensive structure. Six graves were reported to have been seen and covered over. However, the details a very scant and once again more research has to be undertaken.

---

[8] All satellite images are courtesy of Google, DigitalGlobe, MapData Sciences Pty Ltd. PSMA. 2009

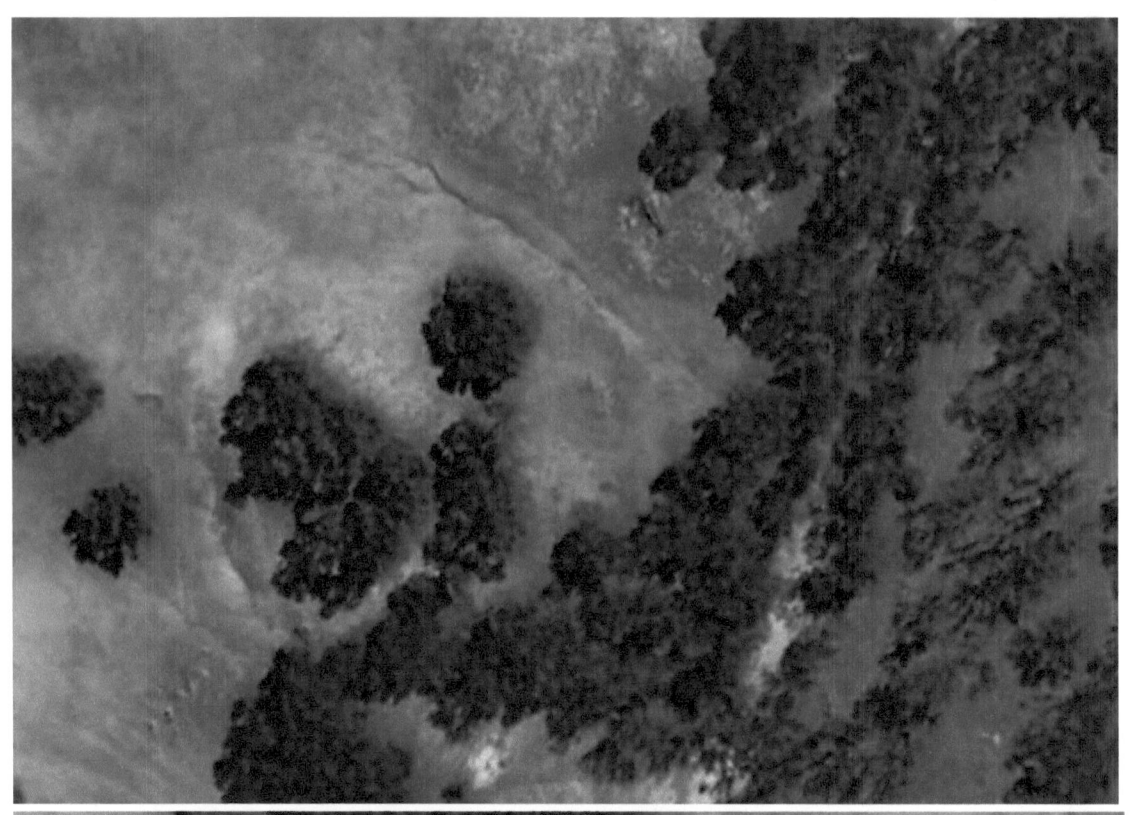
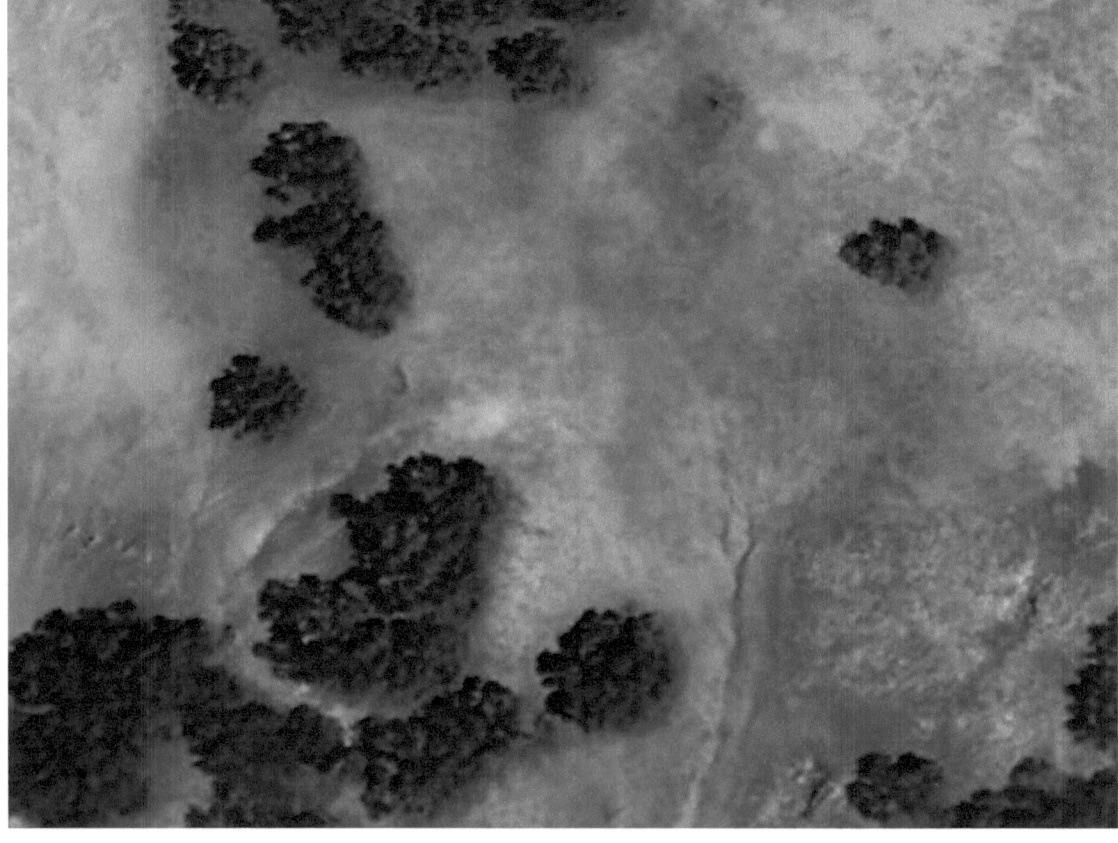

Chapter 8

Legend of the Lost White Tribe

The Beardmen Jugs and a coin necklace from the Vergulde Draeck. Courtesy of the Tim Coleman Collection.

Fight for Survival

Between 1656 and 1832 there is very little evidence to account for what happened to the Lost White Tribe. However, we do get a very brief outline of how they survived as well as why they eventually built a fortified wall and kept mainly to themselves. The slender piece of evidence comes from an extraordinary man, Augustus Frederick Oldfield, a botanical collector with a great interest in Aboriginals.

Augustus Oldfield (1821-1887)

Oldfield was extraordinary because of the extent of his travels throughout Australia. He explored the Huon Valley in Tasmania collecting plant specimens and walked from Sydney to Melbourne. However, he became best known for his major collections in the Western Australian coastal strip from the Murchison River to King George Sound and along the Nullabor Plain to Adelaide.

Oldfield was convinced that a 'superior' race had at one time inhabited the northern area of the Swan River Colony up to Shark Bay. There was something quite distinct, something that separated the northern tribes from all of the Aborigines he had previously encountered across Australia. During his vast travels, he commented on the traditions, culture, religion and differences in the various tribes.

Every tribe in Western Australia holds those to the north of it in especial dread, imputing to them an immense power of enchantment, greater bravery, and superior skill in the manufacture and use of arms, and this seems to justify the inference that the peopling of New Holland has taken place from various points towards the north; for it is reasonable to suppose that such superiority would be accorded to the parent-stock by all its offshoots[1] ...

Oldfield later remarks more specifically upon the spears used in the Shark Bay area which most closely resembled the pike commonly used in Europe during the 17th century.

The natives about the Shark's Bay use a much more powerful kind of spear than is to be found in any other part of the continent. This weapon, which is called the Pil-la-ra, is from 14 to 16 feet [4–5 m] long, and with 8 to 12 pairs of large barbs formed from the solid wood[2].

The art of constructing even the rudest of boats exists only among the most northerly of the Australian tribes, those to the south seldom resorting even to the use of a bundle of bark or of sticks to enable them to cross an arm of the sea ...

At this point I should caution the reader that Oldfield's account should not be read with 21st century eyes, but read with a mind to the era in which they they were written.

That Australia was inhabited prior to the colonisation by the Alfouru, seems probable from the existence of relics of a civilisation far higher than can be claimed by any tribes of the Malay family. These remains of an extinct civilisation consist chiefly of picture-caves and sculptured rocks, works which the present occupants of the soil, far from claiming as their own, ascribe to diabolical agency. As the features and dresses of the figures represented are such as no untutored savage could possibly conceive, and the tools and pigments used are unknown to the existing race, the only just inference we can draw from these facts is, that some more civilised people has been destroyed by the black man, or possibly, in some instances, the two races have blended, a supposition that would

---

[1] Oldfield, Augustus, *On the Aborigines of Australia*, p216

[2] Ibid. p262

enable us to in some measure to account for diversities of characteristics found to exist in various localities. The anomalies for which we thus seek to account exist chiefly among the inland tribes, in which we occasionally meet with physiognomies departing widely from the Australian type; and to reconcile these discrepancies, we are driven to suppose that the fact is owing to the mixture of the blood of a pristine race with that of the Alfouru, for had this blending of races been due to the migration of strangers from the sea-board, traces of their presence would be equally perceptible along the lines of their journeyings[3].

On the western and northern coasts we find the greatest departures from the normal type, and this doubtless is; owing to the advent of strangers among them; those shores, bordering on the much frequented seas, being more likely to have been visited by such than either the south or east coast, which were perhaps never visited until European enterprise led the white man to them[4]...

After coming across Aboriginals that seemed to resemble Europeans in their physical appearance, Oldfield assumed that this was the result of a British ship, the *Calcutta*. He also gave a clue which partly explains the demise of the white tribe with the assertion by Aboriginals in these parts that 'many of their females' were eaten.

That such accidental blending of races should sometimes occur on the shores of much frequented seas is probable from the following facts. At Champion Bay, in WA, I was much surprised to find in **some of the old natives features nearly approaching the European type**, [Author's emphasis], *although those parts have been settled but a few years. I mentioned this fact to a medical gentlemen, who informed me that he had made the same observation, and could account for it in no other way but supposing that a ship which had sailed from Calcutta to Swan River in the early days of the colony, and had never since been heard of, was lost in these parts, and that some of the people who had escaped had mingled with this tribe, a surmise strengthened by the traditions of the natives, who to this day call Perth ... Ca-cut-ta, having probably mistaken the place of departure for that of the destination of the rescued people: added to this, they often asserted that in the event of the departure of the whites from among them, there were many of their females whom their laws would permit them to eat, they having white blood in their veins[5] ...*

Legend of The Lost White Tribe

However, Oldfield's book made a startling discovery told not by one or two Aboriginals but by **all tribes** between the Moore River and Shark Bay.

The following curious tradition is current among **all the Aboriginal tribes** *from the Moore River to Shark's Bay in Western Australia ...* ***A long time ago, there were two tribes living on the banks of a large river, one (black) inhabiting the southern side, and the other (whites) residing on the opposite shores ...*** [Author's emphasis]

The account describes that *for many years the first of the two tribes were on amicable terms, intermarrying, merrymaking ...*

The Dutch survivors could ill afford to make enemies in this strange land that they were now forced to remain abandoned, marooned for the rest of their lives. The limited number of women was a

---

[3] Oldfield, A, *On the Aborigines of Australia*, pp216–218, 1865

[4] Ibid. p218

[5] Ibid. p218 – 19

problem that could only be solved by forming friendly relations with their neighbouring tribe. Intermarriage between the two tribes would have further cemented their relationship. The Aboriginal wives accelerated the learning process in some of the most basic survival skills including gathering food, killing small animals and how the food should be prepared and cooked.

Learning to hunt, make new weapons and tools was also of vital importance to their survival. Initially their small numbers would have posed no threat to the southern tribe. The Dutch sailors eagerly grasped the new Aboriginal technology but improved and adapted European knowledge to design superior weapons. Combined with their knowledge of European fighting techniques such as the fighting formations of spearmen and pikemen, the new white settlers practised fighting drills until they surpassed their Aboriginal teachers.

By and by a change in the sentiments of the northmen took place. These whites were evidently the superior of the two races; for they were more more powerful, athletic and agile than the blacks, and made better spears, boomerangs and other arms, and, what is of greater importance, could use them more efficiently than the poor southmen, as they later learnt to their cost.

We don't know exactly how long this transition took place except that it took many years. It was possibly about 15 to 20 years before their relations became strained. The reason behind my supposition is that the first children of the Lost White Tribe would, by now, be aged between 15 and 20. The southern tribe more than likely believed that since they gave their women to the white tribe, then it was only reasonable that the white tribe should allow the taking of their young white girls as wives for the southern black men.

Augustus Oldfield noted that when unmated Aborigine men *discover an unprotected female, their proceedings are not of the most gentle nature. Stunning her by a blow from the dowak [...], they drag her by the hair to the nearest thicket to await her recovery. When she comes to her senses they force her to accompany them, and as at worst it is but the exchange of one brutal lord for another, she generally enters into the spirit of the affair*[6].

It could also have been a clash of cultures where the Aboriginal law allowed the eating of white European females. However, it is difficult to ascertain exactly when this Aboriginal law began.

... there were many of their females whom their laws would permit them to eat, they having white blood in their veins[7].

Suddenly all of their European culture, tradition and religion rushed to the fore. A decision was made to maintain what was most dearest to them: their family, culture, religion and traditions. Attempts to change the southern tribe met with failure as the Aborigines had no intention of changing their culture and traditions least of all surrender their new white captives.

Their attitude could be compared to that of Robert Lyon, a settler of the Swan River Colony, who spoke passionately and wrote often in the defence of Aboriginals. However, he was highly critical of how their men treated their wives or women in general.

I have found several instances of bigamy; and I believe polygamy is not uncommon. Consequently jealous, the available attendant or such manners, frequently burns like fire in, the breasts of the

---

[6] Oldfield, Augustus, *On The Aborigines of Australia*, p251, 1865

[7] Ibid. p219

men; and, as they have no seraglio to guard the chastity of their wives, the life of the unfortunate female, I fear, too often falls a sacrifice to her imprudence. The practice of spearing the women, whenever they offend them, is cruel, and barbarous. His knowledge of it, I trust, will excite the sympathy of the christian females of Europe. Woman is sate from insult, degradation, and, slavery, no where, but under the shield of christianity[8].

Upon their first arrival at the Karakin Lakes, the Dutch could ill afford to make enemies. There was much to be learnt and a great deal to be lost by warring with their neighbours. However, the strong desire to keep every white female and child within the settlement, led the Dutch settlers to maintain a ferocious defence of their European cultural values.

Unfortunately the area of the Lost White Tribe had been disturbed by settlers since 1851 making it difficult to be absolutely certain if a line of stone was a wall or a natural formation. The satellite photo of the Karakin Lakes does show a line of stone that resembles a wall. However, in an area that was devoid of stone, it would make sense that any settler would use whatever they could find to build their homestead. The farmhouse is less than a kilometre from the Karakin Lakes site. With no other stone available, the home may have been built from the stones of the Lost White Tribe.

At length, proud of their superiority, these northmen refused to hold any intercourse with their southern neighbours, save and excepting in the matter of fighting, in which diversion the advantage was always on the side of these insolent whites.

By this time the Dutch settlers had time to prepare themselves. They were able to find the most suitable site for their settlement that provided water, food, shelter and protection. The bemused Aboriginals must have wondered why this white tribe spent so much time and energy in building a stone wall[9] with stone houses attached.

They lived in houses enclosed all together within a great wall to defend them from black men[10].

Old Settler's hut at the extreme south-eastern end of the Karakin Lakes

---

[8] Lyon, Robert M, Letter To His Honour the Lieutenant Governor in Council. Woodbridge 26 November 26, 1832

[9] Photo of what might have been part of the stone wall at Karakin Lakes. Photo by Henry Van Zanden

[10] Leeds Mercury Newspaper article of the Lost White Tribe

War between the tribes

It may have been after the Dutch settlers raided the southern tribe to rescue their stolen daughters that hostilities commenced in earnest. After retreating behind their stone wall, the southern tribe had to cross a river before they could engage their new enemy. If they made it across the river, the Dutch settlers retreated behind the wall which afforded them protection from any spear attack. Using pikes and spears from behind the wall, the Dutch were able to drive the Aborigines back at great cost.

After the first battle, the Dutch settlers realised that they had to become almost Spartan like in their attitude. Every male had to be trained in not only how to better use their weapons but also how to make them. Thus every male from an early age became both a warrior and hunter.

All the young, from ten up to a certain age, are considered a standing militia, and are armed with long pikes[11].

Pikes[12] were regularly used by European armies since the Middle Ages. It could be used either as an offensive or defensive weapon. Since it was a very long thrusting spear, it was not designed to be thrown. It varied from size between 3 and 7.5 m. Its great length was also its greatest advantage as it allowed for a great concentration of spearheads to be forced upon the enemy. Combined with a great wall to shield them against any spear attack, the new white tribe was able to establish military superiority over the southern black tribe.

[11] Ibid.

[12] Pike Square, re-enactment during the 2009 Escalade in Geneva, by Rama, Wikimedia Commons

As they became more insular with less and less contact with their neighbours, they clung to what remnants of their European heritage they could remember. For example they maintained their European mode of dress as far as the rough manufacture of animal skins would allow.

The young man's dress consisted of a round jacket and large breeches, both made of skins, divested of the hair and bleached as white as linen; and on his head he wore a tall white skin cap with a brim covered over with white down or the small feathers of the white cocatoo. (sic) ... *They are nominal Christians: their marriages are performed without any ceremony: all the elders sit in council to manage their affairs ... they retain a certain observance of the sabbath by refraining from their daily labours, and perform a short superstitious ceremony on that day all together*[13].

Over the 176 years, the Lost White Tribe maintained a system of authority based upon the descendants of a Dutch officer. *The descendant of an officer is looked up to as chief, and with him (whose name is Van Baerle), the party remained eight days*[14]. He must have had both superior and separate living quarters big enough to house both Dale and his party.

It's difficult to believe that Dale did not write more as he remained with the Lost White Tribe for eight days. Somewhere in the missing parts of Dale's 200-page journal is the history of Australia's first settlement. We know that it was brought to England by Governor Stirling along with all of the journals made by every explorer between the years 1829 and 1832.

The Lost White Tribe no doubt thought that they had been rescued for *on our party visiting the white village, the joy of the simple inhabitants was quite extravagant*[15]. They waited expectantly for Dale and a rescue party to return with extra horses, pack mules and perhaps a small waggon. To the three hundred joyous souls celebrating a return to a country they had never seen, to live the stories told over at least six generations, rescue was the one thing that they had all prayed for. They lived a precarious life with each year a challenge depending on the fluctuations of drought, storm, flood and famine. A thousand emotions mixed with excitement, fear and elation spun endlessly in their conversations, hopes and prayers.

Dale had plenty of time to think about what to do about his most amazing discovery as they made their way back to Perth. A pact of silence was made among the party leaving the decision making to Governor Stirling. The consequences of a 17th century Dutch settlement could see the Netherlands claim prior occupation and ownership. The Swan River Settlement could be put into jeopardy.

Stirling, leaving his post, used the Lost Dutch Tribe as leverage for gaining concessions for the Swan River Settlement after releasing an edited version of Dale's journal in the Leeds Mercury newspaper. Fortunately for Stirling, the location of the settlement was too far north for any contact in the immediate future. No further land grants were made in the Karakin Lakes district until 1850.

Governor Stirling, anxious to avoid any contact with the Lost White Tribe, made a proclamation limiting any land survey near the Karakin Lakes. This effectively meant that no land could be settled anywhere close to the Karakin Lakes. None of the properties shown in the map titled *Homesteads* was available for settlement effectively keeping the secret of the Lost White Tribe safe.

---

[13] Leeds Mercury Newspaper article of the Lost White Tribe, DISCOVERY OF A WHITE COLONY ON THE NORTHERN SHORE OF NEW HOLLAND, 1834

[14] Ibid.

[15] Ibid.

The limits of the survey at present fixed extend 20 miles NNW, and 20 miles [32 km] SSE, from the summit of Mount Bakewell, which distance comprises 20 miles of the Avon already surveyed[16].

The law made it impossible for any settlement to occur for at least 50 km from the Karakin Lakes. The problem of a Dutch Settlement was solved for at least the short and medium term.

In 1839, the northern limits of the Swan River colony can be seen in a map of all the available land grants. Its most northerly land grant was at the northern reaches of the Swan River. On the accompanying map, this land grant would have been situated north of Toodyay, Green Mount.

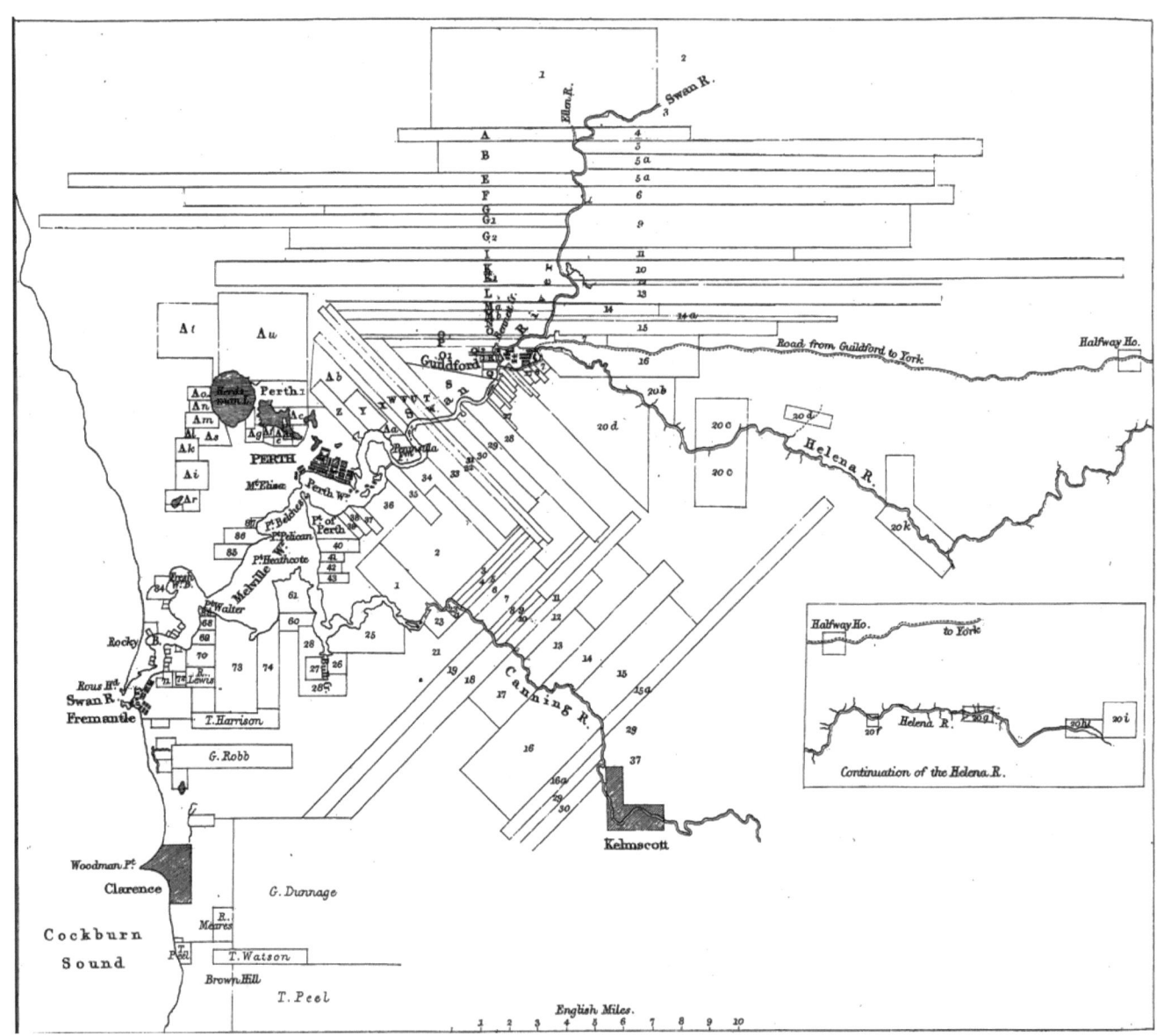

1839 – Swan River Colony Land Grants Map[17]

---

[16] The Western Australian Journal, Saturday November 15, 1834.

[17] Arrowsmith, John. *Swan River Colony Land Grants Map*. Scanned from a reproduction in, Appleyard, RT and Manford, Toby (1979). *The beginning: European Discovery and Early Settlement of Swan River Western Australia*, Nedlands, Western Australia: University of Western Australia Press

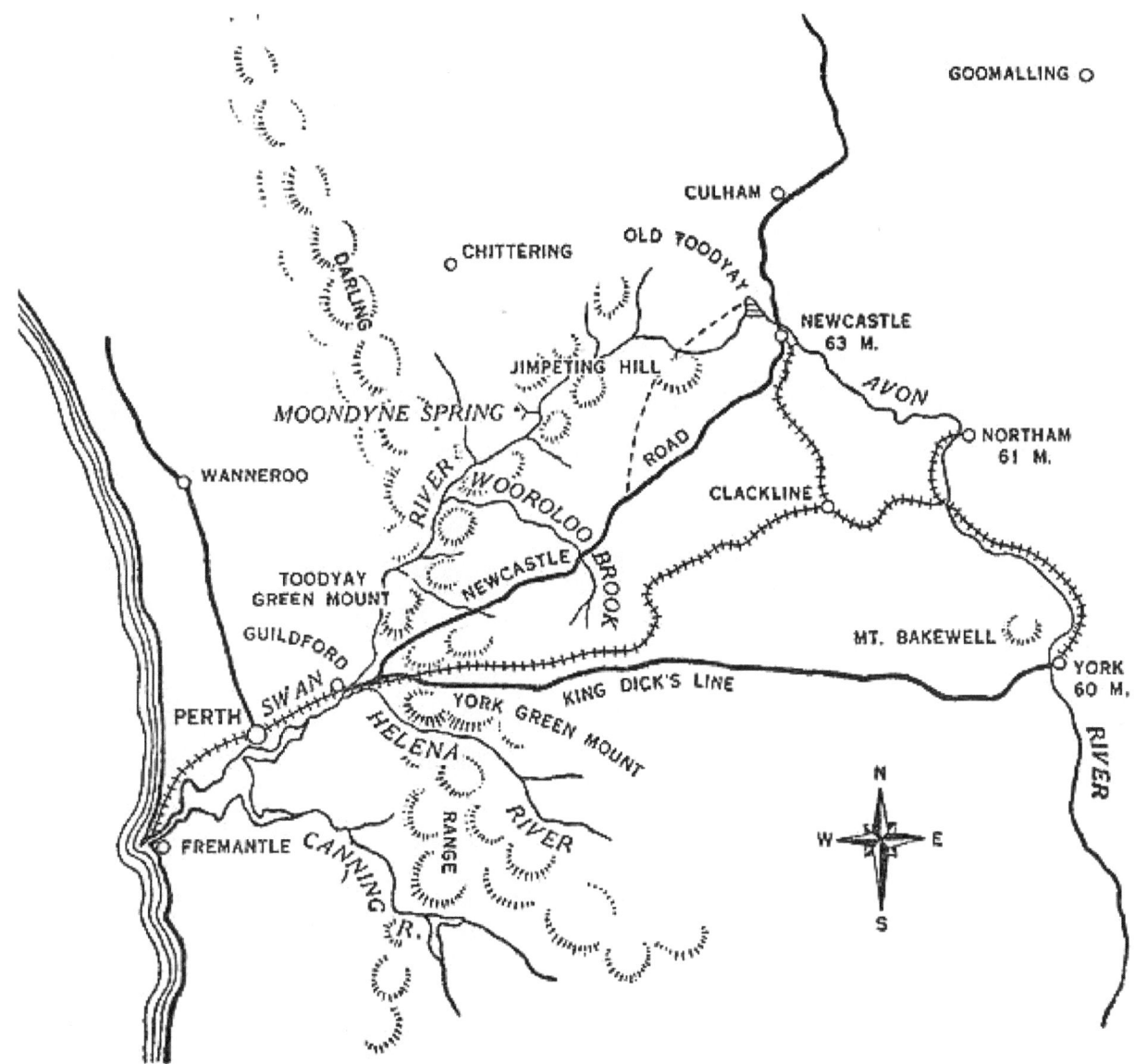

Map of Perth and the surrounding district[18]

Stirling's Land Proclamation
The limits of the survey at present fixed extend 20 miles NNW, and 20 miles [32 km] SSE, from the summit of Mount Bakewell, which distance comprises 20 miles of the Avon already surveyed Mt Bakewell.

Mt Bakewell can seen on the right of the map near York. The 20 mile [32 km] NNW limit had already been surveyed. Coincidentally, the Karakin Lakes were approximately 80 km NNW of Mt Bakewell.

It wasn't until 1851 that the Irish brothers Henry and Robert de Burgh purchased a substantial property at Cowalla on the Moore River which is not far from the Karakin Lakes. By the time the de Burghs had arrived, Stirling was long gone and the Lost White Tribe was forgotten.

---

[18] Department of Lands and Information, From the archives of the Surveyor-General

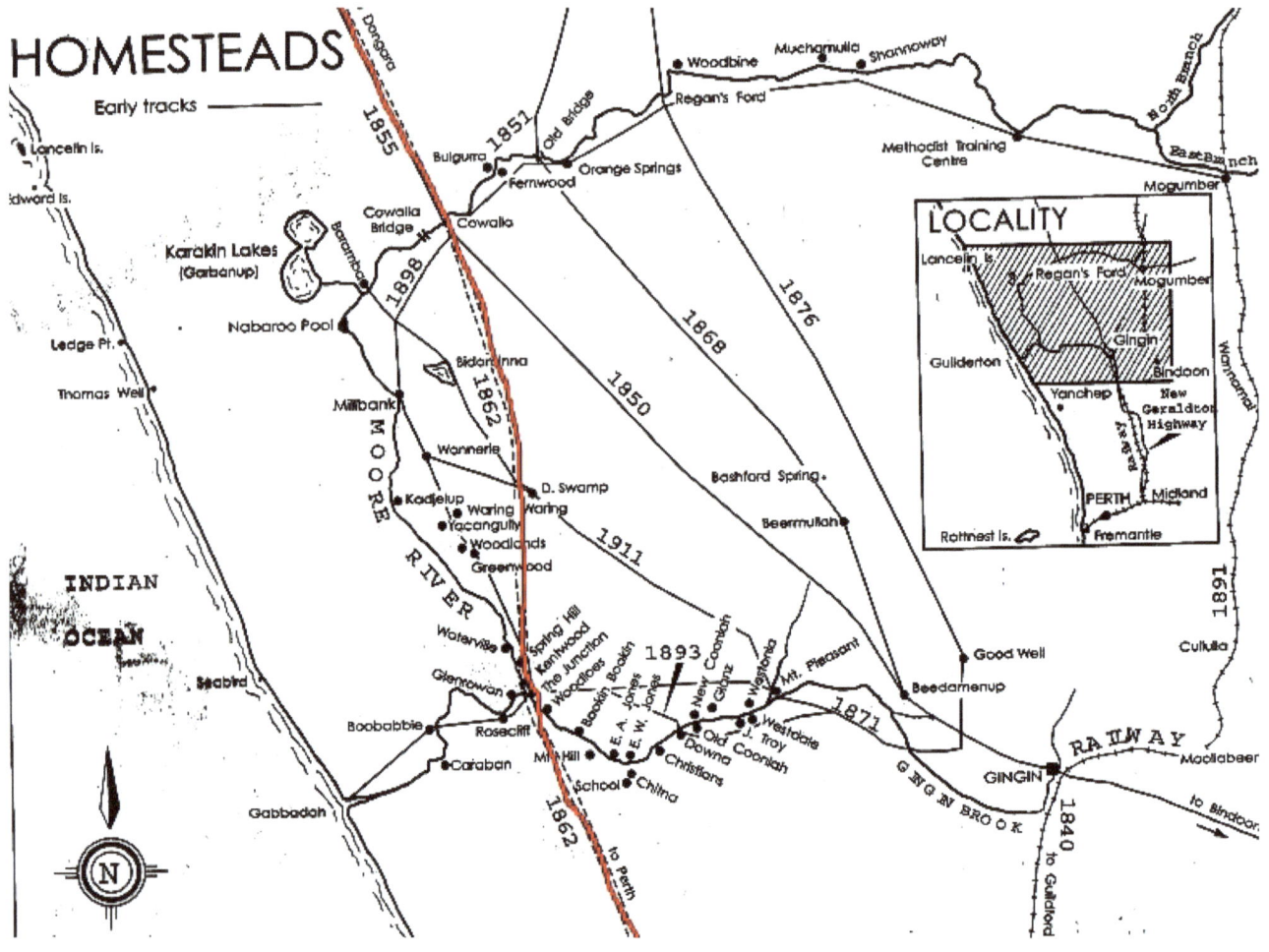

Homesteads

The *Homesteads* map[19] shows how long it took for the first settlers to arrive in the area. The eventual owner of the Karakin Lakes property, a branch of the de Burgh family, did not settle the Karakin Lakes region until 1851 – nearly 20 years after Dale made his discovery. Despite having plenty of water and fertile land, this rich land was out of bounds. Stirling was determined to keep the location of the Lost White Tribe a secret.

Sid and Edith de Burgh are the 5th generation of the de Burgh family. They moved from their original homestead at Cowalla, to live close by the Karikan Lakes. Their 1700 ha cattle farm, called Baramba, borders the Moore River and is about 12 km inland from the town of Ledge Point.

However, it was going to be difficult to keep secret the existence of three hundred Dutch settlers. News of a white settlement to the north began to trickle in by word of mouth from conversations with Aboriginals. In particular, a famous Aboriginal leader named Yagan spoke of the existence of the Karakin Lakes to Robert Lyon, an ex-captain and new settler as early as 1832. Later, in 1834, there were widespread stories of shipwrecked sailors stranded ashore to the north of Perth.
Of particular interest was a region called Waylo's Territory that was inhabited by Waylo men described as either *white men* or *men from the north*.

---

[19] Homestead map courtesy of the de Burgh family and the Gilt Dragon Research Group

Yagan, a warrior chief had confided with a settler, Robert Lyons. He provided Lyons with a great deal of information which included a map of the Karakin Lakes. As a result Lyons was keen to explore the region and wished to furnish Governor Stirling with the newfound knowledge provided by Yagan.

Lyons must have been quite taken aback with the reply. Stirling had requested that Lyons not to write to him any more as he had *ample information on every subject with the settlement*. That is an extraordinary reply to someone who could speak the language well and had spent 6 weeks with the most important and influential Aboriginal leader in the colony.

Waylo Men – *('white men - men from the north')*

The Swan River Aboriginals had an interesting term for white men. They called them Waylo men or men from the north. However, the term Waylo had already been in existence long before the 1829 Swan River Settlement had begun.

Waylo men was also used to describe a particular tribe from the north. This particular tribe had a very different way of speaking. Aborigines described the Perth white people as speaking like the Waylo men from the north. The following was reported by George Fletcher Moore.

April 21st. ... The Perth natives now say that the Perth white men speak "English plenty," meaning broken English, but that I speak like a Waylo man, that is, a man from the North. Waylo is the name of the district we visited. (1835)

Moore had explored the Moore River and came close the Karakin Lakes which the Aboriginals called Waylo's Territory.

After comparing the map[20] made by Lyon based upon Yagan's descriptions, to a modern map, the Waylo territory is clearly in the proximity of the Karakin Lakes area. A diagram of a very large lake was drawn by Lyon using the descriptions given to him by the captured Aboriginal chief, Yagan.

Lyon wrote in some detail of the geographical names of the tribes and areas surrounding the Waylo territory. Words such as *Byer*, *Bookal*, and *Mooler* all have a Dutch sound. For example, the Dutch word, *Bookal*, means cup, goblet or bowl and was perhaps a drinking hole. *Mulle* means loose, sandy earth or loose earth. On one side of the Moore River, the earth is loose and fertile. However, on the high side or the northern side of the river, the soil is hard, stoney and less fertile. The *Bookal* was probably a stream that ran off the *Mooler* River (Moore River.)

---

[20] Part of Lyon's map based on the descriptions of Yagan

Karakin Lakes old Homestead

Chapter 9

Yagan and Lyon

A watercolour painting of Yagan, Chief of the Swan River, by George Cruikshank, 1834, National Library of Australia

Both Yagan and Robert Lyon were extraordinary characters who shared a great understanding and admiration for one another. What drew my immediate attention to Yagan was his name, Yagan, which means *hunter* in Dutch. There is no letter 'y' in the Dutch language. Instead they pronounce the letter 'j' as 'y.' Thus Yagan in Dutch would be spelt *Jagen*. The Dutch dictionary meaning for *Jagen* is 'to hunt, pursue, chase and capture game animals.' A *jager* is a huntsman or was also used to describe a *soldier in the rifles*.

He also had two sons, Willim and Naral – also Dutch names. Their mother's name was Moyren – a European name. They also ate yams most likely introduced by the early Dutch sailors. Only the Aboriginals in the areas associated with the Lost White Tribes cultivated and ate yams.

4th May 1832—Two natives came here to-day: one of them is learning to speak English, and is very intelligent. I discovered the names of more than a dozen who were concerned in the recent murder; among others, two sons of Ya-gan, Naral and Willim, the latter a young imp not more than ten or eleven years of age: we are greatly in their power, and must keep on good terms with them, if possible. One of them had a number of frogs (which I think he called "dweep") nicely packed up in the bark of the tea-tree, and tied with grass; these he signified they roasted for food, with a long white root, growing like a parsnip, which they dig up in wet weather[1].

Olivier van Noort, the first Dutchman to circumnavigate the globe, stopped over at Patagonia before sailing through the Magellan Straits. After spending four months there refreshing their supplies of salted penguin and eggs, his men also fought the local natives. Van Noort called them *Yagans*.

A number of questions come to mind such as how did Yagan get his name? How was it possible for his two sons, Willim and Naral to receive their names *before* the British had arrived in 1829? (They were already between nine or eleven years old in 1832.)

Yagan (1795 – 1833)

The official story of Yagan is that he was the son of the respected Aboriginal elder Midgigoroo of the Noongar people who lived in the south west region of Western Australia. The settlers regarded Midgigoroo as the chief of the district called Beeliar which is an area south of Perth bounded by the Swan and Canning Rivers as well as the sea. According to Daisy Bates and other scholars, the Beeliar people may have been a family subgroup of a larger tribe called Beelgar. The group had customary land usage rights over a much larger area than this, extending north as far as Lake Monger and north-east to the Helena River. The group also had an unusual degree of freedom to move over their neighbours' land, possibly due to kinship and marriage ties with neighbouring tribes.

However, the official story conflicts with what Yagan had told Lyon. Yagan had said that he was the son of Worragonga who was the chief of this district called Worragonga (or Yellowgonga as written by Lyon). This district belonged to the tribe that lived just below the Karakin Lakes area[2]. Yagan and his family, must have had some contact with the Lost White Tribe to the north. The rivers were the natural highways of the bush Aboriginals so it would have been surprising had they not had any contact.

---

[1] Moore, George Fletcher, *Extracts from letter and journals of George Fletcher Moore*, p260

[2] Ibid. p204-5

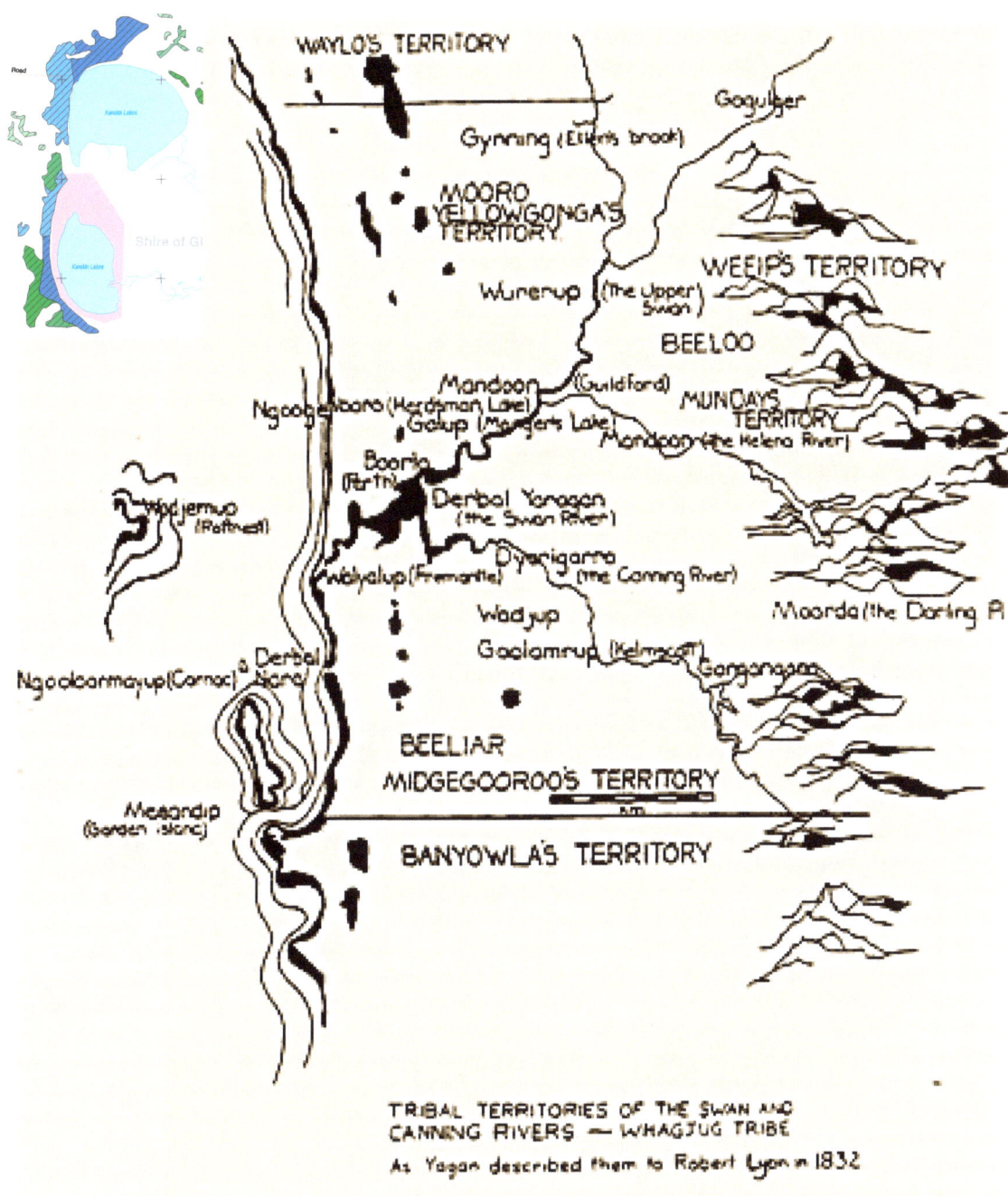

Tribal Territories of the Swan and Canning Rivers and Whagjug Tribe as Yagan described them to Robert Lyon in 1832

Top left inset is a modern map of the Karakin Lakes made by the Department of the Environment and Conservation

It is significant that Yagan describes a large body of water which he calls Waylo's territory. The large body of water resembles the Karakin Lakes. What is remarkable is the accuracy of the map which was based on Yagan's descriptions and what maps were already available. It was the Waylo country that Stirling did not want Lyon to explore for he already has *ample information on every subject with the settlement*[3].

---

[3] Part of a reply to a letter by Lyon to Stirling requesting permission to explore the Waylo country

On the following 1858 map, 'Waylo Country' is located south of the Moore River near a salt lake. The original name of the Karakin Lakes was Lake Garagan and later Garbanup Lake after it was discovered the Garban River (Moore River) flowed nearby the Lake[4]. However, on the map completed by Lyon, Waylo Country is above the Karakin Lakes.

[4] Frank, George, Surveyor-General, 1858

Yagan the Outlaw

Trading fish for bread and flour, the settlers and the Noongar people had been able to coexist without too many problems. However, the settlers became a little alarmed when the Noongar started their annual burning of the land. Tensions arose when their livestock was killed in response to their own dwindling stocks of native animals.

In 1831, the now uneasy coexistence exploded after a Noongar was shot while taking potatoes from a settler's garden. Aboriginal tradition was to seek revenge. It didn't matter too much who was killed so long as someone was killed. As a result, a settler was speared in retaliation. Yagan, who was also known as a warrior, was part of the group.

After another man was killed in June 1832, Yagan was named as one of the men responsible and declared an outlaw. As the attacks grew more frequent, a huge reward of £30 was placed on his head.

When he was finally captured, it was expected that the Governor would order his execution. However, he was saved by Robert Menli Lyon.

Robert Menli Lyon

There was no one more sympathetic and outspoken in their defence of Aboriginals than Robert Menli Lyon. The Scotsman had previously had a career in the army rising to the rank of captain. He arrived in the colony at about 40 years of age but made no claims to military rank preferring to be called by his name Robert Milne. He changed his surname to Lyon and added Menli to his name being an anagram of Milne.

In May 1832, a meeting in Guildford was held by settlers to discuss what was to be done about the damage to farms caused by Aboriginals. They described them as 'truly alarming and disheartening', resulting in strong resolutions to be sent to the Governor. His lenient policy had been criticised by the settlers believing his leniency came at the expense of both their property and safety. Their frustrations were so great that they even threatened that they would be forced to leave the colony unless they were allowed to defend their interests. Stirling refused to change his policy of Aboriginal protection. Lyon was the most outspoken in their defence when he made an impassioned speech.

Gentlemen, have you a Fatherland? So have the Aboriginal inhabitants of this country, Have you the rights of men? What has expunged theirs from the book of nature? Their lands have descended to them from time immemorial and their title deeds require not the wrangling of lawyers to prove them correct. They have the Seal of Heaven, the sanction of Him who divided unto the nations their inheritance ... Reflect! ... Beware ...

Lyon also became Yagan's saviour arguing that he should be treated as a prisoner of war rather than a criminal. Writing to the Perth Gazette, Lyon explained that the two murders that Yagan had been involved in were matters of tribal honour and were carried out with Yagan's repeated threats to take a life.

He must be ranked among the Princes of the country. He has greatly distinguished himself as a patriot and a warrior. He is in fact "The Wallace of the Age [5]*."*

---

[5] Lyon, RM, Perth Gazette, 1832

The commander of the colony's military forces, Captain Irwin, was persuaded to spare Yagan. Although a most severe and stern officer, Irwin was not adverse to helping Yagan. While in England during 1834–36, he attempted to push the cause of Aboriginal welfare with the Church of England Missionary Society. Irwin was a senior member of the Swan River government and was acting governor during Stirling's temporary absence from September 1832 to September 1833. Captain Irwin had a problem: he wanted to foster friendly relations with the Aboriginals but was forced to execute one of the Aboriginal leaders after two white settlers were murdered. Hoping to achieve some reconciliation with the Aboriginals, Irwin freed Yagan.

Portrait of Frederick Irwin (1788–1860), acting Governor of Western Australia from 1847 to 1848 taken from the website of the Constitution Centre of Western Australia. Author Bartletto Studios

There may have been another motive that encouraged Irwin to give the Aboriginal chief his freedom: news of a story of rich new lands. As a result, John Septimus Roe, the Surveyor-General of Western Australia recommended that Yagan and his men should be exiled on Carnac Island, a penal settlement for Aboriginals, under the supervision of Lyon and two soldiers[6].

Lyon had become well respected for his studies in the local customs and languages of Aboriginals. He had learnt in the course of his research that the Aboriginals had told him of rich lands, lakes and rivers to the north. Lyon had already previously written to the Secretary of State for the Colonies offering his services to lead an exploration party providing they paid him £200 per year in expenses.

On 6 November, 1832, Moore wrote of a description of the Karakin Lakes by Aboriginals who were imprisoned on Carnac Island, situated about 10 km south-west of Fremantle between Rottnest and Garden Islands.

It was a desolate, unforgiving rock that barely had a shrub growing. Sea lions and seals were the only welcome visitors.

The natives, who are confined on Carnac Island, have given a rude sketch of some part of the country: they make Lennard's brook identical with the Avon, and represent som large river[7] flowing to the N.W., which has different names in different districts; but they do not seem to know whence it arises, nor where it debouches into the sea; they also sketch a large unexplored lake, [Karakin Lakes] or cul-de-sac, to the north, in the interior, but are not able to give any idea of the distances or relative situations of them.

I understand they were very accurate in describing the rivers which lie to the nrth. Mr. Lyon, who superintended the native prisoners at Carnac, says they describe several rivers to the north; one of them large, and abounding with fish; [Moore River] but they could not be undestood in their description of distances. It seems that the land is all parcelled out into districts among themselves, and that they rarely travel far from their own homes. The chief of this district is called "Worragonga": Ya-gan is the son of Worragonga[8].

---

[6] Green, Neville, *Broken spears: Aborigines and Europeans in the Southwest of Australia*. Pert, Western Australia: Focus Education Services, p80, 1984

[7] Moore River. Although the Moore River flows SW and not NW, it is the only large river there. Moore was also focused on searching for an inland sea.

[8] Moore, GF, *Extracts from the Letters and Journals of George Fletcher Moore*: pp204–205, 184

A modern representation of Lyon's map

In Lyon's map[9], Waylo's territory is above a large lake. It's tempting to name the largest and most northerly lake, the Karakin Lakes. It is even more tempting when we read the following definition Lyon made in a letter to the Perth Gazette in 1833: **Waylo**, *a lake into which the Boora* [Moore River?] *discharges itself*[10]. [Author's emphasis]

The word *waylo* becomes even more interesting when we compare the Dutch meanings of the words *Waal, Walloon* and *wal* or *wallen*. *Waal* means river and *wal* or *wallen* mean rampart, shore, or embankment. However, Walloon is the geographical name for one half of Belgium. In the 17th century, Walloon was under Dutch control so it would not be surprising if there were sailors aboard the *Vergulde Draeck* who had come from that region. The 'o' on the end of Waylo was sometimes added by the Aboriginals to describe a body of water, such as a lake or river, with the addition of an

---

[9] *Copy of Lyon's map by the NSW Department of Education and Training 2008*

[10] Letter by Lyon to the Perth Gazette, 1833

'o' sound. For example, Booneenboro, Perth Water; Dootanboio, Melville Water; Yardelgarro, a large sheet of water and Ngoogenbo, a large lake. Walloon in Belgium has one very large river: the Meuse or Maas in Dutch. It flows through Namur, the capital of Walloon and is surrounded by stone walls on the hillside overlooking the river. The description of the stone walls overlooking the Karakin Lakes sounds familiar fitting very well into the description of the Lost White Tribe in Dale's journal.

Lyon had no idea of course that this area had already been explored by Dale where he had discovered the 'Lost White Tribe.' The Secretary of State did not want Lyon stumbling into the same area finding these Dutch settlers. He therefore wrote back to Lyon the following:

Captain Stirling having since his return, furnished the department with ample information on every subject with the settlement, Mr Stanley thinks it no longer necessary to give you the trouble of continuing your correspondence ...

The ample information Governor Stirling was referring to was Dale's journal and his description of the Lost White Tribe. However, Captain Irwin, who was acting Governor in Stirling's absence, sensibly allowed Lyon to take Yagan to Carnac. After Yagan agreed to teach Lyon his native tongue in return for Lyon teaching Yagan English, he wrote, *I have my hand on the key that will unlock its hidden spring and disclose its treasure.*

For six weeks Lyon, Yagan and three other Aboriginals exchanged their languages, culture and histories. Yagan must have more than once expressed his desire to return to his own territory and family. Lyon would have explained that it was impossible as he would surely be shot.

The subsequent actions of Yagan would seem to indicate that both Lyon and Yagan had hatched a plan of action after his escape from Carnac. According to Lyon, he had carelessly walked past a boat that was at the water's edge. Yagan and the three others later escaped.

Yagan then did the unthinkable. He came to Perth to speak to Captain Irwin in a very good mixture of broken English and his own language. Yagan spoke in terms of a truce where he guaranteed that both black and white people could live in peace. Although Yagan agreed that the white settlers would not have to return to England, he could not agree to the Swan and Canning natives moving to the outer reaches of the settlement.

Yagan seemed to know exactly what to say. He suddenly saw in Stirling that he was his long dead brother. He recognised James Drummond as the reincarnation of a tribal elder and respected Moore as the keeper of law that would serve both black and white.

He offered an agreement to Irwin where his people would receive regular rations in return for their lost hunting grounds. None of his tribe were to be denied entry to Perth or prevented from fishing on their river frontages. Yagan insisted that the rations were to be handed over not as a charity but as a payment for their lost hunting grounds. Yagan would collect the rations himself and distribute it amongst his people. In return, his people would no longer have any need to raid gardens or spear the stock of settlers. Despite the already existing food shortages, Irwin agreed and the colony entered a short period of peace. Given the length of time Yagan and Lyon had spent together, as well as his well-known sympathies towards Yagan and his people, it's hard not to come to the conclusion that they had worked everything out together.

Sealing the deal, Yagan was given a red soldier's coat whenever he was in town. He gained a lot of appreciation from the townspeople after sometimes chopping wood or fetching water for people whom he regarded as friends. He even once organised his own people to save a burning house. These events were recorded in the Perth Gazette.

Relations continued to improve into the first quarter of 1833. Whenever game was plentiful, Yagan exchanged kangaroo and other wild game for wheat, rice and bread. However, the settlers did not always keep their side of the bargain. When food was particularly scarce in April, Yagan's brother, Domjuim, decided to steal a loaf of bread at the Fremantle store in 29 April. Domjuim was shot at by the caretaker and died a few days later in gaol. Vowing vengence, Yagan gathered a party of 50 to 60 Noongar warriors at Bull Creek where they intercepted a party of settlers who were loading carts. Both John and Thomas Velvick were killed. Their supplies that they had been carting were also taken. The reward for Yagan's capture was increased to £30, dead or alive.

Although a truce was arranged, it only lasted until May 1833. A visitor, driving a cart, was unacquainted with the excellent relations that had now been built between the two cultures, foolishly shot at a group of inoffensive Aboriginals killing or wounding every member of the group. An enraged Yagan with fifty other warriors followed the tracks of the cart and killed them. However, Yagan had more suffering and heartbreak to come. His father was captured and tried for at least four murders. Yagan made it known that should his father be killed then he would take three lives in retribution. Despite the threat, Midgigoroo was discreetly shot. Settlers were warned to keep the execution a secret lest Yagan should carry out his terrible promise.

Despite having a huge reward for his capture and having a fearsome reputation, there were many settlers in the upper Swan River area who still regarded Yagan as their friend. Continuing to visit his friends, he would press them as to any knowledge they might have of his father. Of course they feigned ignorance on the matter. After Yagan interviewed Moore on the matter, Moore interpreted Yagan's response as follows: *You came to our country; you have driven us from our haunts and disturbed us in our occupations; as we walk in our own country we are fired upon by the white men; why should the white men treat us so?*

Eventually a settler did reveal to Yagan that his father was dead. Within a week two soldiers were killed by Yagan. However, he still kept the company of many of the settlers trusting that they would not be tempted into betraying their friendship for the reward.

Unfortunately, two young apprentices to the settler Mr Bull, James and William Keates, came across a group of Aboriginals. Instantly recognising Yagan, they suggested to the group that they should get their rations of flour while Yagan stayed with them. It was during this time that the teenage brothers decided to kill Yagan for the reward money. At their first attempt, the gun stopped mid-cock. It took them some time to muster up enough courage to make another attempt but by now Yagan was anxious to join the rest of the returning party.

Yagan refused to go any further with the Keates ... and when he became threatening and began to raise his spear, William Keates cocked his gun and shot him, while James shot Keegan, another native, who was throwing his spear. James then ran for his life down to the river where he plunged in out of sight, and turned to see four natives driving their spears into his brother[11].

James returned with some armed settlers where they discovered Yagan's body as well as the Aboriginal that James shot. However, he was still alive but his brains were hanging out. They shot the poor man to put him out of his misery.

---

[11] Hasluck, A

The thirteen-year-old brother James was able to escape to claim the £30 reward. Understandably James was promptly sent back to England. Yagan's head was later cut off by soldiers and preserved by smoking it in the hollow of a tree for several months. Thus the artistic depiction of Yagan by Dale, bears little resemblance to the real Yagan.

There was no glory in the killing of Yagan. The Perth Gazette was scathing in its criticism of his death describing it as 'a wild and treacherous act and that by this act the whites had taught the native to exercise towards them deceit and treachery which in him had been the subject of daily reproof.'

The retaliation was swift. Yagan's mother, Moyran, ordered the firing of crops and outbuildings. Stock was speared and settlers feared for their lives. By the time Stirling had left to England, the settlement had lost 3,600 people. Less than five hundred of the original 4,000 strong settlement remained. For most, the promise of wealth never eventuated. Too many settlers arrived with too few skills, too little money on too much land. Faced with constant hardships, food and labour shortages, attacks by Aboriginals, most of the original settlers returned to England.

The news of the discovery of 300 Dutchmen living only 100 km north of Perth had put the whole question of the legality of the Swan River Settlement into question. Combined with the raids by Yagan's tribe and the food shortages, the settlement's existence never looked more uncertain.

Sketch of Yagan[12]

---

[12] Sketch drawn by George Fletcher Moore in his unpublished handwritten diary July, 1833
The digital image was obtained by scanning Figure 18.1 of Fforde, Cressida (2002) Chapter 18: Yagan, in Fforde, Cressida, Hubert, Jane and Turnbull, Paul (eds) *The Dead and Their Possessions: Repatriation in Principle, Policy, and Practice*, pp 229–241, London:Routledge.
This above source credits "Courtesy Battye Library — Private Archives 263A" for the photograph.

Appendix: Letter[13] by Lyons to Lieutenant Governor Irwin
To His Honor the Lieutenant Governor in Council. Woodbridge 26 November, 1832
Sir,
Yon will probably desire to know how far the plan lately adopted with regard to the Native
prisoners, promises to lead to any amelioration of the condition of the native tribes, I am happy to be able to state for your information, that so far as the opportunity was afforded of carrying the plan into effect, it was attended with complete success. Up to the very evening on which they made their escape, the experiment was more and more satisfactory ...

I have acquired a small portion of the native language, the geographical names of all places of any consequence within the Settlement; the names of the chiefs of all the tribes with whom we are more immediately connected; together with the boundaries of their respective districts. I have also acquired some important geographical information, beyond the present boundaries of the Colony. The country to the Southward has been partially explored. But of the countries to the North and the East, we are entirely ignorant. To these quarters I therefore directed my attention.

To the North is a stream called the Gyngoorda. It seems to be the outlet to the lake into which Lennards brook or the Boora, discharges itself; and the Boora seems to be a continuation of the Avon, called in the native language the Gogulger. The Gyngoorda is probably Bannisters river. **To the North and next to the Gyngoorda, are the Bookal and the Mooler, which apparently unite after the manner of the Swan, and the Canning. Some of the government stock have found their way to the banks of the Mooler. These rivers abound with fish; and the timber on their banks is said to be lofty.**

To the West of the Mooler and almost adjoining the coast, is the Yardlegarro; a large sheet of water, described to be fresh, and very deep. Indeed the whole of the country, in the vicinity of the Bookal and the Mooler, appears to abound with lakes. [Author's emphasis] But the existence of a large river passing the Settlement on the East and the North, will be a discovery of the greatest importance. This river, which bears three different names? accordingly to the countries through which it passes, rises in Goodengora, under the name of the Wilgy. Passing Bargo, where there is a chief called Wulbabong, it assumes the name of the Gatta; and, after a circuitous course through a great extent of country, it is approximate. I am not certain that in either case, there is a continuation. It takes the name of the Margyningara; after which, turning westward it falls into the ocean, some where to the North of the Mooler.

To the North of the Margyningara, is the Narnagootin, of which I know nothing beyond the name. I am rather at a loss to form a correct estimate of their ideas of distance and magnitude. But after making all the allowances on this ground which I conceive to be necessary, I have reason to believe the information here communicated will be found to be perfectly correct.

Such are the results of one month's intercourse with the native prisoners, taken at Point Belcher. I mention this not from any feeling of vanity, but to demonstrate the practicability of acquiring the native language.

---

13 [13] Lyon, Robert M, Letter To His Honour the Lieutenant Governor in Council. Woodbridge 26 November 26, 1832

There is in fact no obstacle whatever to the civilizing of the native tribes; unless it be foundin the backwardness of the local Government. But I trust the reins are in the hands of men, who will do honor to themselves and the country they serve. A niggardly policy will not only sacrifice the peace, of the Settlement for years, but will cost the Government and the country an expense hereafter, of which they have no conception. Thirty thousand pounds, if I am correctly informed, will not cover the expenses of a sister colony, during the last three years only, in pacifying the natives – not to mention the great sacrifice of human life in the sanguinary conflicts which so repeatedly occurred between them and the settlers-and all in consequence of the unwise policy originally pursued.

I must not forget to observe, that the natives of this Country, are naturally possessed of all the finer feelings that, when cultivated, adorn the human character. I am therefore bound to contradict the statements that have gone abroad upon this subject. On this point Colonel Hanson was in error. That gentleman must have received his information from those who knew nothing of them. Yagan, allowed by every one to be, of savages the most savage, wept with gratitude after I saved his life, and expressed his sense of the kindness shown to him in the strongest terms. Yet this is the man who, in the midst of his guards, on a small island, where his life must have been the forfeit, could seize his spear; and, erect in all the pride of his native independence, determine to sell his life dearly, rather than submit even to an insult. Such are the men you have to deal with in the natives of Western Australia. I need not add, that your best policy is to make peace with them, before they get a knowledge of your manners and tactics.

I would strongly recommend exploring parties to the East and the North, And my services are at the command of the local Government for this purpose. Indeed I am desirous of going that I may have an opportunity of communicating with the native tribes in those quarters, before the country be contaminated with the visage of European immorality. [Author's emphasis]

My vocabulary is ready to be presented to the the Council; and I shall be happy to read it, and answer any questions you may desire to ask of me.
I have the honor to be Sir,
Your obedient Servant
P.S.
LYON.
I am ready to join Captain Ellis and Mr. Norcott; and under proper arrangements, to prosecute the work of making peace with the natives, either on Melville water, the Canning, the Murray, Ellen's brook, or the Avon ; or, for a time to go into exile on the Boora, the Gyngoorda, the Mooler, or the Margyningara. And I have no doubt, under the blessing of the Most High, that in the course of one twelve month, I shall be able to present one, if not more of the native tribes, at Perth on Sunday to attend divine service and benefit by the Ministerial labours of the Colonial Chaplain. In the mean time I earnestly intreat that a stop be put either by proclamation or otherwise, to the wanton and unprovoked attack upon the native tribes at all convenient opportunities by our own people. The tribe of the quiet and inoffensive Yellowgonga, was lately fired upon while fishing on the river, driven into the bush and plundered of their fish. The cry of this deeply injured race must be heard by the judge of all the earth; and their blood will assuredly call for vengence. I would suggest that the proclamation strictly forbid them to be molested; while peaceably encamping, travelling, fishing, or hunting. They are called British subjects; and rewards ought to be offered for the apprehension of those who want only and wilfully murder them, without any provocation.

Chapter 10

Aboriginal stories of a White Settlement

Swan River Settlement 1858 by Weller / Edward. Karakin Lakes is written as L. Garagan.

Story One – shipwreck

The story of a white settlement came about after Billymera was captured by the soldiers for killing settlers. Billymera's son, Weeip[1], found a way to entice the Governor to free Billymera. After having speared a soldier to death, Weeip was also a wanted man. He recounted a story of a ship that was wrecked possibly as far as Shark Bay. Weeip knew that the Governor would be a lot more interested if he thought that it was an English ship with a 'large quantity of money ... lying on the shore.' Weeip[2] didn't claim first hand knowledge of the shipwreck, but had said that a tribe called the 'wayl-men' that lived much farther north, told them that white men, women and children were living there. It's worthwhile taking a closer look at the whole episode as told by Moore.

1834 – Friday, July 11 — To-day I find that a great sensation has been created in the colony by rumours which have come to us, only through the natives, of a vessel that was wrecked nearly six months ago[3] (30 days journey, as they described it) to the North of this, which is conjectured to be about Sharks Bay. Further enquiries have been made from the natives; they say that "wayl-men" – men from a distance to the North – have told them of it, and that there are men and women and children still alive, inhabiting two larger and smaller tents made of poles and canvas; that the ship is quite destroyed by the sea; and that a large quantity of money, like dollars, is lying on the shore. Here is a matter of most painful and absorbing interest. There have been great discussions among the members of the Government about what is the best course to pursue, in which discussions I have been in some respects a participator.

The story seemed sufficiently convincing for Lieutenant-Governor Stirling to send off a search party via ship. At the same time, a message was also to be delivered to the castaways by native couriers at the suggestion of Moore.

An expedition by land with horses was first thought of, but, from the great price of horses, &c., it was found that it would require nearly £500 to equip such an expedition. It is now determined to send off a vessel direct to Sharks Bay, and thence to commence a search north and south along the coast – which is of such a nature that it cannot be approached from sea except at two or three points all the way up there. It is awful to contemplate the sufferings of the wretched survivors. All here have been anxious about them, and I myself have not been idle so far as my thoughts and powers went; but I shall explain this in due order.

In the midst of our discussions, I suggested the possibility of forwarding a letter to the sufferers by means of the natives, and to get the Government to authorise me to offer the liberation of Billymera (Weeip's father) who is now in prison, as an inducement to any of them who would carry a letter there and bring an answer back.

Moore went to some trouble to find Weeip. Luckily he came across some natives who knew him. Taking Moore into some thick bush, the natives stopped, whistled and called out Weeip's name.

Like a spectre, Weeip appeared from behind a bush, and came smiling to meet me, with his hand outstretched. I could not refuse it, and coming at once to the point with him, I related to him, in his own language and manner, that "black man" had told "white man" that other white men, our friends, were sitting on the ground at a distance, crying, and that the ship which had walked with

---

[1] Weeip's Territory according to map by Lyon and Yagan.

[2] Weeip has also been described as a 'mountain chief'

[3] Six months could mean an old shipwreck was revealed after a tsunami had hit the north-west coast in 1833.

them over the sea from England was broken upon the rocks, that the white men here were sorrowful, and that I would give black fellow a "paper talk," that black fellow should give that "paper talk" to the white fellow at a distance; that my "paper talk" should stop there, and that the white man at a distance should give another "paper talk" to black fellow, who should come back soon and give it to Mr Moore, and that Billymerra, his son, would then be a friend, and Governor would say, "walk away, friend"[4].

Weeip agreed with Moore and took his friend Tomgin with him to deliver a letter to the survivors of what Moore believed to be a British ship.

After sailing past Kalbarri and as far as Shark Bay, the ship returned without sighting any evidence of a wreck. They were unable to see the well-hidden wreck of the *Zuytdorp* which literally crashed into the cliffs now named the *Zuytdorp* Cliffs. We now know from more recent research that survivors from *Zuytdorp* did come ashore and coins were recovered in the water at the base of the cliffs.

Weeip and Tomgin also returned after making exhaustive enquiries from tribe to tribe before arriving at the same conclusion that the story had been a 'lie properly.' However, according to reports in the Perth Gazette, Weeip did not go far enough as he was unable to cross the Bannisters River due to flooding.

The Bannisters River should not be confused with the river south west of Perth. It was most likely either the Toodyoy River[5] or a northerly tributary of the upper reaches of the Swan River. In either case, Weeip was a long way from completing his mission.

Perth Gazette 9 August 1834
RETURN OF WEEIP
WEEIP, the proscribed native, who, with the prospect of obtaining his own pardon and the Liberation of his son, Jiill-yoo-merry, undertook to convey a letter to the white people who were supposed to be Wrecked to the Northward, returned on Monday last, after an absence of about 22 days. It appears he did not go so far as was expected: probably not further than Bannisters River, which it is imagined impeded his progress.

No one suggested that the Swan River tribes had lied but had simply interpreted a word of mouth story that was based on what happened centuries ago. They realised that chronology was of little consequence where a year ago or a century ago were interpreted the same as 'the time past.' Despite the lack of success of Weeip's mission to Shark Bay, Weeip received a full pardon from Sir James Stirling and Billymerra was released from custody.

It was either a very clever ruse by Weeip or he was relating the story of a shipwreck of either the *Vergulde Draeck* or the *Zuytdorp* where survivors from both ships had made it safely ashore. It would be easy to dismiss the story as fanciful and a product of Weeip's scheming imagination. However, it is more likely that Weeip had the best intentions of reaching the white settlement which was rumoured to be as far as Shark Bay, but simply could not make his way through the recent flooding. Weeip was still a long way from the Karakin Lakes and even further from Shark Bay.

Just 15 days later, another story appeared of a Lost White Tribe living north of Perth.

---

[4] Moore, G.F. *Diary of ten years eventful life of an early settler in Western Australia and also a descriptive vocabulary of the language of the aborigines.* Chapter 9, *The Colony*

[5] See map at start of chapter, *Map of the Swan River Settlement 1858* by Weller / Edward.

Story Two – A Lost White Tribe

The following was reported in the Perth Gazette, 26 July, 1834.

Another version of the wreck to the northward has been communicated to us by Mr F Armstrong; the substance of the information is as follows:-

I have this week, for the first time, been able to make inquiries of the Upper Swan Natives respecting the supposed wreck, – my information is small but, perhaps, sufficient to throw some light upon the subject. The natives tell me that about two and a half day's walk from here – say about 50 miles, [80 km] or, perhaps, not more than forty – **are several white people living***: they have not been there very long; some of the natives whom I know, belonging to the second Northern tribe, have been to them. The white people, they say, go out catching kangaroos; they are on friendly terms with the natives, and have given them food, as well as white 'money'. They don't know what they have come for, neither do they say that they have either women or children. I described to them that a vessel had been sent in that direction; but they said, on my pointing out the distance to which she ordered to extend her search, that* **it was too far, and that they would miss the white people, as they were settled rather inland.** [Author's emphasis]

The knowledge that Mr Armstrong possesses of the native language, induces us to place every reliance in his statement. ... It may be interesting to know that the natives have intimated to know that they are aware that Weeip is gone to see the white men, and they say he has promised to bring some of them 'white money'[6].

Apart from the distance, Mr Armstrong's interview compares very well to the location of the Karakin Lakes. Anyone travelling up the coast would certainly miss the Karakin Lakes as it is too far inland. The *Vergulde Draeck* survivors had settled inland. From the above information, it seems as though they did take some money with them. Coins from the wreck have been found as far east as Mogumber or further east than the Karakin Lakes settlement. It is also just one more confirmation of a white tribe living north of Perth.

Despite Weeip not finding any traces of white people to the north, he maintained an insistence that there was ' *"money plenty" on the shore just where the waves beat on the beach; that the pieces of money lie on the top of one another, and he indicates that they cover a good space of ground*. He was most likely referring to the 1712 shipwreck of the *Zuytdorp* which literally crashed into the cliffs just north of Kalbarri but south of Shark Bay, the site most deemed to be the location of the white castaways. (Story One)

Apart from the versions told to Moore and Armstrong, there was still a third version of events also told by Tomgin and Weeip. It was the first time the story had been told. Stephan Parker, a farmer who lived about 10 km north-east of Perth, was the first to receive the news of wreck.

They spoke of a great deal of 'white money' (silver coins), that were scattered for about 30 m along the shore in front of the wreck. The ship had been torn apart ('broke'), and it had three masts, with 'blankets' (sails) flapping around.

Parker was told that those who had survived included **tall white men, with women and children**. Relations between the survivors and the Aboriginals were said to have been good. They had given the Aboriginals food ('biscuit'), and received spears and shields in return. [Author's emphasis]

---

[6] Perth Gazette and Western Australian Journal, 9 August 1834

Initially the survivors had built five 'houses' – two large and three small – constructed of wood and canvas, situated on the open coast. The authorities at that time, had assumed that the wreck was most likely situated in the Shark Bay area which is not far from where the *Zuytdorp* was wrecked. However, Parker was told that the survivors included women and children which means that these survivors were most likely from the *Vergulde Draeck*.

The historian Phillip Playford[7] believed that the story had been handed down from generation to generation until it had eventually reached the Swan River tribes.

In 1927 the *Zuytdorp* site was discovered and later in 1964, a dive team literally discovered a 'carpet of silver' very close to the shore line below the cliffs.

The variations of the different stories can be also be explained in another way. All the stories were true except that two different white settlements became entangled and interpreted within the same story. That is, the *Vergulde Draeck* and the *Zuytdorp* survivors became the one white tribe instead of two distinct white tribes.

The dates of these stories of white tribes are important. Suddenly in 1834, the stories begin to emerge. The white tribes were on the move thus coming into direct contact with other Aboriginal tribes who were also on the move. The end of the chapter will reveal the reason why there was a mass movement of tribes in the second half of 1833.

Story Three – Description of the Lost White Tribe

Explicit references to a white tribe or people were later made by Tomgin who had returned from the north after going into voluntary exile for slaying a man. He had gone a considerable distance. Had Moore included the following interview with Tomgin in his diary, he may well have been able to link the story to the one told by Weeip. Instead Moore included Tomgin's account in his journal[8].

When he returned in 1835, Moore asked what strange things had he seen. Tomgin spoke of seeing *a man called Mannar who said he had gone a long way to the north east till he had gone to Moleyean; that it was very far away 'moons would be dead.' (Meaning more than a month) before you would arrive at it; that you walked over a great space where there were no trees; that the ground scorched your feet and the sun burned your head; that you came to very high hills; that standing upon them, you would look down upon the sun rising out of the water beyond them –* **that the inhabitants were of large stature;** *and that the* **women had fair hair, and long as white women's hair;** *that all the people's eyes were "sick"; that they contracted the eyelids and shook their heads as they looked at you*[9].

If you are looking down at the sun rising out of the water, then he could only be on the east coast of an island or watching the sun rise over a large lake. Tomgin had frequently spoke of Moleyean and pointed to the north-east. On further investigation, Moore found from a Mr Armstrong who helped to interview Tomgin, that *the natives seem all to be aware that they are living on an island, and Tomgkin* [Tomgin] *appears to be speaking of the other side of the island*. Looking across a very large lake, there may be parts that would seem like an island.

---

[7] Playford, Phillip, *Carpet of Silver, The Wreck of the Zuytdorp*

[8] Moore, GF, *Evidences of an Inland Sea*, published in 1837

[9] Possibly a symptom of conjunctivitus

Moore had two months earlier made an excursion that followed a river course to a spot about 160 km from Perth in a NNE line. Moore asked a native, where the waters of the east of the river went. The native replied, *The waters there go to the east, and out at Moleyean.* There is only one place where the waters could have flowed into: The Karakin Lakes. The Karakin Lakes[10] are about 160 km in a NNE line from Perth and the waters of the east or the Moore River, flowed into them.

Despite not finding the elusive Moleyean, Moore still believed of its existence and continued to write to the Perth Gazette to convince the colonists that a large inland sea or lake surrounded by good land was real. However, Moore had to contend with the problem of conflicting stories of Moleyean by different Aboriginals from different tribes. Some had proclaimed that Moleyean was east of the Wongan Hills while others believed it to be north east of Perth. Moleyean appeared also to have several meanings.

What is interesting about the 1880 and 1833 maps is how the Karakin Lakes are drawn in relation to the Moore River. These maps had drawn the Moore River as flowing into the lakes whereas maps from other years show the Moore River clearly bypassing the lakes. If the 1880 and 1833 maps are true to scale, then the lakes extended a further 2 to 3 km.

THE MOLEYEAN. Saturday 24 September 1836

To the Editor of the Perth Gazette.
Sir,-With reference to the question of the existence of a large body of water lying to the eastward in this Colony, it is very desirable to ascertain, if possible, the precise meaning of the word "Moleyean," the use of which term by the native first gave occasion for the conjecture of such a probability. This word Moleyean has been interpreted in various ways, having been supposed to signify "the other side of the island" – "the ocean" – "the strange water" – "the muddy water of inundation" – "the furtherest place known;" – and, again, several directions very widely apart have been pointed to as indicating its situation. It appears so difficult to establish the character and fix

10 The Moore River and Karakin Lakes (spelt L. Garagan) Map by John Bartholomew, 1880

the position of this "Protean Ubiquity," that, although very desirous to give it "a local habitation and a name," I candidly confess myself to be as yet quite at fault in this respect[11].

However, it was Moore's letter to the Perth Gazette a few months earlier that provided the greatest interest. He wrote of his native friend Tomgin who had returned from the north in 1835. Tomgin made reference to the inhabitants of Moleyean as been of **large stature** with the women having **long fair hair** as long as **white women's hair**. Although Tomgin had not seen these people first hand, he had been told of their existence by *a man called Mannar* who had gone a *long way to the north east*. [Author's emphasis]

Letter to the Perth Gazette

Saturday 25 June, 1836
To the Editor of the Perth Gazette:
Much scepticism appears still to prevail as to the existence of a large body of water at no great distance in the interior, as I have before ventured to assert. As this is a subject of much importance to the Colony, I am desirous of mentioning all the progressive steps of Information by which I have advanced to such a conclusion, in order that others may not only have the means of judging of the reasonableness of the conjecture, that such a thing does exist, but also may be able to form some idea of its situation, distance, extent, and direction. It is known to all, who converse with the natives here, that their knowledge of the localities of the country beyond the bounds of their own immediate district is extremely limited and imperfect. A visit to some friend in a neighbouring tribe comprises, in general, the extent of their travels; the occasions are rare and urgent when they transgress these limits.

*Tomgin is a native of much shrewdness of observation, and some reflection. Having upon one occasion gone into a sort of voluntary exile for the slaying of a man, he had proceeded to a considerable distance, principally northward. On his return, nearly a year ago, I had been inquiring what strange things he had seen or heard of during his absence; and it was then that he first told me, amongst other things that he had seen a man called "Mannar", who said he had gone a long way to the north east, till he had gone to Moleyean ; that it was very far away – "moons would be dead," (meaning more than a month), before you would arrive at it; that you walked over a great space where there were no trees; that the ground scorched your feet, and the sun burned your head; that you came to very high hills; that, standing upon them, you would look down upon the sun rising out of the water beyond them; – that the **inhabitants were of large stature, and that the women had fair hair, and long as white women's hair**; that all the people's eyes were "sick"; that they contracted the eyelids and shook their heads as they looked at you. Dreaming much of this to be the mere exaggeration of a traveller's story at the time, I laughed at it; when he said, "Well, friend, do you ask Mannar, I do not tell you that I saw these things: I tell you what Mannar told me."* [Author's emphasis]

From my imperfect acquaintance with the language at that time, I was not sure whether he meant that Mannar himself had seen all the wonders, or only heard of them; but he frequently mentioned the word Moleyean, and pointed to the north-east, in explanation of it.

Explanation for the confusion
If the huge flood had occurred in late 1833, then the Lost White Tribe from the *Vergulde Draeck* were on the move, travelling north and highly visible to the northern or 'Waylo' tribes who were

---

[11] Moore, GF, *The Moleyean* Perth Gazette, Saturday 24 September, 1836 pp.767, 768

also forced to move from their familiar hunting grounds. The rising waters sent both humans and animals to seek the highest ground. Inevitably this drew both the black and the white tribes together.

With their houses, walls, and crops wiped out at the Karakin Lakes, a northerly migration was the only possible route as it was physically impossible to travel south into the floodwaters and low lying land. After such a catastrophic event, weakened by hunger and exhausted from their trek to the north, the Lost White Tribe could not sustain such a large nomadic population. Smaller groups remained where sustainability allowed or chose different northerly routes in the hope of finding an ideal location to found a new settlement. However, as the white tribe dissipated in their northerly trek, they could no longer maintain their separate entity and were forced to accept the terms of assimilation from the northern tribes.

Meanwhile, in 1834, a year after the white tribe embarked upon their great trek north, a story had been told by Aboriginals of white people shipwrecked north of Perth. So convinced were the authorities that both a land a sea excursion were sent to bring back the survivors.

Chapter 11
Aboriginal Legend of a Lost White Tribe and the Great Flood

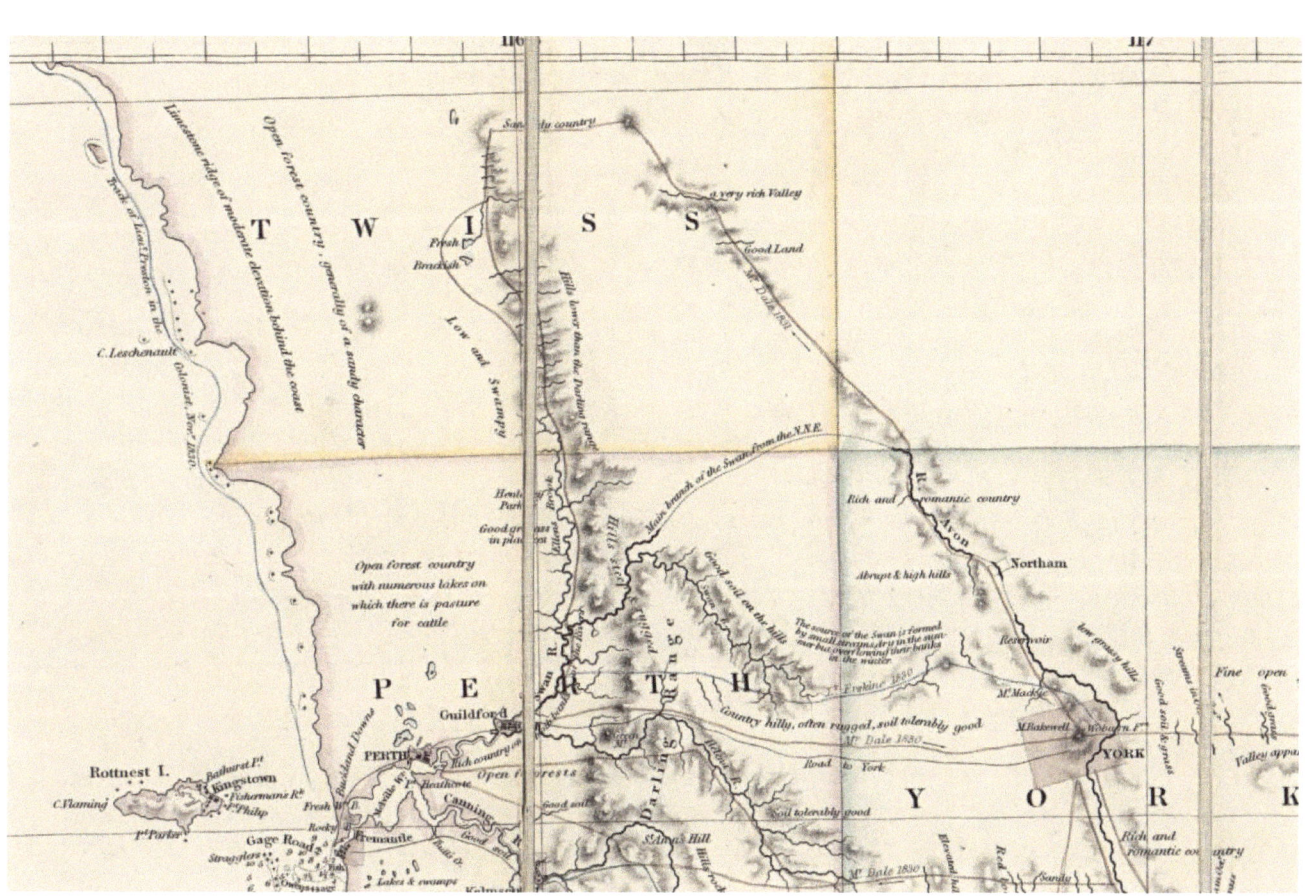

Early map of Western Australia by J Arrowsmith, 1833

Story Four – Aboriginal Legend of the Lost White Tribe

With so many white settlers in the region one would expect that Aboriginal tribes in the area and even the early explorers must have come across some evidence of this Lost White Tribe. Although Oldfield's account of a Lost White Tribe, has been dissected in chapter 8, it is worth revisiting in the context of the great flood which wiped out many of the settlers and forced the survivors to trek north. Oldfield gave a clear description of a 'white' tribe that existed on the northern shores of a river while the Aboriginal tribe lived on the southern side. When we compare Oldfield's story to The Leeds Mercury, the evidence is compelling. Here are two pieces of evidence independent of each other both corroborating the same facts.

One important fact was the exact location of the Lost White Tribe. The Leeds Mercury article refers to the Dutch as having settled on the northern side of the river. The Aboriginal tribe who lived to the south of the river, were called the Southmen. The white tribe were called Northmen or Waylo-men.

Augustus Oldfield's account of a Lost White Tribe

The following curious tradition is current among all the Aboriginal tribes from the Moore River to Shark's Bay in Western Australia, each claiming to be the one referred to. **That the people of the other tribe were white** *may be looked upon as a recent innovation which has only arisen since the settlement of the country by the English; for, as the blacks have evidently lost all remembrance of the race in question, knowing only that it was distinct from their own, it is but natural that they should consider as identical with the only race of which they have not any knowledge. It is not unlikely that this tradition refers to the pristine inhabitants of New Holland, of whose existence some traces are still extant ...* [Author's emphasis]

I now proceed to relate their legend which was given rise to the foregoing remarks:

A long time ago, there were two tribes living on the banks of a large river, one (blacks) inhabiting the southern side, and the other (whites) residing on the opposite shores. For many years the two tribes were on amicable terms, intermarrying, merrymaking, and fighting with each other, and so it continued, until by and by a change in the sentiments of the **northmen** *took place. These whites were evidently the superior of the two races; for they were more powerful, athletic and agile than the blacks, and made better spears, boomerangs and other arms, and, what is of greater importance, could use them more efficiently than the poor southmen, as the latter learnt to their cost. At length, proud of their superiority, these northmen refused to hold any intercourse with their southern neighbours, save and excepting in the matter of fighting, in which diversion the advantage was always on the side of these insolent whites.*

Things continued in this state for a vast number of years, till one day **it began to rain, and poured incessantly for many months,** *and the river overflowing its banks the blacks were forced to retire before the rising waters, and this way they were driven far away from their own country. The flood was long in their ebbing as it had been in rising, and thus it was long ere they regained their old hunting grounds, as they had to follow the subsiding waters; but arrived there, what was to their astonishment to find, in place of the fordable river they had left, that the* **impassable sea** *rolled to the north of them, and that their late haughty neighbours had entirely disappeared, and they were never to be seen or heard of by the black men*[1]. [Author's emphasis]

The *large river* was the Moore River and the *impassable sea* was the now flooded Karakin Lakes. Although there are other large rivers between the Moore River and Shark Bay, the Moore River is the only river with a large lake nearby.

---

[1] Oldfield, A, *The Aborigines of Australia*, in the *Transactions of the Ethological Society of London.* p232–5

The Great Flood

The whole story is uncanny as it also explains what happened to the Lost White Tribe. A great flood not only destroyed the entire settlement, the white tribe was forced northwards as that was the only high ground that provided a safe escape. This would also explain why the majority of the evidence of European influence, both written and archaeological, lies north of the Karakin Lakes especially between the Irwin River, Geraldton, and as far as Shark Bay. The flooding must have been widespread as the logical thing to do would be to wait out the flood and return to rebuild their settlement. The widespread flooding forced the white tribe to travel north until they arrived at an area that provided fresh water, shelter and a food supply.

It's impossible to work out how much time the white tribe had in readying themselves for a possible evacuation. However, it is not hard to imagine how difficult it would be for 300 men, women and children to wind their way through flooded plains, rivers, gullies and ditches.

Oldfield mentions *an impassable sea*. Here is Moore's inland sea and Moleyean. It also explains why there were so many differences in the location of Moleyean. The inland sea must have encompassed a massive area. This is supported by Daisy Bates in her reference to a *great flood that covered all the land except certain hills*.

Story Five –'A Great Flood which covered all the land'

The Great Flood legend is given more credence when we refer to one of Australia's most important anthropologists, Daisy Bates, who lived amongst the Aboriginals for some considerable time. She wrote: *There were vague traditions extant amongst some of the South-western tribes of **a great flood which once covered all the land except certain hills** … In the Gin Gin district, it is said that a long time ago there was a great flood which once covered all the land except Mindangup Hill and on this hill all the animals took refuge. The people also went to the top, but they were afraid to kill the kangaroos until they became very hungry. After some days the water went down and the kangaroos and the people spread themselves over the country*[2]. [Author's emphasis]

According to the Aboriginal traditional stories, the flood was extremely widespread. Although we can question the timeframe of the flood, the location of the flood is quite specific: the Gingin [Gin Gin] district which is in close proximity to the Karakin Lakes settlement. Mindful of the flat terrain of Western Australia, I asked Steve Caffery, a local with expertise in Environmental Management, how widespread a flood could be in that area of Western Australia

'A flood of only two metres could submerge huge tracts of land in Western Australia. We are a very flat state after all.'[3] He gave me the recent example of the 1999 flooding of the Moora district which coincidentally connects with the Moore River. According to Caffery, 'It is not inconceivable that the Karakin district could also flood as a direct result in harsher wetter times.'

To illustrate how low lying the land is along parts of the mid-west coast, Steve Caffery sent me three photographs. Two of the photographs show the north and south hummocks. Steve speculated whether these two peaks were the ones left untouched by the great flood. I also wondered if some other outside factor influenced the unusual rain pattern of the latter half of 1833. Three catastrophic events occurred in 1833 that may have triggered the great flood: the eruption of nine Indonesian volcanoes, earthquakes and the resulting tsunami.

---

[2] Bates, D, *The Native Tribes of Western Australia*, p226

[3] Caffery, Steve. (BSc Environmental Management), The Gilt Dragon Research Group

North and South Hummocks located between Jurien Bay and Lancelin. The two hummocks are the two high points on a massive flood plain.

'The area around the North and South Hummocks is unusual even today due to the large tracts of exposed sand. An exposed sand dune can take up to 100 years to recover (if ever). There's no reason why a vast area of exposed sand could not represent an area recovering form an 1833 flood[4].

---

[4] Caffery, Steve, *(BSc Env Man)* Interview with author October 2012

Story Six – Second Aboriginal Story of a Great Flood

On 16 February, 1842 yet another story of a great flood emerged in the *Inquirer* which reported a story told by William Nairne Clarke[5]

There is one legend current amongst the natives of the interior which is rather remarkable. **They say that one man and one woman came from a far away country long ago**. *The direction to which they point is north and north by west. The part of the earth which the man and the woman inhabited was suddenly covered with water and they fled to a very high mountain, and on the fall of the water, descended into the plains, where they found plenty of tu-buck (i.e. native yam), and, being almost dead due to the pangs of hunger, ate plentifully ... Mr Drummond states, 'They [Aborigines from the York district] say that the earth was at one time covered with water, when one black man and woman found themselves on a rock on top of a very high mountain. They were reduced to the extremities of hunger but the water retiring, left the roots of the wyrang exposed. They had nothing to do but gather them and eat. In the process of time it spread over the country, but got deeply imbedded into the earth, and now they require much labour to dig them out*[6]. [Author's emphasis]

There are a few very interesting points in this report. The man and the woman came from a 'far away country long ago' in a 'north and north by west' direction. From the district of York the Karakin Lakes are in a NW direction.

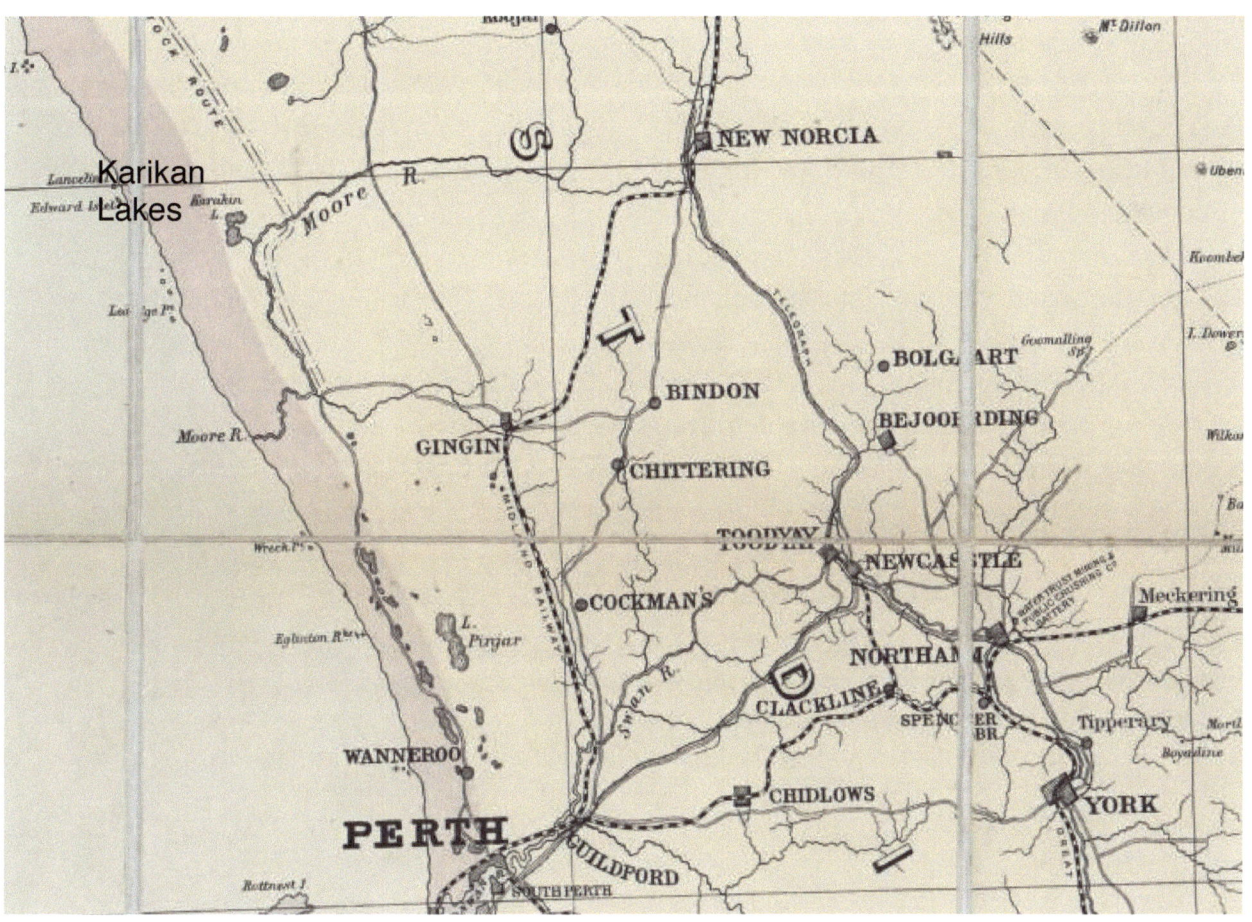

---

[5] Clarke, William Nairne (1804–1554) was a lawyer and publicist. Newspaper proprietor of the *Swan River Guardian* in 1836–38. Explored South Western Australia between 1840–42.

[6] Clarke, WN, *An Inquiry Respecting the Aborigines of South Western Australia in the Inquirer 16 February, 1842*, p5 Also Gerritsen p99,9

1833 – The year of Extreme Weather Events

1833 was not just a cataclysmic year in Indonesia, but all over the world. So severe and extreme were the weather events in that year that it sparked some debate as to the causes of the hurricanes, floods and earthquakes that occurred throughout 1833 and 1834. Rev W.B. Clarke wrote a detailed paper in 1835 discussing the extreme climate change events of 1833 and 1834. Clarke believed the severe changes were linked to volcanic eruptions and possibly meteor strikes. Mount Vesuvius in Italy had erupted on 7 August.

Europe not only suffered from severe storms and floods. Between 31 August and 13 September, earthquakes were felt all over Scotland. England had earthquakes in Oxford and Gloucester in November 1833 and in October, Ostend had the highest flood it had ever known. 103 British vessels were lost during August and September 1833. From 'April 2 to 6, there were violent hurricanes off the coast of Egypt[7].' In May 1833, a hurricane of the most furious intensity destroyed thousands of lives in both Calcutta and New Orleans.

In NSW a drought was not broken until March 1833. *Hurricanes and rain commenced in NSW at the end of April 1833; in Bengal in June, when they ceased till September; in China, in July; At the Cape of Good Hope in August; whilst in Europe they commenced in October. In August the rains in India were dreadful ... in Dhoola they had continued rains for 20 days. In China, the rains, which subsided on July 24, were still more dangerous; the rivers were overflowed and thousands of lives were lost: the crops were ruined, and thousands of lives were lost; villages carried away, and trade suspended ... Immense flooding in India August 1833 – up to 40 ft deep, [12 m]. Villages and towns were carried away, bridges destroyed*[8]. The flooding continued from August 1833 until June 1834 in China, Bengal and Surat.

1833 was also the year of the most intense Indian Ocean cyclone. 'The lowest barometric pressure actually measured in the Bay of Bengal was during a severe cyclone in 1833 when the British vessel SS Duke of York reported a measurement of 891 mb while passing through the eye of the cyclone[9].' An estimated 50,000 deaths resulted from the cyclone in India and Bangladesh. In December 1833, and January 1834, dreadful floods occurred in the Maine, the Moselle, the Rhine, in Holland and France. On 2 January the Seine was higher than known since 1740.' December 1833 also saw violent hurricanes in London to Liverpool. On the 29th there were hurricanes at Mauritius and also on the 26th at Trieste.

The westerly gales... intensity and frequent hurricanes character, in 1833, point to some great modifying cause. Certain of those gales can, I think, be traced to a connection with volcanic influence. Now, it certainly proves this to be no haphazard calculation, that the years 1833 and

---

[7] Clarke, Rev. WB, Magazine of Natural History, Vol 8, *On certain recent Meteoric Phenomena, Viccissitudes in the seasons, prevalent disorders, and contemporaneous in supposed connection with Volcanic Emanation, p14*

[8] Ibid. p149

[9] Burt. Christopher C, *Weather Extremes: Tropical Storm Superlatives for Australia and the Indian Ocean.*

1834 answer the conditions required: since, independent of volcanic outbreaks, the whole of the world has been visited by a drought of long continuance, which has dried up the rivers[10].

Extreme weather events occurred across the entire globe and on every continent in 1833. Western Australia was not spared. Evidence of extreme and unusual weather conditions occurring between August and October, 1833 in the Swan River Settlement would confirm 1833 as the year of the Great Flood. In the same month in 1833 the ship *Mercury* disappeared after leaving Calcutta.

1833 Flood

George Fletcher Moore recounted the flood events in his diaries. Below are some of his excerpts detailing the poor weather conditions.

DESCRIPTION OF THE TERRITORY OF WESTERN AUSTRALIA, FROM DOCUMENTS IN THE OFFICE OF THE HON. J. S. ROE, ESQUIRE, SURVEYOR-GENERAL [11]

August 5th. Last nights' rain having rendered the country insecure traveling for the horses, we had a great difficulty in proceeding a mile easterly from our bivouac, when our course was interrupted by the last mentioned stream flowing northerly, on penetrating a short distance down its course with the expectation of crossing it, we were obliged to return to nearly where we had forded it last night, where, owing to the wet and hollow nature of the ground, we had to unload the horses, before they could approach the margin; having carried the baggage across we attempted to remove it to a hill opposite the ford, but our progress was again arrested by a broader stream flowing to the North, the channel of which was too deep to ford ...

August 7th ... we ascended a hill, and at its base again fell in with the brook on the banks of which we tested last night, and which here intercepted our course, owing to its turning abruptly to the North; it being too rapid and also too deep to attempt to ford it ...

They managed to ford the brook by making a bridge. Continuing in a ESE direction, there came a river which they named the Avon which they described as *a considerable stream.*

August 8th ... to avoid passing over the hill we ascended yesterday, which we found, too much saturated with rain for the horses to attempt to traverse, we continued our course down the right bank of the brook in a North and North-Easterly direction ... when we had the gratification of arriving at the considerable stream we noticed yesterday running towards the NW – it had evidently overflowed its banks, the apparent channel or bed of the river being about 60 yards – the water discoloured and muddy with a rapid current, and enclosed between banks moderately clothed with trees and shrubs.

August 9th ... We advanced this forenoon 2 miles up the left bank of the river, but with considerable difficulty owing to the soft and yielding nature of the soil in the neighbourhood of the river, caused apparently by excessive rain ...

August 10th – Finding it impossible to make any further progress with our horses ... we were fortunate this night in finding shelter from the rain, which was pouring down in torrents... the flats bordering the river being mostly flooded, we were unable to judge of their general character. The soil on the uplands and hills being chiefly composed of a light sandy loam, with a stratum of clay

---

[10] Ibid. p3

[11] Perth Gazette and Western Australian Journal, Saturday 7 September, 1833

about a foot underneath the surface, rendered the travelling from the late excessive rains rather fatiguing, as we were obliged to tread on tufts of grass to avoid sinking in many places to some depth in this wet and hollow ground.

August 11th – Having only brought two days' provisions with us, we regretted now being obliged to retrace our steps to where we had left our horses ... Mount Bakewell ... as we reached the summit it was obscured completely by the dense state of the atmosphere, and by the heavy rains which then set in. ... On rejoining our men, we found they had encountered so much difficulty in urging on the horses whilst loaded, owing to the excessive wetness of the ground, that they had been obliged to unload them, and carry the baggage themselves.

August 12th – After walking about 7 miles, [11 km] we arrived at the northern side of the range, but were much disappointed in not being able to obtain a view of the plain, as, directly we reached the summit it was obscured completely by the dense state of the atmosphere, and by the heavy rains which then set in (Mount Bakewell area) ... On rejoining our men, we found they had encountered so much difficulty in urging on the horses whilst loaded, owing to the excessive wetness of the ground, that they had been obliged to unload them, and carry the baggage themselves.

August 15th .... one of our horses, became so exhausted, that he sank to the ground, in which situation we were obliged to leave him till the following morning.

August 31 — We have had much rain during all the last week and strong winds ...
Wednesday — There has been a long spell of rainy and stormy weather ...

The heavy rain continued into October and November after *a further attempt at exploring the region to the north was made in late October / November by J.S. Roe, Surveyor-General with six volunteers and five horses ... Mount Caroline, and the southern Mount Stirling, after my fellow traveller, Mr W Stirling.*

Monday — There came on a very severe storm on Saturday night. Thunder, lightning, and heavy rain; ... An expedition ... is delayed for some days longer to let the ground dry sufficiently before they start.

October 10th – Tuesday – There has been much rain, and the river is considerably swollen in consequence. I had some trouble in riding through it; the mare was all but swimming ...

Friday – There has been experienced in the York district **a hail shower of extraordinary severity, such as has not been seen nor dreamt of in this colony before.** *The hailstones are described to have been as large as pullet's eggs. Some sheep are said to have been killed by the storm, and some of the crops beaten all to pieces.* [Author's emphasis]

Monday — Much rain, thunder, and lightning, which are unusual at this time of the year.

From explorers' reports, there is ample evidence that the 1833 flood extended as far east as the Avon River. This would also mean that the flooding of the Moore River would have occurred closer to its source and well before it reached the proximity of the Karakin Lakes.

From subsequent explorer reports such as F Gregory in 1858, there is evidence that the flood extended all the way to the upper Murchison and Gascoyne rivers.

Upper Murchison
... the river runs in a deep channel from 80 to 100 yards [73 to 91 m] *wide in ordinary seasons, but when in flood must exceed 300 yards,* [274 m] *and the rise of the water, judging from the rubbish drifted up in former years, must exceed thirty feet.*

Gascoyne River
... the river keeping a general course of west-north-west, its channel deepening to sixty feet, and maintaining an average width of 400 yards. ... the accumulated waters of the late inundations having been confined to one channel, had risen to the height of forty-eight feet, carrying away many of the largest timber trees, as also much of the soil from the banks, leaving a scene of devastation exceeding anything of the kind I had hitherto witnessed[12].

Rain, storms and flooding were certainly unusual for that time of the year as the records show from the Bureau of Meteorology which has records dating back as far as 1876. Normally June and July have the highest rainfall throughout the year. Then there is a sudden drop in rainfall especially in the months September to November. Thus unusual heavy rainfall over a few months after the two wettest months of the year, would have compounded any flooding.

The highest record Perth rainfall figures for the months June to November between 1876 and 2010 are listed below:

June	July	August	Sept	Oct	Nov
176.7 mm	169.9 mm	134.1 mm	80.9 mm	52.4 mm	22.2 mm

These records unfortunately don't go far enough back to record the 1833 figures. If it did, then the record for October would appear to have been easily broken. Still, even if there had been records for Perth in 1833, the Karakin Lakes are at about 120 km north of Perth where the weather pattern could have been even more severe given its closer location to the northern cyclones. As late as 1926, Aboriginals still spoke of the 1833 flood.

The natives of the past used to speak of a great flood that covered everything except two peaks[13].

Two Western Australian meteorologists, Joe Courtney and Miriam Middlemann recently completed a study of the meteorological hazards in Western Australia. After studying the floods of 1926, 1945, 1963 and 2001, they concluded that the most devastating floods occurred after accumulated rainfall over an extended period. They based their research on a 70-day period of the above flood events. *Indeed rainfall can be important as much as 12 months prior to the event.*

The rivers were already swollen as early as 1830. *Their want of knowledge of the climate, however, caused a good deal of suffering during the wet season. The winter rains of 1830 were particularly heavy, so much so that the river overflowed its banks and brought considerable loss and damage to*

---

[12] Gregory, F. *Mr Gregory's Report*, Perth 1858

[13] *Sunday Times The Avon Valley The story of York 1829-1834* (Perth, WA Sunday 24 October, 1926)

those who were temporarily residing on the flats waiting for their grants, or who had elected to build permanent homes on the lower levels[14].

Courtney and Middlemann also found that the unusual rain events occurred when a *decaying tropical cyclone interacts with a cold front into an intense fast-moving system. These systems can produce a range of destructive phenomena* including intense rainfall ...

Cyclones in the southwest can move at speeds greater than 70 km/h, in contrast to the average speed of 10-165 km/h in the north. The structure of the cyclone changes as it accelerates so that the regions of dense cloud and heavy rainfall are displaced towards the right quadrants of the system (when looking on the direction of the track), leaving the left quadrants largely free of significant cloud. As a result the **heaviest rainfall, for example, would occur when a cyclone crosses the coast near, and to the north of Perth, as in March 1934**[15]. [Author's emphasis]

A combination of high winter rains followed by unusual rainfall events from August to October changed the destiny of the Lost White Tribe forever. An enforced trek north also meant that any chance the white tribe would be brought back to Perth and sent back to the Netherlands, was gone. The story of the Lost White Tribe remained a secret: no embarrassment, no complications, no headlines, no Lost White Tribe.

---

[14] Striling, E, *Brief History of Western Australia Volume 1*, p5

[15] Courtney, Joe and Middlemann, Miriam. *Meteorological Hazards* Bureau of Metoerology, WA Regional Office and Geoscience Australia 2002

Chapter 12
Relocation of the Lost White Tribe

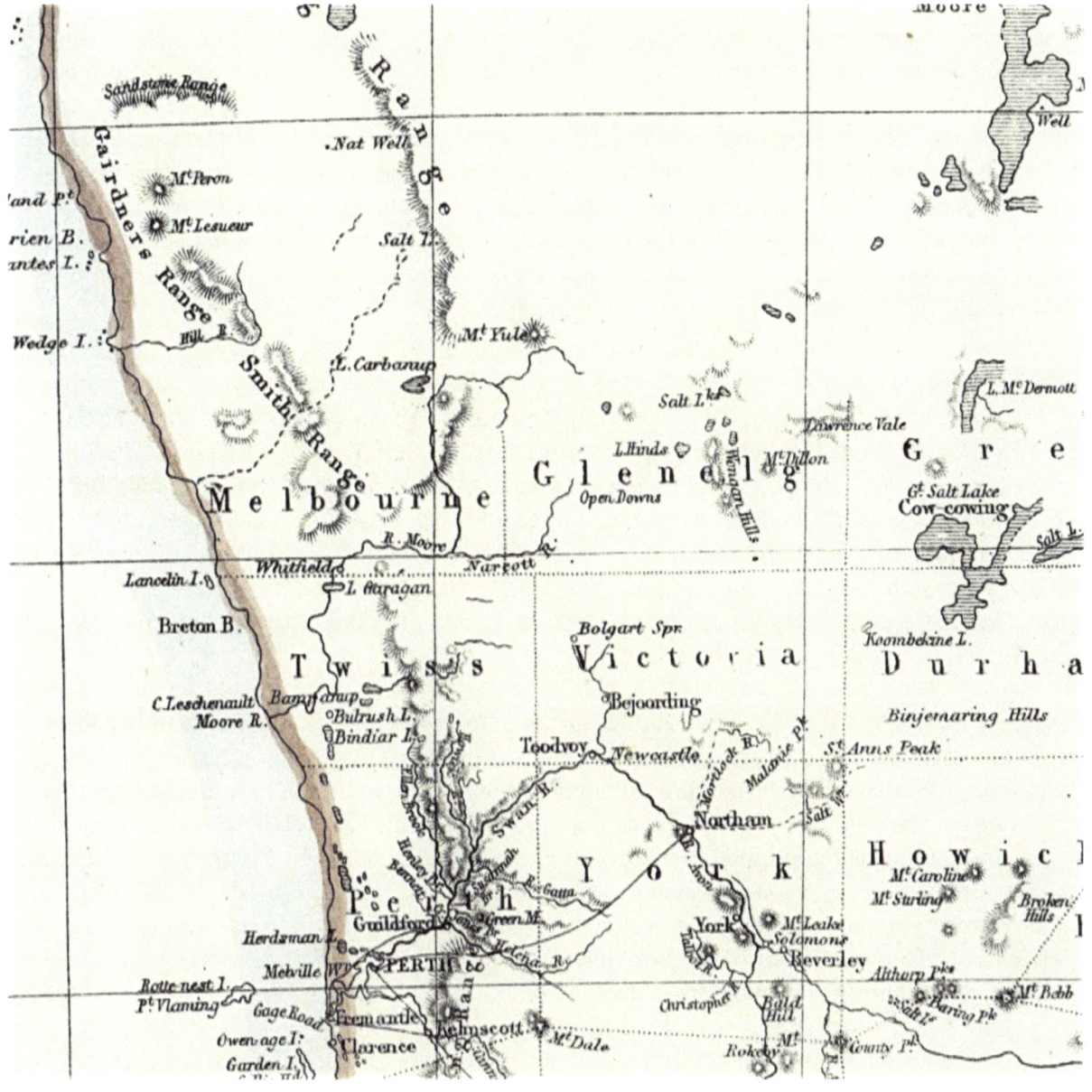

South Western Australia 1871-5, Cassell, Petter & Galpin

Note the Karakin Lakes are marked as L. Garagan. During a huge flood, the most likely way north was along the Gairdners and Smith Ranges

The Great Trek North

To understand what had happened to the white tribe after the catastrophic flood of 1833, we must realise that *all* of the 300 members were born and bred in Western Australia before any other European settlers. Their fathers and grandfathers had also been born around the Karakin Lakes. All they knew of Europe were the stories passed down from generation to generation.

This new white tribe of Western Australia had conquered and adapted to their new surroundings. Combining their new found knowledge they had acquired from neighbouring tribes with their European knowledge of tools, houses and weapons, they created a permanent settlement surrounded by a stone wall, a river and a vast lake.

127 years of settlement had preceded their forced trek to the north. Generations of the white tribe had already experienced and survived drought, storms and floods. The higher ground was to the north. There was no way south except across kilometres of low lying ground. However, on this occasion they were to witness a flood that no one, including their ancestors, had ever experienced.

Although preparations for a temporary move north would have been made well in advance, the possibility of a catastrophic flash flood cannot be discounted. If they did have time to prepare, food, tools and weapons may have been gathered and placed into receptacles for easier transport. Perhaps they used a canoe to carry their supplies. Each family gathered enough yams to help sustain their temporary evacuation. There had to be enough supplies to last at least a week before they could return and rebuild their settlement.

The 1833 Flood

The flood was far worse than anyone could have imagined. It had extended as far inland as the Gingin district. Daisy Bates had been told by Aboriginal tribes that *a great flood covered all the land except certain hills … In the Gin Gin district, it is said that a long time ago there was a great flood which once covered all the land except Mindangup Hill and on this hill all the animals took refuge. The people also went to the top, but they were afraid to kill the kangaroos until they became very hungry. After some days the water went down and the kangaroos and the people spread themselves over the country*[1]. Gingin is quite close to the Karakin Lakes situated approximately 20 km further inland in a south-easterly direction.

Fortunately for the white tribe, a ridge of higher ground stood north of their settlement but there were no mountains. The dips and valleys in the terrain would have made it impossible to make an immediate return. However, the terrain did not significantly increase in height until they reached inland from Jurien Bay and Green Head. Once they passed the Hill River, they could gain respite on a number of mountains that continued in a northerly line. Situated between Jurien Bay and Green Head, Mount Benia (257 m), Mount Lesueur (312 m) and Mount Peron all offered some respite from the devastating floods. East of these mountains, the terrain is quite high varying between 200 and 300 m above sea level. We know they travelled along the Gairdner Range towards the coast because a reported sighting was made by Aboriginals[2].

With three hundred men, women and children competing for food, it became obvious that they

---

[1] Bates, D, *The Native Tribes of Western Australia,* p226

[2] Salvado, Rosendo, *The Salvado Memoirs: historical memoirs of Australia and particularly of the Benedictine Missions of New Norcia and the habits and customs of the Australian natives*. Translated and edited by EJ Stormon. Nedlands, WA. University of Western Australia Press, 1977. Mission natives told Bishop Salvado, that, '*four days journey north of New Norcia there were other white men.*'

could no longer survive together as a separate entity in the one location. The weak, injured and sick settled with a few families at locations that could at least sustain a small population. Alongside the white tribe on these hilltop islands, other animals such as snakes, kangaroos and small reptiles competed for life. Although at first there may have seemed to be a plentiful food supply, once it ran out, there was nothing left except, perhaps, the next hillside. Thus the white tribe became fragmented on its trek north which would, in part, explain the wide sightings between the Irwin River and Geraldton's Champion Bay area.

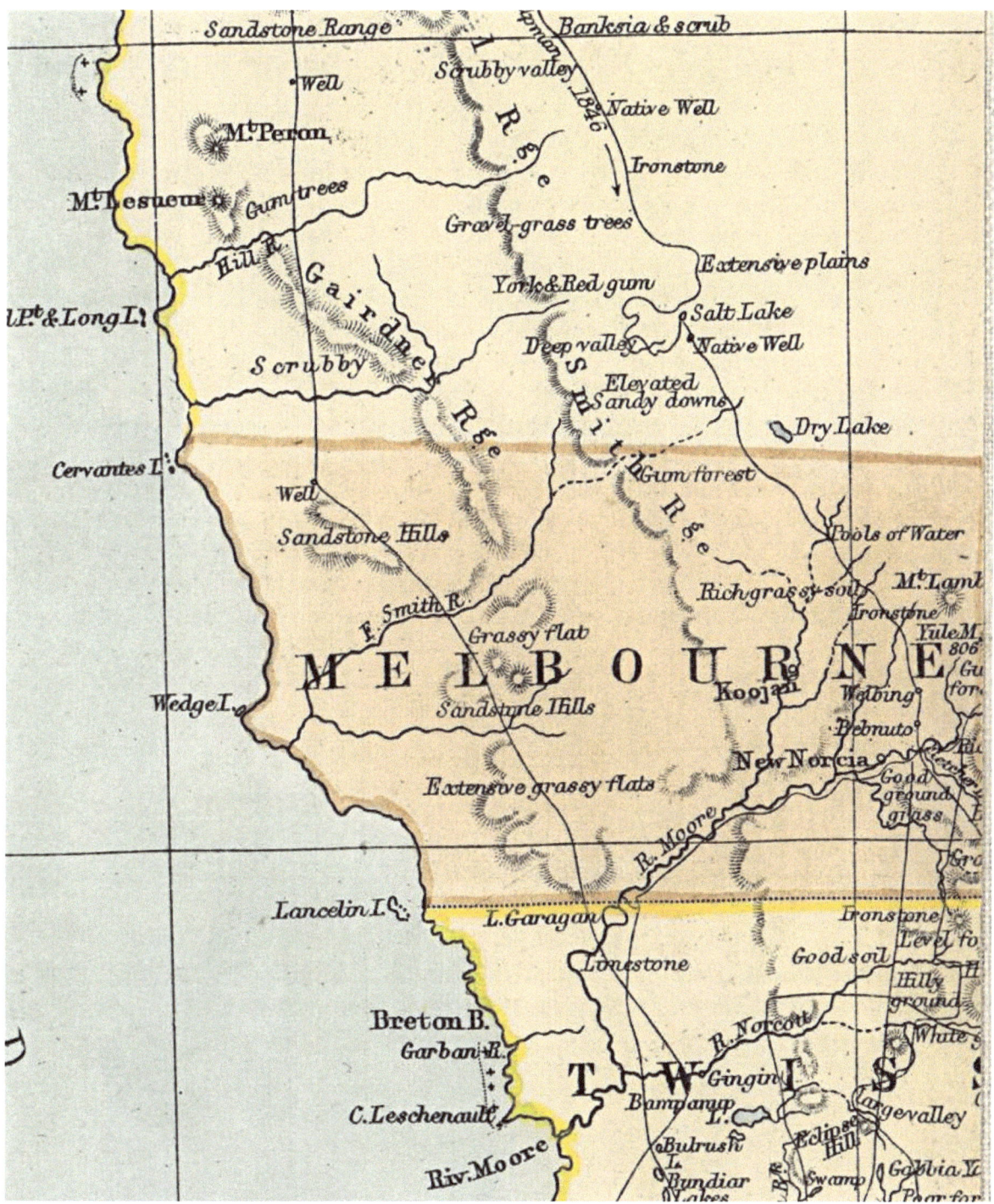

The above map[3] shows the ridge line from the Karakin Lakes (shown as L. Garagan) to Gairdner Range, Mount Lesueur, Mt Peron and finally to the Sandstone Range

---

[3] Bartholomew, J, *Map of Western Australia 1880*

Accounts of a 'white tribe' north of the Moore River
Fortunately we are able to trace the route of the white tribe based on the accounts of explorers, anthropologists and settlers who either saw the remnants of the white tribe or the results of intermarriage between local Aboriginal tribes. The question over where the Lost White Tribe finally settled is somewhat clouded by the existence of other shipwrecked sailors who had come ashore north of Geraldton. However, there was one significant difference: the Lost White Tribe had remained separate, for the most part, from all Aborigines. The Dutch sailors in the north assimilated into the northern tribes but their influence proved to be enormous.

Story Seven – 'White people shipwrecked north of Moore River'
Mary Durack wrote about rumours of white people possibly shipwrecked sailors. *Not long after, rumours were circulated by the natives that a number of white people had been shipwrecked on the coast somewhere north of the Moore River. No one at that time suggested that the story might be a true enough account of a bygone happening perpetuated by word of mouth and interpreted, on the last reaching the Swan River Tribes, as a contemporary incident. Chronology was of little consequence in an Aboriginal context, in which one year ago or a century ago were simply the time past. Wrecks had been many on that treacherous coast. One of them, the Dutch vessel Gulden Draak [Vergulde Draeck] had gone down some 60 miles [97 km] north of Perth on 1656. The story, as told by seven survivors who reached Batavia in a small boat, was those 75 men, women and children had made ashore, though subsequent search parties never found no trace of them. Then there was the Zuytdorp, wrecked 56 years later north of the Murchison River, which must also have a place in Aboriginal memory* [4].

The survivors of the *Zuytdorp* made it ashore just north of Kalbarri in 1712. Over the next 121 years, their influence crept steadily northwards as far as Shark Bay, the Murchison, Gascoyne and Ashburton Rivers. Therefore, somewhere around the Champion Bay district the Lost White Tribe came into contact with Aboriginal tribes that had already had a significant Dutch influence.

The first physical piece of evidence that showed where the Lost White Tribe had come and which direction they were heading, came in the form of a 'Ring of Stones.'

Ring of Stones
A ring of stones was found by two surveyors, Alfred Burt and Harry Ogbourne, about 30 km north of Green Head and about 'one or two miles [1.6 to 3.2 km] from the coast[5].' They kept their secret for 58 years until Burt revealed their find to a newspaper in 1933.

In the year 1875 – 58 years ago – Mr Burt, then a young man, was camped at Woodada Well 45 miles [72 km] SE of Dongara. Starting out with provisions to take to the coast for Captain Archdeacon, he was accompanied by Mr Ogbourne, since dead. Near the ocean a dense thicket was met with. Cutting their way through they found a cleared spot, some 14 feet square, [4.2 m] in the centre of which was a complete circle of stones. Mr Ogbourne before his death recalled that there were no other stones nearby[6].

---

[4] Durack, Mary, *To be their heirs forever*, p118

[5] Gerritsen, R. *And Their Ghosts May Be Heard*, p 237

[6] *The Mirror*, 21 January, 1933. Gerritsen, p237

The wattle scrub was so thick that it prevented the two surveyors from making any progress. After setting fire to the thicket, they discovered the stone arrangement after proceeding inland. According to Malcolm Uren, the stone arrangement was located at 29° 56' 43"S, 115° 5' 46" E or on the enclosed map between the Salt Lakes and Stockyard Creek.

The ring of stones also had a line of stones pointing in a north by north east direction. I have included this particular map because it shows the natural stock route from Hill River to the Upper Irwin River. Stock naturally follow the easiest and most natural path and the one that provides the best feed and fresh water. It's interesting to note that the stock route veers north north east until it reaches the Upper Irwin. Not only does the line of stones point in the direction of the Upper Irwin, but that is precisely the location of sightings of 'fair skinned' Aboriginals.

Others had also either seen the ring or other strange stone formations near where the ring was sighted. Mr William Stokes of Greenough had claimed to have seen the ring. In 1932 Mr F King of Three Springs had discovered a 'strange formation of limestones placed at intervals of about 150 yards [137 m] apart over a mile of ground, pointing towards the vicinity in which the "Ring of Stones" was first seen.' Constable Loxton of Dongara, one of the participants in the two Burt expeditions, claimed the line of stones actually extended 'four miles[7].' [6.4 km]

The discovery of the Ring of Stones intrigued the readers. Many believing that the stones marked the location of the treasure of the *Vergulde Draeck*. In December 1938, two Dongara men, Jack Hayes and Gabriel Penney, embarked upon a treasure hunt.

---

[7] Gerritsen, R, *And Their Ghosts May Be Heard*, p237

All they had to do was rediscover the Ring of Stones[8] and dig. The first part, finding the Ring of Stones, was easy. However, the second part was impossible. They managed just 5cm when they struck not gold, but limestone bedrock. However, they still didn't give up hope as they noticed that the stones were placed in such a way as to be pointing at something or in a direction. Still no gold but Hayes wrote a detailed description as well as a rough plan of how the stones were represented. Uren, a journalist, interviewed Hayes.

Hayes described the Ring of Stones in the following way: *There are three groups of stones in a clear area ... One was in the form of a ring and the other two were rectangular in shape, situated on each side of the circle. One of the rectangular areas had a base line of about 22 yards [20 m] in length with sides about three feet long.[0.9 m] The other had a base line of about 15 feet [5 m] and sides of about the same length as those in the formation. One was set straight in relation to the circle and the other was slanting. In front of the ring there was a much larger rock with a tree growing from its base[9].*

In the sketch[10] that Hayes had provided Uren, he showed that the circle of stones was about eight feet [2.4 m] in diameter. In one part of the circle a small tree was growing. To the north of the circle was a large stone which he marked on his sketch as perhaps 'a pointer'. In a line with the north-east diameter (but apparently not strictly in line) there were projected lines of spaced stones, that on the east being about 45 feet long [14 m] and that on the west about 15 feet long. [5 m]

The Ring of Stones photographed in 1939 and touched up for clarity

---

[8] Gerritesen, R, *And Their Ghosts May Be Heard*, p238

[9] Uren, M. *Sailormen's Ghosts: The Abrolhos Islands in Three Hundred Years of Romance, History, and Adventure* pp39-40. Published 1940 Public Domain

[10] The sketch made by Hayes has never been found.

Man-made stone wall

According to Gerritsen, the most likely place that the lines were pointing to was 'a local high point, Woodada Hill, about 8 km away.' From the top of this hill, the white tribe would have been able to see the Arrowsmith River and Arrowsmith Hill which are about 13 to 14 km NNE. 'If this route was taken they would have eventually found themselves at the head of a sloping valley which is dotted with springs, running directly north to the Irwin River in the vicinity of the Yardarino Flats, 42 km away. Upon reaching there it would seem they then turned once again in a north-easterly direction up the Irwin River,

finally stopping, exhausted by their forced march, north of its headwaters[11].'

After undertaking a number of expeditions, in June 2009, Rupert Gerritsen discovered what appeared to be a man-made wall overlooking a shallow valley. Gerritsen believed that the structure was either a lookout or a defensive wall[12].

---

[11] Gerritsen, R. p. 243

[12] Man-made stone wall, Gerritsen, Rupert, June 2009

Although I have been unable to visit the site, it would appear that the building of a permanent structure meant that the new settlers had either spent a considerable time there or were forced to erect a defensive wall to defend themselves against Aboriginal attacks. Unlike the stone at the Karakin Lakes, this wall is still largely intact. Satellite photos of the lakes, however, did show what looked like a line of stones that could be interpreted as a wall.

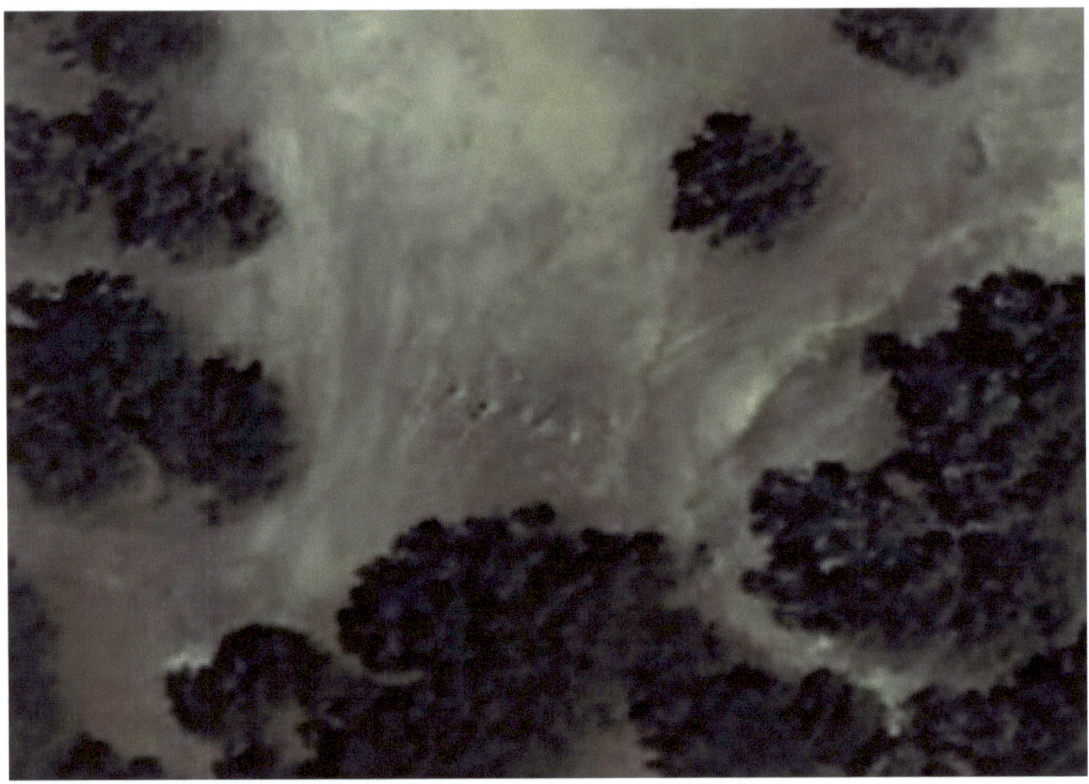

Satellite close up of a line of 5 stones at the Karakin Lakes

Two satellite[13] photos of the Karakin Lakes showing a row of stones or mounds that may have been the remnants of a wall.

Story Eight – Bishop Salvado

Further evidence that the white tribe had settled in the Irwin River Valley comes from Bishop Salvado, a Benedictine monk, missionary and author from New Norcia. This is the only town in Australia founded by monks. Salvado arrived in 1846 where he established a mission for the training of Aboriginals and their conversion to Catholicism.

Salvado from the New Norcia mission wrote in the 1840s that:
They told me through one of the mission natives that near the coast, four days journey north of New Norcia **there were other white men.** *After looking into this matter I came to the conclusion that these could well be the descendants of the mutineers Captain Pelsaert left behind*[14]. [Author's emphasis]

According to Gerritsen, four days journey for an Aboriginal would equate to 220 km. This would mean that the Lost White Tribe or groups of the white tribe, settled in the Irwin River Valley.

As for the Australian natives' hair, I have noticed that in the west it is not wooly but straight, and often fair enough to make a European envious[15].

As the white tribe travelled north the escape the flood, small groups perhaps too exhausted to continue, were left behind. No doubt some of them died. However, Aboriginals who were also suffering from the flood, may have adopted these stragglers into their own tribe. Unfortunately he doesn't reveal how old the natives with the hair **straight and often fair** are. However, it may have also been the result of contact between the Karakin Lakes white tribe and their neighbouring tribes despite the claim that they had remained homogeneous. It is hard to believe that in 177 years no intimate contact had been made between the white tribe and their neighbours.

This is borne out by his further statement that Aboriginal women's hair *is in fact abundant, and is sometimes fair and sometimes black*[16]. Salvado[17] often combed and washed their hair thus giving him the perfect opportunity to examine their hair. He also remarked on the baldness of some Aboriginal men from the west although he admitted to only have seen one completely bald Aboriginal[18].

---

[13] Courtesy of Google Earth, Digital Globe, 2009

[14] Salvado, Dom Resendo, *The Salvado Memoirs* p75

[15] Ibid. p112

[16] Ibid. p117

[17] Salvado, Dom Resendo, *The Salvado Memoirs*

[18] Gerritsen, Rupert, *And Their Ghosts May Be Heard*, p76

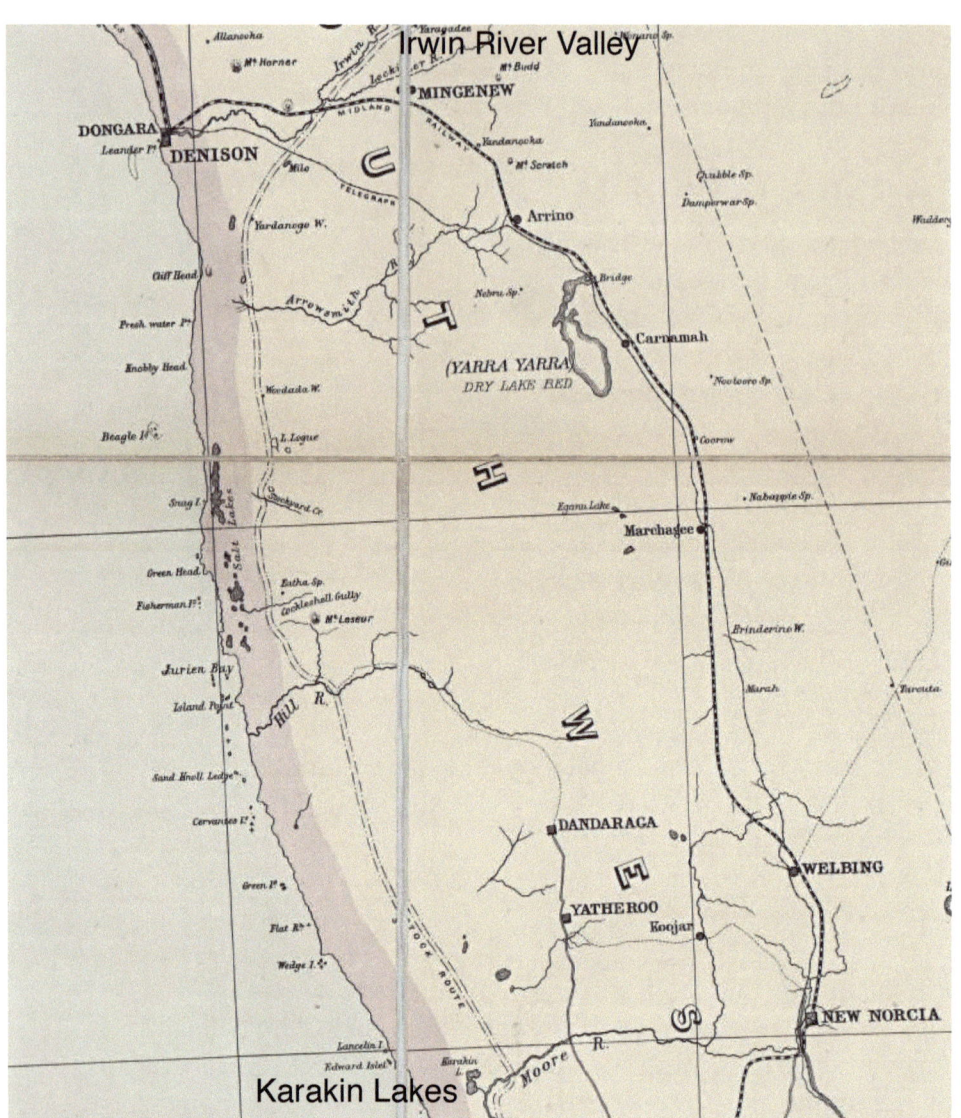

Goldfields Map (1896) showing the Karakin Lakes, New Norcia and the Irwin River Valley

Irwin River Valley[19]

---

154   [19] Photo courtesy of Hans Emmenegger

Chapter 13

The Irwin River Valley Settlement

The floor of the Irwin River Valley, Coalseam National Park. Photo courtesy of Hans Emmenegger.

The Upper Irwin Settlement

The Perth Gazette 9 August, 1861 commented on a tribe *who differ essentially from the Aborigines* on the upper Irwin River area[1]. The bold type in the newspaper article is the author's emphasis.

Below the blue dotted line on the 1869 map of Western Australia, is the route taken by the explorers, Augustus and Frank Gregory.

General Intelligence.

From Champion Bay we hear that a tribe of natives have made their appearance at the easternmost sheep stations upon the north branch of the Upper Irwin, who differ essentially from the aborigines previously known, in being **fairer-complexioned, with long light-coloured hair** flowing down upon their shoulders, fine robust figures and handsome features; their arms are spears ten feet in length, with three barbs cut out of the solid wood, long meros with which they throw the spear underhanded. A gentleman, who some months since explored the country to a distance of 100 miles north-east of the Irwin, informs us that he found these natives residing there, they were very friendly and gave, through a native interpreter, serviceable information as to the country in their neighbourhood.

[1] Petermann, August Heinrich, *John Forrest's Reise im Innern von West Australien*, 1869

There is an area in the Upper Irwin valley[2] that is extremely fertile with permanent water and high hillsides. The whole area is more than a kilometre long offering protection from the elements, fresh water, and an obvious hunting ground for game. In fact it is the *only* green, fertile area in the Upper Irwin. A 'mysterious gentleman' who wrote to the Perth Gazette, described a tribe in the Upper Irwin River area as one, *that differed essentially from the Aborigines ... in being **fairer complexioned, with long light coloured hair** flowing down upon their shoulders, fine robust figures and handsome features*[3] ...

This *mysterious gentleman, who some months since explored the country to a distance of 100 miles [160 km] north-east of the Irwin,* was the highly distinguished explorer, Augustus Gregory who had explored the area south of Champion Bay to Irwin River.

From the photo above, a fertile river valley, high hills and cliffs can be seen that must have sent torrents of water gushing into the river valley below during storms and floods. Given that the white tribe had just been evicted from their settlement at the Karakin Lakes because of a catastrophic flood, any permanent structures must have been built either high enough or far enough away from the flood zone. However, they may have also become semi-nomadic, exploring the course of the Irwin River into Champion Bay in search of food or water in times of drought.

---

[2] *The Irwin River.* Photo courtesy of Hans Emmenegger.

[3] Perth Gazette, 9 August, 1861

The photo[4] of the Irwin River above was taken much closer to the coast. It is logical that in times of water shortage, the white tribe would follow the river until they found sufficient fresh water.

Gregory described the river in the following way: *...struck the river, running north through beautiful grassy flats timbered with York and white-gums and wattles; there were many fine pools of water, which appeared to be permanent*[5].

Lieutenant Helpman, 1846, Irwin River, south of Geraldton.
We here met with the first native hut; it was well plastered outside and the timber which formed it was about 6 inches [15 cm] *in thickness, about 6 ft. high* [180 cm] *and capable of containing ten persons easily*[6].

The reports of superior huts and weapons, different dialects and traditions, continued further north to the Champion Bay or as it is known today, the Geraldton area.

---

[4] *The Irwin River*. Photo by S & D Elliot

[5] Gregory and Gregory, *Journals of Australian Exploration,* p15

[6] Helpman, Lt, *Champion Bay to the Coal on the Irwin River* in Exploration Diaries, Vol 4, p9, 9 December, 1846

Chapter 14

Champion Bay

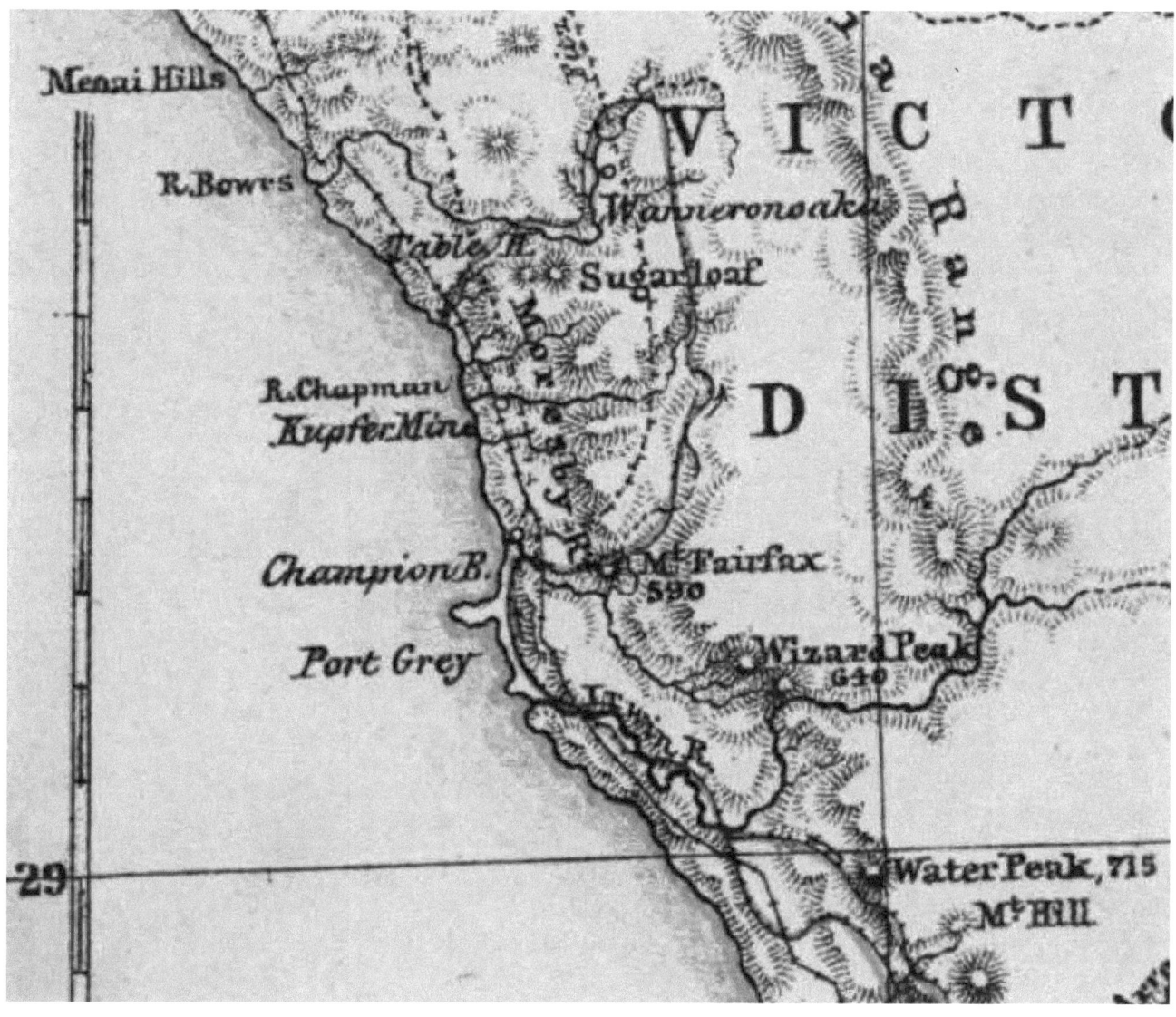

John Forrest's Reise im Innern von West Australia[1]

---

[1] Petermann, August Heinrich, *John Forrest's Reise im Innern von West Australien,* 1869

Numerous accounts by explorers, settlers and anthropologists describe the northern tribes of Champion and Shark Bay as different, very different from the southern tribes. Their dialects, weapons, huts and even some traditions were different. However, the most surprising difference of all was their appearance. This led to many theories as to the origin of the Aboriginals. Augustus Oldfield for instance believed that some of the Aborigines from the Champion Bay area were the remnants of the Alfouru race, a *civilised people that had been destroyed by the black man*. Only the results of the blending of the two races remained. The 19th century writers were not always culturally sensitive and Oldfield's speculation of *a pristine race* would not be acceptable today. However, we have to look through the eyes of a European educated in the belief that the English were the most civilised 'race' on the planet.

The hottest issue of discussion in the scientific world at that time was Darwin's theory of evolution. In his book *On the Origin of Species,* he introduced the idea that populations evolved over many years through a process of natural selection. It is worth noting that one of the full titles of his book was, *The Preservation of Favoured Races in the Struggle for Life*. Oldfield must have been a supporter of Darwin's belief in the transmutation of species which was an idea already current in the early 19th century. Transmutation meant that any species, even humans, could be changed or gradually evolve into either a more developed species or an entirely new species. Oldfield seemed to be an enthusiastic supporter of this highly controversial theory and he applied it to the northern tribes that lived in the Champion and Shark Bay areas.

Every tribe in WA holds those to the north of it in especial dread, imputing to them an immense power of enchantment, greater bravery, and superior skill in the manufacture and use of arms, and this seems to justify the inference that the peopling of New Holland has taken place from various points towards the north; for it is reasonable to suppose that such superiority would be accorded to the parent-stock by all its offshoots[2].

The art of constructing even the rudest of boats exists only among the most northerly of the Australian tribes, those to the south seldom resorting even to the use of a bundle of bark or of sticks to enable them to cross an arm of the sea[3].

Although bark canoes were popular on the east coast of Australia, significantly, the Aboriginals only began to use canoes along the coastal regions of Western Australia around the 17th century. 'Along a large part of the south and west coast the natives of Australia seem to have possessed no means of conveyance by water ... On the west coast the raft is recorded on the mouth of the Gascoyne River ... It is recorded that in the western and southern area not only the art of navigation but even that of swimming was unknown to the natives[4].'

Oldfield believed that there once was an advanced civilisation living in the north west of Australia basing his belief on some of the cave paintings and rock sculptures explorers such as Grey had discovered. In 1837, George Grey led an expedition of exploration into north-west Australia. Two years later he became the first European to explore the Gascoyne River.

That Australia was inhabited prior to the colonisation by the Alfouru, seems probable from the existence of relics of a civilisation far higher than can be claimed by any tribes of the Malay family.

---

[2] Oldfield, Augustus, *On the Aborigines* (1864), p216

[3] Ibid. p217

[4] Thomas, NW, *Australian Canoes and Rafts, The Journal of Anthropological Institute of Great Britain and Ireland 1905, (Royal Anthropological Institute of Great Britain and Ireland)* 35: 56–79

These remains of an extinct civilisation consist chiefly of picture-caves and sculptured rocks, works which the present occupants of the soil, far from claiming as their own, ascribe to diabolical agency. As the features and dresses of the figures represented are such as no untutored savage could possibly conceive, and the tools and pigments used are unknown to the existing race, the only just inference we can draw from these facts is, that some more civilised people has been destroyed by the black man, or possibly, in some instances, the two races have blended, a supposition that would enable us to in some measure to account for diversities of characteristics found to exist in various localities. The anomalies for which we thus seek to account exist chiefly among the inland tribes, in which we occasionally meet with physiognomies departing widely from the Australian type; and to reconcile these discrepancies, we are driven to suppose that the fact is owing to the mixture of the blood of a pristine race with that of the Alfouru, for had this blending of races been due to the migration of strangers from the sea-board, traces of their presence would be equally perceptible along the lines of their journeyings[5].

Wandjana paintings reproduced in Grey's Journal

Oldfield was referring to some amazing cave paintings[6] discovered in 1838 by George Grey in north Western Australia[7]. During this expedition, Grey described *light coloured men* who led groups of Aboriginals in battle against Grey and his men. Grey referred to them as *individuals of an alien white race*. Grey's discoveries will be analysed in greater detail in Part Two of the *Lost White Tribes of Australia*.

Oldfield believed that the arrival by people from countries overseas, such as Africa and Europe, had changed the characteristics of many of the Aborigines living in the area from Shark Bay to Champion Bay. Oldfield had assumed the

---

[5] Oldfield, Augustus, *On the Aborigines (1864)* p217-8

[6] Cave paintings discovered by Grey in 1838 near the Glenelg River, Western Australia

[7] Location Map of Windjana Gorge in Western Australia, Wikipedia Commons

European influences were the result of a shipwreck of an English vessel that had sailed from Calcutta. However, there is no record of any ship sunk off the Western Australian coast since the *Zeewijk*, a Dutch VOC merchant sailing ship, in 1727 until 1963 when the *Alkimos*, a Greek merchant ship sank. The only missing ship at around the date, 1832–3, was the *Resolution*, which was lost somewhere between Launceston, Tasmania, and Twofold Bay, NSW. No other ship was missing anywhere close to Western Australia or the Indian Ocean in the 1830s. However, there is a great deal of speculation about the following ships: the *Fortuyn*, a VOC ship had left the Cape of Good Hope in January 1724 and was never seen again. Wreckage had been sighted in the Houtman Abrolhos, not far from Champion Bay, by survivors of the *Zeewijk* in 1727. The *Beagle*, the ship that had taken Grey to the Murchison River, had also sighted wreckage in 1840. Under similar circumstances to the *Fortuyn*, the *Ridderschap van Holland* and the *Aagtekerke* went missing in 1694 and 1726 respectively. However, it was most likely the *Ridderschap van Holland* as the crew of the *Zeewijk* had discovered the remains of a ship of approximately the right age on their island. Numerous artifacts, such as bottles, had also been found which suggested that some of the 300 strong crew and passengers had survived. As no skeletal evidence was found on the island, it is possible that they had made it to the mainland, Champion Bay. Unfortunately, the remains of the wreckage have long since been destroyed by guano mining on the island in the early 20th century.

Oldfield had observed that the older natives at Champion Bay had *features nearly resembling the European type*. He also gave a grisly clue to why some of the white tribe did not survive. When the white men had departed from the tribe, perhaps in search of other survivors, the white females were eaten because they had *white blood in their veins*. The killing of the white females would dramatically reduce the number of the white indigenous tribe over time. Inevitably those of the white tribe allowed to live assimilated into the black tribes but left some distinguishing physical features of their ancestors. Oldfield had no doubt that Europeans had lived amongst the people from Champion Bay area resulting in European type physical characteristics

On the western and northern coasts we find the greatest departures from the normal type, and this doubtless is; owing to the advent of strangers among them; those shores, bordering on the much frequented seas, being more likely to have been visited by such than either the south or east coast, which were perhaps never visited until European enterprise led the white man to them. The tribes inhabiting the country from the Murchison River to Shark's Bay possess more of the characteristics of the Negro family than do the Aborigines of any other part of Australia; and as some of their proper names are similar to those used on the opposite coast of Africa, we may assume that there has been a recent mixture of Negro blood with that of these Western Australian tribes[8].

That such accidental blending of races should sometimes occur on the shores of much frequented seas is probable from the following facts. **At Champion Bay, in WA, I was much surprised to find in some of the old natives features nearly approaching the European type,** [Author's emphasis], *although those parts have been settled but a few years. I mentioned this fact to a medical gentlemen, who informed me that he had made the same observation, and could account for it in no other way but supposing that a ship which had sailed from Calcutta to Swan River in the early days of the colony, and had never since been heard of, was lost in these parts, and that some of the people who had escaped had mingled with this tribe, a surmise strengthened by the traditions of the natives, who to this day call Perth ... Ca-cut-ta, having probably mistaken the place of departure for that of the destination of the rescued people: added to this, they often asserted that in the event of the departure of the whites from among them, there were many of their females whom their laws would permit them to eat, they having white blood in their veins. This approach to the European type features I have also observed among the natives about Geographe Bay ... While botanising the*

---

[8] Oldfield, Augustus, *On the Aborigines* (1864), p218

country about the Murchison River (1858-9), I was desirous of making a journey to Shark's Bay, and to that end sought of the natives all the information they could give respecting the nature of the country between these two points.[9]

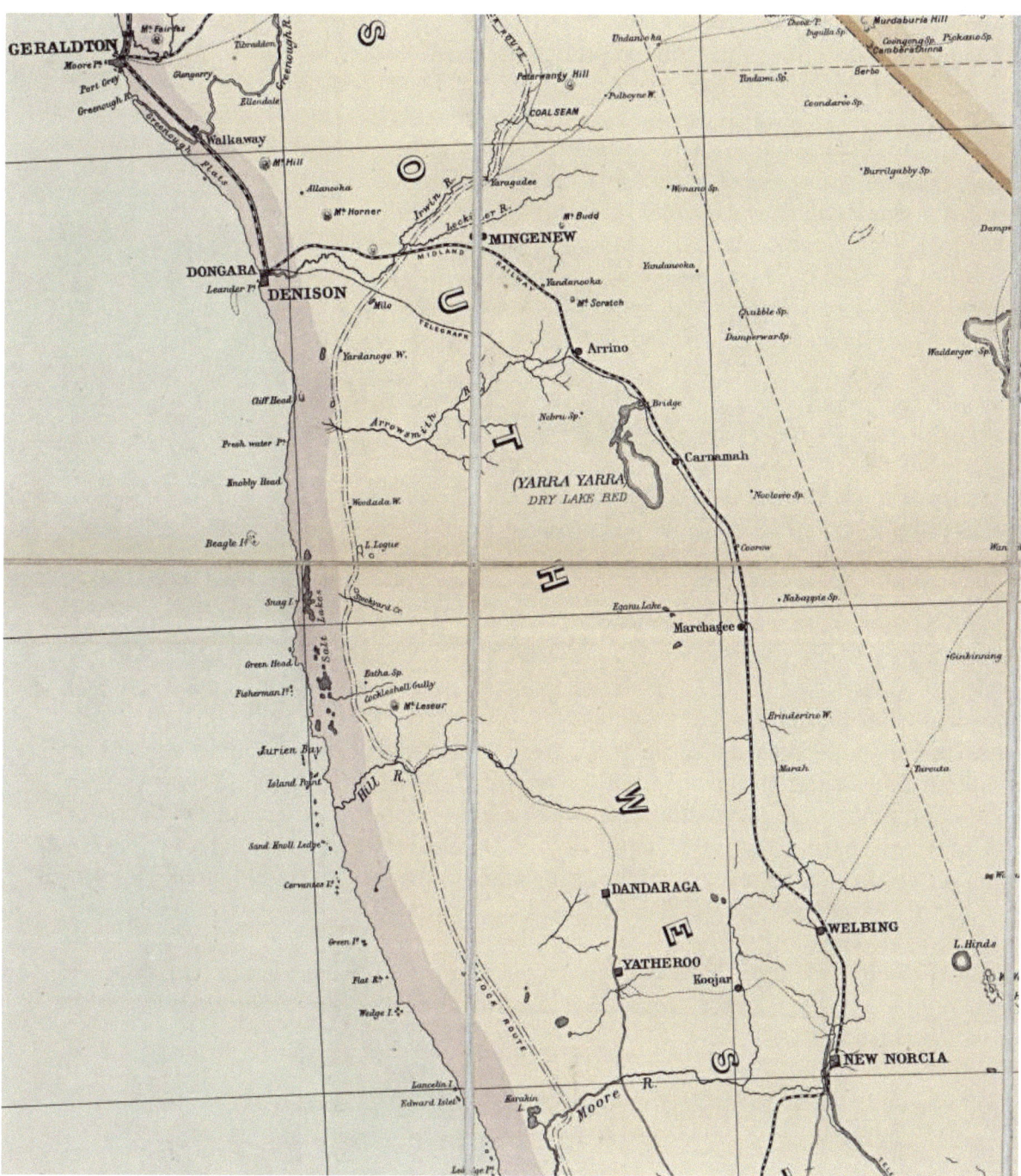

Four days journey north of New Norcia near the coast would most likely be between Dongara and Geraldton[10] or between the Irwin River and the Murchison. The Karakin Lakes can be seen just off the Moore River.

---

[9] Oldfield, Augustus, *On the Aborigines* (1864) p. 218-9

[10] Gold Fields Map 1896, *London and West Australian Exploration Company*

1848 – Augustus Gregory (1819–1905)
Champion Bay and Hutt River Settlements

In an address to the Queensland Branch of the Royal Geographical Society in 1885, the explorer, A Gregory had stumbled across remnants of the Lost White Tribe in the Champion Bay area just north of the Irwin River.

In 1848 I explored the country where the Dutchmen had landed, and found a tribe whose characters differed considerably from the average Australian. Their colour was neither black nor copper, but that peculiar colour which prevails with a mixture of European blood; their stature was good, with strong limbs, and remarkably heavy and solid around the lower jaw. Their dialect was scarcely intelligible to the tribes farther south.[11]

I was much surprised to find some of the old natives [at Champion Bay] *features nearly resembling the European type, although these parts have been settled but a few years*[12].

Gregory, in reference to the *Dutchmen had landed*, was speaking about the two sailors marooned on the mainland after the *Batavia* mutiny. However, two sailors could hardly have changed the skin colour of a whole tribe. A much greater influence was needed.

One would think that the sighting of a tribe that had a strong resemblance to Europeans might be something that Gregory would consider writing down in his journal in 1848. After reading it three times, I discovered Gregory had made no reference to the above despite writing in detail every encounter they had with Aboriginals. Gregory possibly wrote to the Perth Gazette in 1861 requesting his name not to be revealed. Or he may have waited another 37 years before revealing what he had seen in the Champion Bay area. Thus a possibility exists that the Western Australian Government still did not wish to reveal the existence of a Lost White Tribe. Gregory's encounter with this tribe may have been expunged from the record. By 1885, Gregory no longer felt the need to remain quiet on the matter and revealed his startling story to the Queensland branch of the Royal Geographical Society in the first year of its existence.

However, Gregory did remark upon the very different dialect spoken in the Champion Bay area:
... we could not obtain any other useful information, as their dialect differs considerably from that spoken in the settled districts ...[13]

Gregory is also quoted by Bates as remarking upon the lightness of the eyes of the Aboriginals in the Shark Bay area. However, the original source has been lost.

The third and the least numerous race ... were fairly proportioned with rather small heads covered with light flaxen hair, the eyes approaching the colour of the same, the features flat and wanting in character[14].

---

[11] Gerritsen, R, *And Their Ghosts May Be Heard*, p107

[12] Gregory, AC *Inaugural Address* p23. Gerritsen, R, *And Their Ghosts May Be Heard*, p71

[13] Ibid. p106

[14] Quoted from Gerritsen's book, *And Their Ghosts may be heard*. AC Gregory, MSS held by Dr J Park Thompson, quoted in Bates Archives, 'Origin of the Australian Race' MS, p31

In 1885, during his Inaugural Address, Gregory also remarked upon the advances in agricultural science by stating that, *Agricultural science seemed to have made some progress, as they never dug a yam without planting the crown in the same hole, so that no diminution of food supply should result*. The proliferation of yams or warran grounds seemed to be a feature of the Lost White Tribe wherever they settled. By following the warran grounds, we are also following the footsteps of the Lost White Tribe.

Further sightings of a 'white tribe' in the Champion Bay area

Daisy Bates, an Irish Australian journalist who spent 35 years of her life studying Aboriginal life, history and culture, commented on the Aborigines in the Dongara and Geraldton areas where she noticed the following differences: *The prevalence of the **fair-headed** natives far eastward of Dongara, etc, where the **changes of dialect** are so noticeable, may be due to the same cause. **Light, curly, wavy and straight haired natives** have been met with as far eastward as Meekatharra*[15]... *Eastward of Dongara* where Bates sighted 'fair-headed natives' is also where the Irwin River Valley is located.[16] [Author's emphasis] Daisy Bates also makes mention of the distinctive dialects.

Champion Bay district – Dongara (spelt Dongarra), Arrowsmith, Greenough and Irwin Rivers

The dialects of Dongara, Geraldton and the Northampton district show such marked differences towards their eastern and southern neighbours, that it can only be conjectured that the original people who introduced the dialect variations came by sea, or were wrecked on that part of the coast.[17]

---

[15] Bates, D, *The Native Tribes of Western Australia*, p107

[16] GW Bacon & Co. *Map of Western Australia*

[17] Ibid. p109

Daisy Bates[18], an expert on Aboriginal languages and their different dialects, had no doubts about where this 'white tribe' originated. ***The original people ... came by sea or were wrecked on that part of the coast.*** [Author's emphasis]

In regards to comparing the dialects of South Australia, New South Wales and Western Australia, Grey came to the following conclusion:

Having thus traced the entire coast line of the continent of Australia, it appears that a language the same in root is spoken throughout this vast extent of country, and from the general agreement in this, as well as in personal appearance, rites and ceremonies, we may fairly infer a community of origin for the Aborigines[19].

Explorer, Edward John Eyre agreed with Grey's conclusions in regards to dialects in Western Australia.

... the whole of the distance intervening between these places, [Swan River, King George's Sound, Cape Arid] *and extending fully six hundred miles in straight line along the coast, the same language is so far spoken, that a native of King George's Sound, who accompanied me when travelling from one point to the other,* [950 km] *could easily understand, and speak to any natives we met with. This is, however, an unusual case, nor indeed am I aware that there is any other part of Australia where the same dialect continues to be spoken by the Aborigines, with so little variation, for so great a distance, as in the colony of Western Australia ...*

... In Western and South-western Australia, as far as the commencement of the Great Bight, the features and character of the country appear to be but little diversified, and here, accordingly, we find the language of the natives radically the same, and their weapons, customs, and ceremonies very similar throughout its whole extent; but if, on the other hand, we turn to Eastern, South-eastern, and part of Southern Australia, we find the dialects, customs, and weapons of the inhabitants, almost as different as the country itself is varied by the intersection of ranges and rivers[20].

In other words, he believed that there was a common root in language, appearance, weapons, rites and ceremonies across Australia. In particular he noted that 'the same dialect was spoken, with so little variation,' across most of Western Australia. However, the Champion Bay area was different not only in dialect and appearance but also in how they lived.

The natives we took from Swan River, never could understand any of those we met on the North-west coast ...[21]

---

[18] Photo of Daisy Bates, from *The Passing of the Aborigines*, 1938

[19] Grey, G, *Journals of Two Expeditions of Discovery North-West and Western Australia During the years 1837, 38, and 39*. Vol.ii, p216 Project Gutenberg E Book Library

[20] Eyre, Edward John, *Journals of Expeditions of Discovery into Central Australia and Overland from Adelaide to King George's Sound in the Years 1840-1: Sent By the Colonists of South Australia, with the Sanction and Support of the Government: Including an Account of the Manners and Customs of Aboriginals and the State of Their Relations with Europeans. Vol 2*, Project Gutenberg Ebook Library

[21] Stokes, John Lort, *Discoveries of Australia Vol 1*, published 1846

Light-coloured people with light-coloured hair

Curious about these strange light-coloured people with fair hair, Bates interviewed an old Aboriginal, Edward Cornally, who grew up around the mouth of the Hutt River in the 1850s. While he was still very young, he became a shepherd in the Champion Bay area in the late 1850s[22]. Although he was an old man when she interviewed him in around 1909, he clearly remembered a *white fellow* gave them help as well as sighting members of the white tribe describing them as *men, women and children with light-coloured hair* and even children with *white hair*.

*Cornally asked an old nigger where they came from. They came from the north. At first there was nothing to eat, no fire and they didn't know what to do. An old man like a **white fellow** appeared to them and said, "You've got no fire, nothing to eat. I'll make you kangaroo and game and vegetable and I'll tell you what to eat," which he did and there was plenty of game but they only had a stone and a stick and couldn't kill them. He came again and made spears and dowarks [clubs] but they had to eat them raw as they didn't know the use of fire. Presently about three weeks after, a young man appeared to them, and they told him their trouble, and he made them a fire and when they asked him who he was, he said that he was the old man's son and that his father had sent him to them. They then asked him where he lived and he told them he lived in the moon*[23].

*The first half-caste child whom Cornally remembers seeing in Champion Bay was also stated by the mother and mother [sic – brother?] to come from the moon and when asked why the child was a **different colour** they stated that this was not uncommon amongst them.*[24] [Author's emphasis]

*Cornally has seen men, women and children with **light coloured hair**. The women have often had **very light brown hair**. He rarely saw them with jet black hair. He has seen children with **white hair**. They are as a rule **straight haired** people although some have curly and other wavy hair.*[25]

Over time, the white tribe had settled in the Champion Bay area and mixed with the local Aboriginal population bringing new technology and food introducing vegetable (yams) to their diet. The *white fellow* sent his son to the Aboriginal tribe to teach them how to make fire. It would appear that Cornally and his tribe were suffering from hunger and were rescued by the white tribe. That he also saw white children, men and women, would indicate that assimilation gradually occurred between the white tribe and the local Nanda tribe.

Bates also wrote the following confirming her belief that there was distinct Dutch influence in the Aboriginal tribes as far north as the Gascoyne and Murchison Rivers.

> *.... **also found traces of a type distinctly Dutch**. When Pelsaert marooned two white criminals on the Mainland of Australia in 1627 [sic], these Dutchmen had been probably allowed to live with the natives, and it may be that they and their progeny journeyed far along the river highways, for I found these types as far out as the headwaters of the Gascoyne and the Murchison. There is no mistaking the **flat heavy Dutch face**, curly **fair hair**, and heavy stocky build*[26]. [Author's emphasis]

---

[22] Gerritsen, R, *And Their Ghosts May Be Heard*, p293

[23] Ibid. p159

[24] Bates Archive, *Section VI Pt 1 3a: Legends: Champion Bay East – Cornally Informant*, p64

[25] Ibid. p73

[26] Bates, D, *The Passing of the Aborigines*, 1938 *p209*

During an overland cattle drive in Western Australia, Bates had a meeting where a *prospector named McPhee found his* **albino aborigine**[27]. However, nothing was revealed as to where the albino Aborigine was found.

Tom Carter, a jackeroo from the Gascoyne area confirmed Bates' observation of a light coloured, fair haired tribe. *Some of the natives at Boolbarty, especially three of the young women, were quite* **light coloured** *with regular features and* **light brown hair**, *and doubtless had a* **strain of white blood** *in them derived from Europeans shipwrecked at some time*[28].[Author's emphasis]

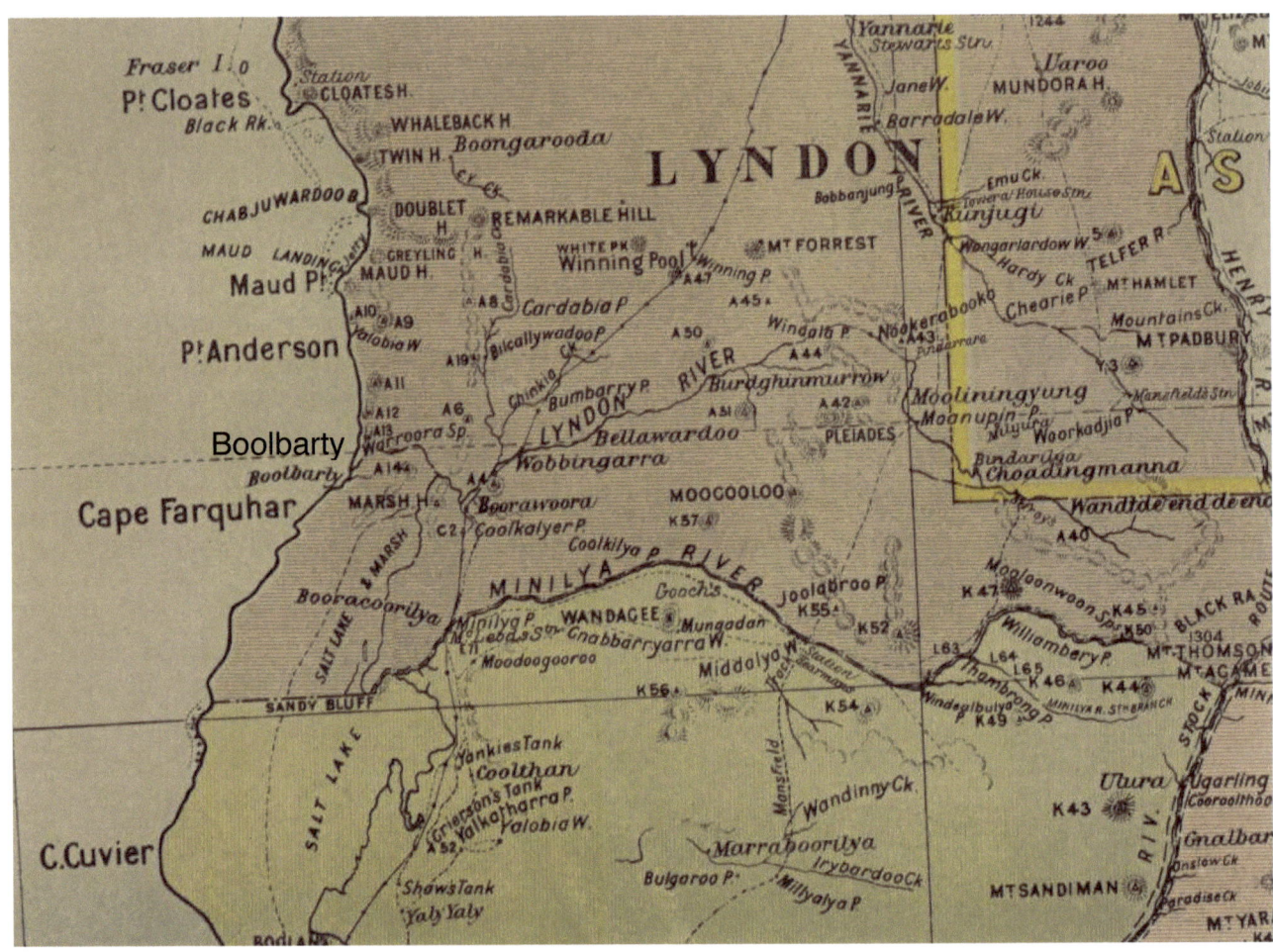

Boolbarty – site of a possible light-coloured and light brown haired tribe[29]

Note that Boolbarty is mistakenly written as Boolbarly on this map.

---

[27] Salter, Elizabeth, *Daisy Bates*, p105

[28] Carter, V, *No Sundays in the Bush An English Jackeroo in Western Australia 1887-1889: from the diaries of Tom Carter*, p123

[29] From the Daisy Bates Map Collection

Chapter 15

Dioscorea hastifolia

Photography by TJ Alford & JF Smith. Image used with the permission of the Western Australian Herbarium

Dioscorea hastifolia (Warran yams)

The botanic term for the yams is *Dioscorea hastifolia* and they are only found in the southern part of Western Australia along the coastal regions as far north as Shark Bay and south of Perth to the Murray River. The yams grow large roots and tubers which are harvested by digging up part of the roots or tubers.

Wherever *Dioscorea hastifolia* or native yams have been found, so too have there been reports of fair-skinned natives or as Stokes described them, *an almost white race*.

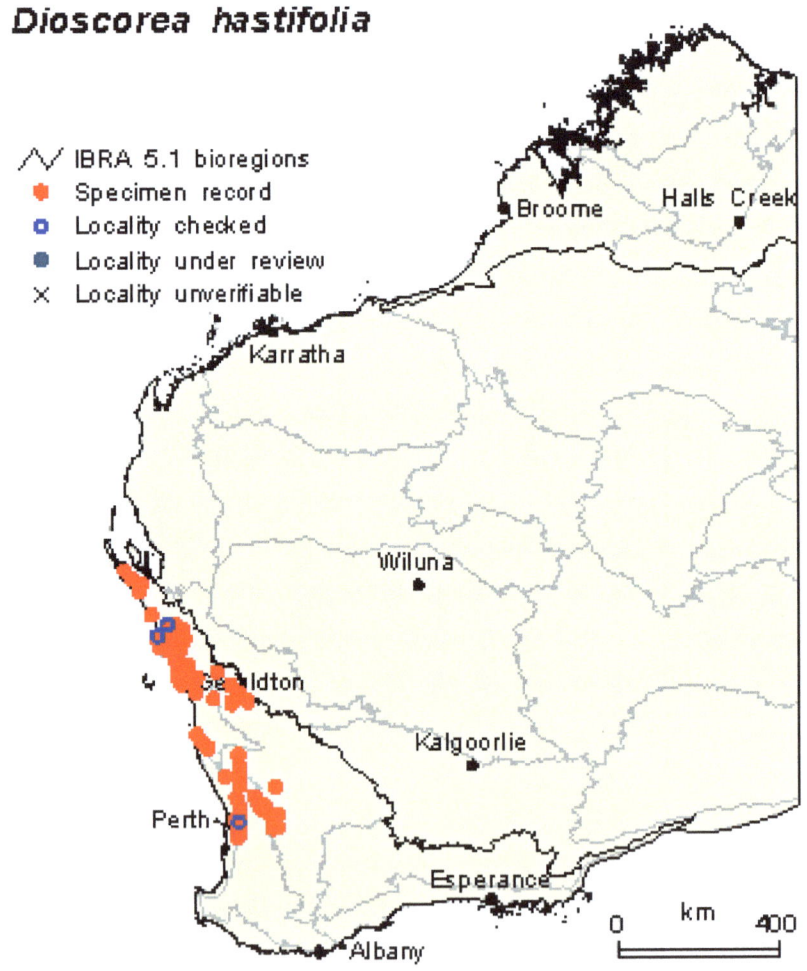

Cultural Influences

If there was a Dutch influence, then one would expect a Dutch or European cultural influence over the native Nanda tribe. Any significant cultural influence would be found in the construction of their housing; a more permanent or village-like settlement; introduction of agriculture to sustain a permanent settlement; a more European social organisation and a change of significant influence in the language. Lieutenant George Grey and later J. Lort Stokes wrote in great detail about a strange tribe they had come across described by Stokes as *almost a white race*.

Permanent Native Villages

Before reading Grey's account of two Aboriginal villages, it's worth comparing his account with that of Lort Stokes, an explorer who wrote the following in regards to native habitation:

The natives, in all parts of the continent alike, seem to possess very primitive notions upon the subject of habitation; their most comfortable wigwams hardly deserve the name: not even in the neighbourhood of English settlements are they beginning in any degree to imitate our European notions of comfort. Among these northern people, the only approach to anything like protection from the sky influences that I could discover, was a slight rudely thatched covering, placed on four upright poles, between three and four feet high. [1 m]

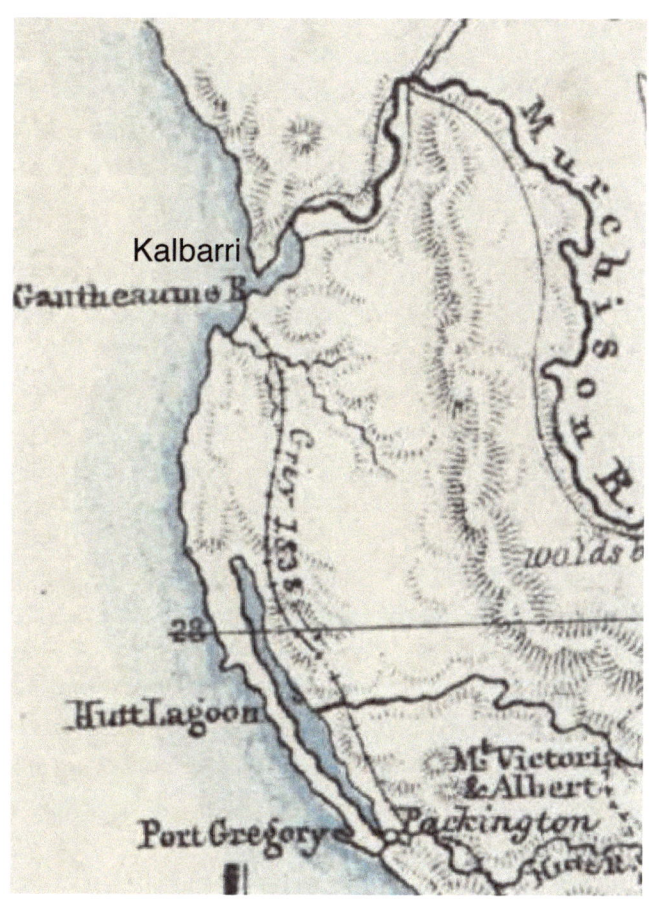

This is in stark contrast to Grey's description of two permanent settlements he had stumbled across during his fourth expedition. After a failed attempt to land two boats at Gantheaume Bay[1], north of the Hutt River and with both boats wrecked beyond repair, Grey and his men had little choice except to walk to Perth on foot.

Grey's Fourth Expedition, 1839

1 April 1839, George Grey embarked upon his fourth expedition to explore the country between Shark Bay and Fremantle. After setting out in three whale boats from Carnarvon they miscalculated the massive tides and high winds when they attempted to land just south of present day Kalbarri. Losing both his boats and his stores, Grey had no choice but to make a forced march southwards to Perth. Fortunately, Grey had with him an Aborigine called Kaiber whom he had befriended on his third expedition. Originally Kalbarri was named Kaiber but over the years the pronunciation changed. For the most part, Kaiber had been able to negotiate a safe passage with some of the local tribes and provide sustenance for Grey and his men. After arriving at the Hutt River, north of Geraldton, Grey described the permanent nature of two native villages and the organised agriculture that enabled the permanency of the villages. Surprised by the breadth and frequency of the paths, Grey also noted the superior construction of wells. It is close to the site of the Dutch shipwrecks, the *Batavia* and *Zuytdorp*. While we know the *Zeewijk* was wrecked on the Abrolhos

---

[1] Petermann, Augustus Heinrich, *J. Forrest's Reise im Innern von West Australien,*1869

Islands and twelve men attempting rescue with the ship's long boat were never heard of again, other Dutch ships may have also came to grief there such as the *Fortuyn* (1724), the *Aagtekerke*, (1726), *Zeelt (1672) Ridderschap van Holland (1694), Zeewijk (1727), Zonnestein (1768), Zeeduin (1785)*.

SUPERIOR NATIVE PATH AND WELLS

*April 4 1839: ... the native path ... now became wide, well beaten and differing altogether by its **permanent character**, from any I had seen in the southern portion of the continent ... The path increased in breadth and its beaten appearance, whilst along the side of it we found **frequent wells**, some of which were ten and twelve feet deep, [3 to 3.6ms] and were altogether executed in a superior manner*[2]. [Author's emphasis]

NATIVE WARRAN GROUND. PLAINS ABOUNDING IN THE WARRAN PLANT
We now crossed the dry bed of a stream, and from that emerged upon a tract of light fertile soil quite overrun with <u>warran</u> plants [original emphasis] the root of which is a favourite article of food with the natives. This is the first time we had seen this plant on our journey, and now for three and a half consecutive miles [5.6 kms] traversed a piece of land, literally perforated with holes the natives made to dig this root ...
It is now evident that we had entered the most thickly populated district of Australia that I had observed, and ... More had been done to secure a provision from the ground by hard manual labour than I could have believed it in the power of uncivilised man to accomplish. After crossing a low limestone range, we came upon another equally fertile <u>warran</u> ground [original emphasis] ... The native path about two miles [3 km] further on crossed this latter range, and we found ourselves in a grassy valley, about four miles wide, [6 km] bounded seawards by sandy downs. Along its centre lay a chain of reedy freshwater swamps, and native paths ran in from all quarters to one main line of communication leading to the southward ...

As they continued their long march south to Perth, *a large party of natives suddenly appeared.* However, Grey could not induce them to come any closer remaining approximately 250 to 300 m away from the party. Instead they *began to shout out to their distant fellows, and again cooeed to others still farther off, until the calls were lost in the distance, whilst fresh reinforcements of natives came trooping in from all directions ...*

Grey's party became alarmed fearing hostile intentions by the natives whose numbers continued to grow. In order to stop his own men from firing their rifles, Grey, with his rifle cocked and pointed, charged towards the natives. Although they withdrew each time he charged, they followed after Grey returned to his party. Unfortunately on one occasion his gun snapped. The Aborigines mimicked the snapping noise and made faces at Grey. This time, with his second gun, Grey fired at a heap of dead bushes just a few metres from the natives. The resulting explosion of dead branches forced the Aborigines to flee in confusion. After this show of force, the Aborigines avoided any contact. This also meant that Grey was unable to gain any knowledge of any possible white tribe living in the area.

Estuary of the Hutt River. Description of 'towns' and 'superior huts'

*April 5 1839: ... The estuary became narrower here, and shortly after seeing the natives, we came upon a river running into it from the eastward; its mouth was about forty yards wide[36 m]... and it flowed through a very deep ravine ... Being unable to ford the river here, we followed it to a SE direction for two miles, [3.2 km] and in this distance passed two native villages, or, as the men termed them, **towns** – the huts of which they were composed differed from those of the southern districts, in being built, and being very nicely plastered over the outside with clay, and clods of turf,* *so that although now uninhabited they were evidently intended for **fixed places of residence**. This again showed a marked difference between the habits of the natives of this part of Australia and the south-western portions of the continent; for these **superior huts, well marked roads, deeply sunk wells, and extensive warran grounds**, all spoke of a large and comparatively-speaking resident population, and the cause of this undoubtedly must have been the great facilities for procuring food in so rich a soil ... [Author's emphasis]*

The Hutt lagoon and Hutt River Estuary

The location of these 'two villages' or 'towns' was the mouth of the Hutt River,[3] the same location that two Dutchmen were marooned in 1629. Wouter Loos and Jan Pelgrom de Bye were Australia's first white settlers after they were put ashore for their role in the mutiny on the *Batavia*.

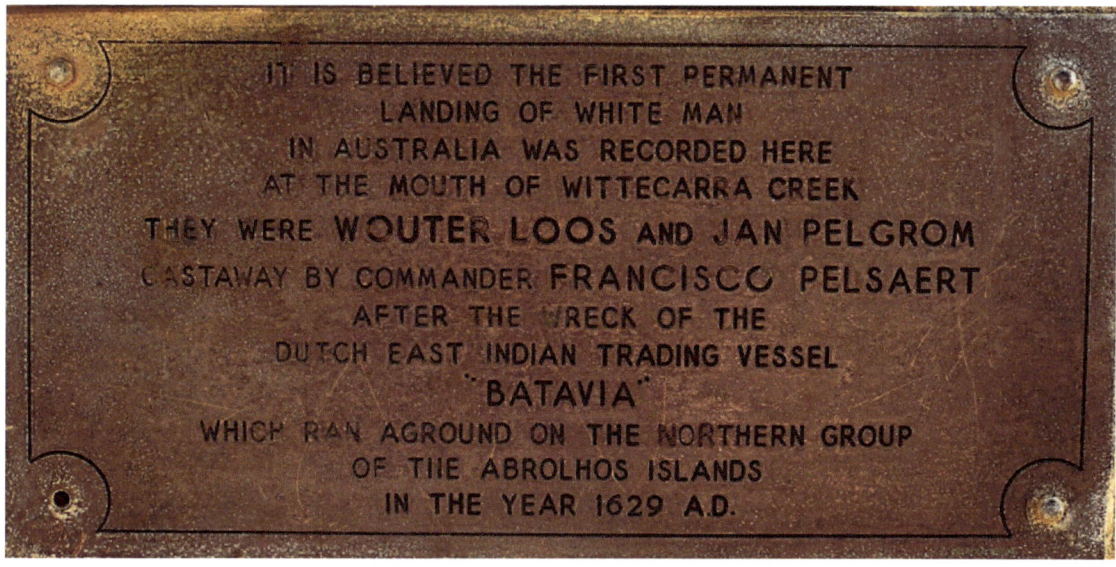

Plaque on a rock near Wittecarra Creek, Kalbarri

---

[3] Hutt Lagoon, Jody Taylor photographer. The Hutt River was the site of the native towns.

These two extremely fertile young men have been blamed for every 'white' Aboriginal sighting ever since. Typical of this claim is one made by the editor of the newspaper, The Shire of Northampton, AC Henville who wrote: *The first white men to settle did so reluctantly as they were the two sailors of the 'Batavia' marooned for their part in a mutiny in 1629, which could account for the **natives with fair hair and blue eyes** reported by our pioneers.*

A more plausible explanation would be a combination of groups from the two marooned sailors, the Lost White Tribe and the survivors from the *Zuytdorp* who had landed north of Geraldton (Champion Bay) near Kalbarri or perhaps an unknown wreck(s).

Native huts at the Bowes River

After their confrontation with Grey, the Aboriginals deserted their villages and kept away at a safe distance. However, they followed Grey's group of exhausted and starving men who slowly become weaker and weaker. Emboldened by this sight, the Aboriginals were encouraged to contemplate another attack.

Arriving exhausted at the Bowes River, Grey noted the same huts of 'superior construction' as those they had seen near the Hutt River. Once again the village was deserted. Grey discovered such a number of huts in a valley along the Bowes River, that he thought *the district must be very densely populated. The huts were of the same superior construction as those which we had seen near the Hutt, and the traces were very recent, but the natives themselves were either at a distance or kept carefully out of our way* ... So impressed was Grey with the extensive fertile country, that he named the area the Victoria District and the mountains the Victoria Range[4].

... being now certain that the district we were in was one of the most fertile in Australia I named it the Province of Victoria. There is no other part of extra-tropical Australia which can boast of the same number of streams in an equal extent of coast frontage, or which has such elevated land so near the sea.

[4] Petermann, Augustus Heinrich, *J. Forrest's Reise im Innern von West Australien,* 1869.

The Victoria District, Western Australia

The Bowes River[5] and the surrounding fertile country is significant. Any wandering tribe or individual searching for a stable source of food and water would logically be drawn to an area 'as one of the most fertile in Australia' as the Bowes River and Victoria District. It's therefore no accident that there were so many sightings of fair-skinned Aboriginals in the Victoria District.

The Bowes River was an obvious place to settle as water and a steady food supply was plentiful. George Fletcher Moore explored the area in 1847 and wrote:

Our position being about 40 miles [64 km] from Champion Bay, and the same distance from the sea coast to the westward, this is probably a branch of the Bowes River, and gives promise of awarding lower down much good soil and feed for stock, as the best land we found in the district was afterwards observed on the lower branches of the Bowes, and the country improved thence eastward kangaroos and emus were numerous as well as that beautiful variety of the cockatoo known as the chokel yokel, but our sportsmen did not succeed in adding any of them to our larder, nor did we see any natives, although their traces and pathways abounded, and gave evidence that the country yielded them a subsistence.

Moore not only literally stumbled across an extensive warran field, but also found well constructed native paths and huts.

... many wild ducks, and two black, swans were disturbed on its waters, and the banks were closely and deeply perforated by large holes dug by the natives in search of their favorite food, the "warren" root, which grows here in great abundance.

Native paths and huts were also numerous, the latter well constructed and plastered over with tenacious red soil. The Bowes has the largest extent of good land upon it, and in its vicinity.

Grey continued to find more native huts *of the same permanent character* along the larger rivers as he marched further southward towards Perth. What took Grey's attention the most though was the discovery of two groups of houses that must have *contained at least a hundred and fifty natives* about 10 km south of the Greenough River.

We passed a large assemblage of native huts of the same permanent character as those I have before mentioned: there were two groups of those houses close together in a sequestered nook in a wood, which taken collectively would have contained at least a hundred and fifty natives ...[6]

Grey continued under enormous difficulties of thirst, hunger, heat and even extreme cold. On his 483 km forced trek to Perth, Grey discovered and named two more rivers: the Irwin and the Arrowsmith. Unfortunately they were both dry. However, Grey could see some very distinct signs that a massive flood had once occurred in the Arrowsmith. This was possibly the 1833 flood.

---

[5] During my first expedition to Western Australia in 2001, I was fortunate enough to stay at Horrocks Beach Caravan Park located between Kalbarri and Geraldton. It was also not far from the Bowes River. The owners, Syd and Kaye Barnes were fascinated with my quest to find the Lost White Tribe. They had already heard of stories from drovers about a white tribe that had dammed the river to maintain a permanent water supply. Unfortunately we neither had the time nor the resources to fully investigate the story. Kaye later sent a photo of the dam but there appeared to be modern interference which would have made it difficult to discern the exact age.

[6] Grey, George, *Journals of Two Expeditions of Discovery*

THE GREENOUGH RIVER.⁷ MORE NATIVE HUTS

He also *saw numerous tracks of natives* and described *the whole of this valley was an extensive warran ground in which they had that very morning been digging for their favourite root.*

... we ascended, out of a dry watercourse, a rise rather more elevated than the others we had met with in crossing the valley; and from the summit of this a curious sight met our view: beneath us lay the dry bed of a large river, its depth at this point being between forty and fifty feet, and its breadth upwards of three hundred yards; [275m] *it was at times* **subject to terrific inundations**; *for along its banks lay the trunks of immense trees, giants of the forest which had been washed down from the interior in the season of the floods; yet nothing now met our craving eyes but a vast sandy channel which scorched our eyeballs as the rays of the sun were reflected back from its white glistening bed.'* [Author's emphasis]

Grey was forced to divide the party into two leaving behind those that could no longer continue. Even Grey found it difficult to continue on. *A disinclination to move pervaded the whole, and I had much the same desire to sink into the sleep of death... My Life was not worth the magnitude of the effort that it cost me to move; but other lives depended on mine, so I rose up weak and giddy, and by degrees induced the rest to start also.*

The Greenough River had two other massive floods since the area was settled. In February 1888, heavy cyclonic rain created a raging, destructive torrent. After four people were drowned and much of the property and animals were destroyed, many left the region. In a similar way the 1833 flood forced the Lost White Tribe to leave the Karakin Lakes area.

As soon as Grey reached Perth in 21 April 1939, search parties were organised to rescue the rest of the party. Frederick Smyth, a cousin of Florence Nightingale, who came out all the way from England with the purpose of joining Grey in his adventures, was the only man to have died.

Thus three very important facts emerge from Grey's journal: the existence of what Grey described as *fixed places of residence* of what his men called *towns* with *superior huts*, *well marked roads*, *deeply sunk wells, and extensive warran grounds;* and the obvious evidence of an enormous flood causing the Arrowsmith River to swell to a *depth ... being between forty and fifty feet,* [15ms] *and its breadth upwards of three hundred yards.* [91 m] The sheer force of the flood forced *immense trees, giants of the forest* to be *washed down from the interior.* The extensive warran (yam) grounds continued in the Champion Bay area into the early 20th century.

A combination of explorers, surveyors, settlers, government officials and officers had provided similar reports to Grey. Lieutenant Helpman described the huts in the Irwin River area in the following manner:

We here met with the first native hut; it was well plastered outside and the timber which formed it was about 6 in. [15cm] *thickness, about 6ft.* [1.8m] *high inside and capable of holding ten persons easily*[8].

When describing the Aboriginals he described them as, *a fine race of men but seem to depend entirely upon warran and gum, of which they have great abundance*[9].

The massive flood that occurred in 1833 drove the Lost White Tribe out of their Karakin Lakes village and forced them north where their influence could be found in the nature of the villages and the planting of yams. Had Grey been able to make to communicate with the tribes of the Hutt and Bowes Rivers, the Lost White Tribe may have been discovered before they had assimilated into the local tribes.

YAM :CULTURE;
To the Editor.
Sir,– As so much of the land in Western Australia is suitable for yam (sweet potato) growing where water can be applied, and amongst the people whose staple food it is, if also in America where it is cultivated and appreciated at its true value it can be made to take the place of as much bought food, it might be looked to for partly solving'-the problem, of "How to Settle People on the Land." The yam patch once started on land free from couch grass is there for years, and yields all through the hot season. Even the man with "that tired feeling" need not suffer hunger or the humiliation of' asking more industrious people for help, if he is not too dead-beat to go and dig up and boil a few yams, while the children would ask for nothing better. An experimental plot at each pumping station along the Coolgardie water-pipe track would be a good object lesson.-
Yours, etc., :
SPARTAN NO. 2.
Champion Bay, Jan[7]

Stories of large populations of natives in the Champion Bay area were not limited to Grey. AC Gregory gave a rough estimate of the high numbers that he though had lived there.

On first landing at Champion Bay in 1846, we found the natives in considerable numbers, about 1000 within a radius of 50 miles[10]. [80 km]

His opinion was supported by the Government Resident, William Burges, who made the following report,

It is impossible at present to give a correct opinion of the natives in the District but they are far more numerous than in any other part of the Colony[11].

Although Grey did not come across any white people or 'Aborigines of European appearance,' as others had done outlined in the previous chapter, he did uncover their houses, villages, wells, roads and yam plantations. However, the French explorer, Louis Freycinet reported seeing *two or three*

---

[8] Helpman, 1846: 9

[9] Helpman, 1849 b:3

[10] Gerritsen Rupert, *And Their Ghosts May Be Heard*, p86 – AC Gregory MSS held by Dr J Park Thompson in Bates Archives, *Origins of the Australian Race* MS p30

[11] Gerritsen, p86, W Burges to Acting Colonial Secretary. 9 June, 1851

racial hybrids[12] around Shark Bay during his 1801–3 expedition under the command of Nicolas Baudin.

Almost every commentator and explorer who had passed over the district, also remarked upon the sudden language difference between the tribes of the Champion Bay district and all other Western Australian tribes. Fair-haired and fair-skinned natives were also sighted in the Shark Bay, Murchison and Gascoyne Rivers.

The *Vergulde Draeck* wasn't the only Dutch ship that sank with survivors off the Western Australian coast. At least two ships, the *Zuytdorp* and the *Zeewijk*, brought more stranded sailors to the Shark Bay area.

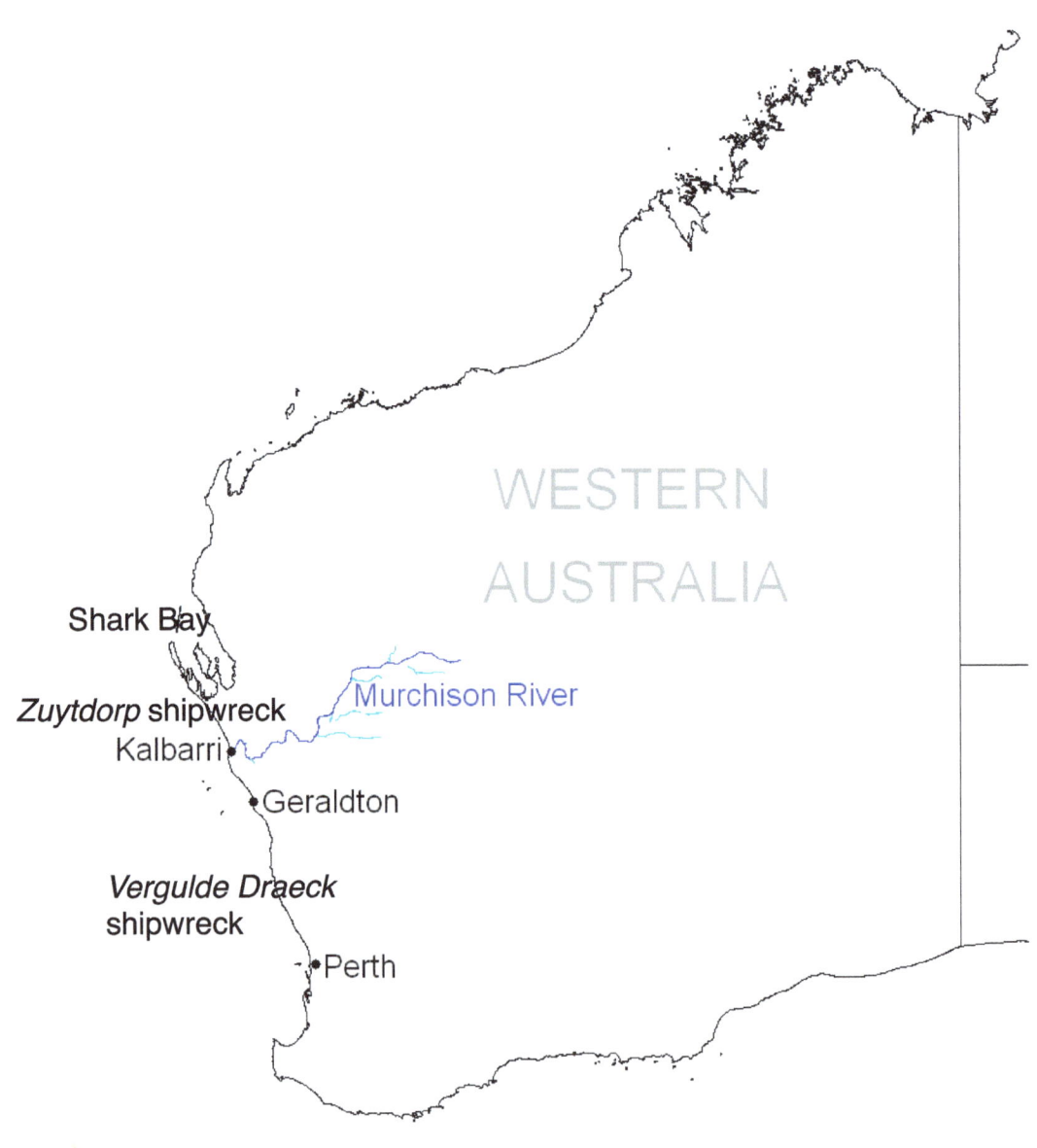

---

[12] Zaborowski, M, *Bulletin and Memoriale Societe d'Anthropologique de Paris* Vol. 8 (1907) pp384-93 quoted in Gates, p32 and Gerritsen, p81.

Chapter 16
The Zuytdorp
1712

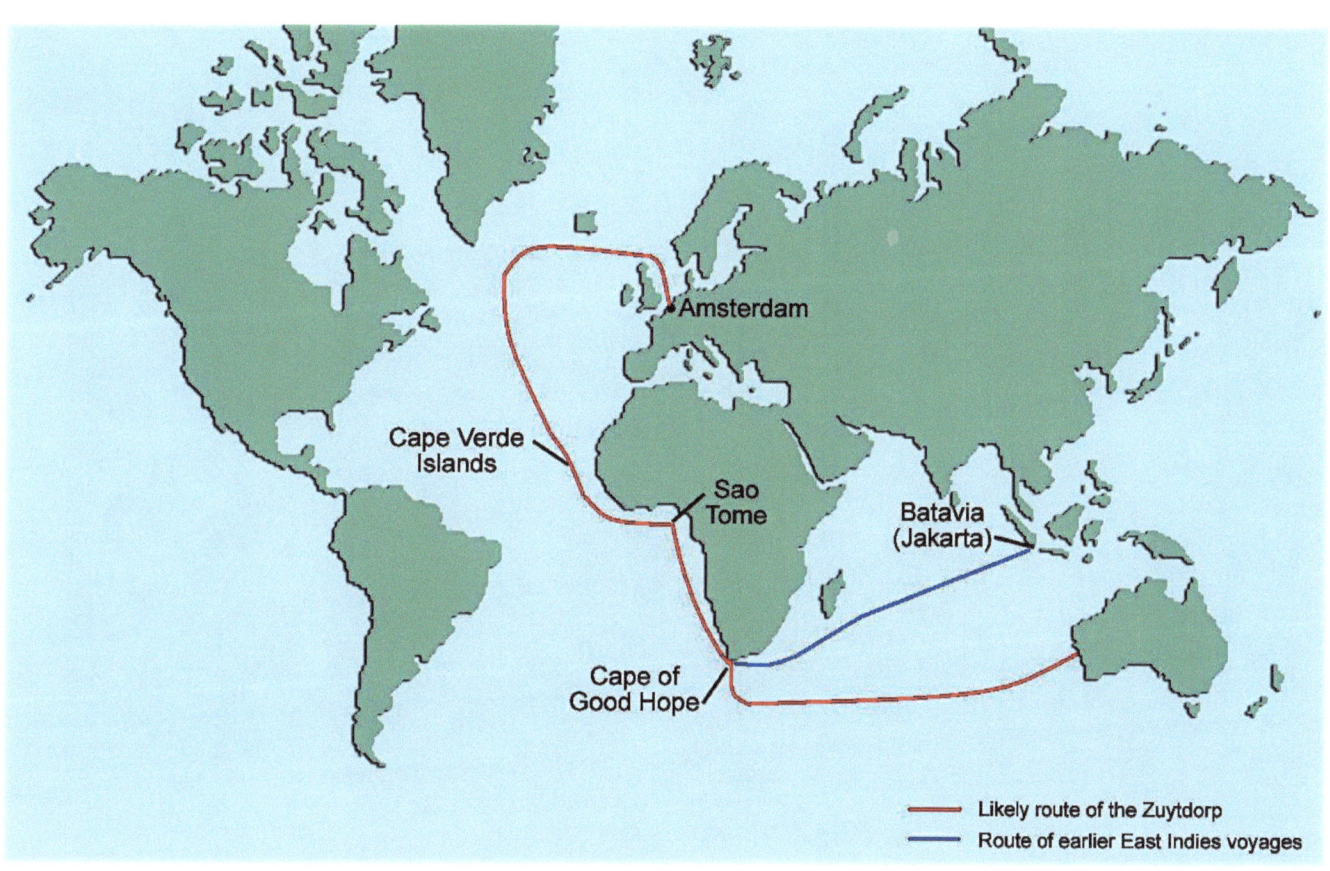

Route of the Zuytdorp from the Shark Bay Organisation

The wreck of the *Zuytdorp* complicates the picture even further as there is a possibility that many of the survivors who made it safely ashore assimilated into the surrounding tribes. Two Aboriginals, Tomgin and Weenat were the first to report of the wreck to a farmer, Stephen Parker, and his sons who lived on a farm 10 km north- east of Perth. According to the historian Phillip Playford, the story had been handed down from tribe to tribe until it had eventually reached the blacks in the Perth area. They spoke of a great deal of *white money* (silver coins), that was scattered for about 30 metres along the shore in front of the wreck. As the surf retreated, 'the Wayl-men would run forward and pick up coins. The ship was ... torn apart (*broke*), and surf surged between the ruptured sections. It had three masts, with *blankets* (sails) flapping around and one of the later informants indicated (by repeatedly tilting his woomera) that the ship had been lying on its side when it was driven ashore[1]'.

The Zuytdorp Cliffs [2]

Parker was told that those who had survived included tall white men, with women and children. Relations between the survivors and the Aboriginals were said to have been good. They had given the Aboriginals *biscuit* (food), and received spears and shields in return.

Initially the survivors had built five *houses* – two large and three small – constructed of wood and canvas, situated on the open coast. The authorities at that time, had assumed that the wreck was

---

[1] Playford, Phillip, *Carpet of Silver, The Wreck of the Zuytdorp,* p78. First published 1996, University of Western Australia Press.

[2] Zuytdorp Cliffs , Creative Commons, Wikipedia

most likely situated north of the Murchison River or where the *Zuytdorp* was wrecked. It's worth remembering that Grey had discovered ***seven native huts built of large-sized logs, much higher and altogether of a very superior description*** north of the Gascoyne River. [Author's emphasis]

The Wreck of the *Zuytdorp* – 1712

The *Zuytdorp* (south village) left for Batavia in August 1711 but unfortunately never made its destination, crashing instead into the high cliffs between Kalbarri and Shark Bay. The *Zuytdorp* was a large East Indiaman carrying about 286 men with 40 cannon. In fact it was probably one of the largest ships of her kind in the world. She was also carrying a fortune in treasure: 250,000 guilders.

On only its third voyage, the captain, Dirck Blaauw, struggled against the extremes of weather to nurse the *Zuytdorp* on a torturous seven and a half month voyage to Cape Town. First they were struck by severe storms, thrashed by winds and tossed by soaring seas. Then, nothing – absolutely nothing. Not a breath of wind – just heat, hot air: they were becalmed. The slow, mad death of scurvy killed 112 men. Spotty skin, spongy gums were the first signs. Just about everyone suffered. Depression was the next stage with the sailor barely able to move. He started to bleed from just about every human orifice imaginable: the nostrils, the ears, the genital area and the anus. He knew that he was almost dead when the open wounds turned yellow with pus and his swollen red bleeding gums finally gave up their teeth. Even if he had fresh fruit, it was almost impossible to eat. With his eyes sunken, and his nails now falling out, bleeding nose and uncontrollable diarrhea, a quick death was often preferable to a slow, painful recovery. Twenty-two survived death but were very sick.

After arriving at Cape Town on 23 March, 1712, the survivors and the crew needed an entire month to recover. The ship departed for Batavia on 22 April, 1712 with two other ships but became separated somewhere in the Indian Ocean. The VOC could not mount any credible search because they simply did not know what had happened or where it was wrecked. They didn't know that the *Zuytdorp*[3] had crashed into the cliffs of New Holland.

However, the *Zuytdorp* survivors had scrambled ashore hungry, hurt and humbled by a harsh environment.

It seems probable that the survivors travelled 50 km north. The largest and most important Aboriginal encampment and waterhole near the *Zuytdorp* wrecksite was at a well known as Wale well[4]. The Aboriginals had called the white men, Wayl-men.

More than 200 years later, in 1927 the legendary stockman, Tom Pepper, and Aboriginals Ada and Ernest Drage and Charlie Mallard were trapping dingoes at a place called Tamala Station in the Hutt

---

[3] Model of the *Zuytdorp* by Jim de Heer. Image courtesy of the Western Australian Museum

[4] Playford, P, *Carpet of Silver, The Wreck of the Zuytdorp*, p81

River district which is just south of Shark Bay but north of the Murchison River. The story was that they found some green glass bottles. cooking pots and evidence of large campfires on the cliff. They were sure that no European had ever been there before so he scrambled down to the reef platform below the cliff face where he found a large wooden figure, coins dated about 1711, several breech blocks from an old cannon (firing mechanism for small bronze cannons) before news of his discoveries leaked out. The cliffs were later called the Zuytdorp Cliffs after the artifacts were identified as to have come from the *Zuytdorp*.

For the next few years, Pepper and his friends visited the Zuytdorp cliffs collecting whatever they could find until news was leaked to the West Australian on 5 February, 1931. Many expeditions were undertaken before the wreck was finally identified. One of the finds was particularly interesting: breech blocks. Pepper was interviewed in the Daily News in 1954 and told the paper that the breech blocks *appeared to have been placed in a circle and in the centre of the circle was an instrument of some type, a sextant I think*[5]. This was exciting news because it meant that survivors of the *Zuytdorp* had made it ashore and left a message for any would be rescuers.

Scuba divers uncovered the mysterious wreck in 1958 at the foot of the Zuytdorp Cliffs[6]. The artifacts recovered proved that she was the *Zuytdorp*. It appeared that the ships sailed directly into the cliffs. This may seem an odd thing for a captain to do but if we think about it logically it may have been the best thing to do. With all of the ship's anchors at work, by crashing head on, the ship may have sustained less damage than if it hit the shore on its side. It probably gave the occupants more time to get off the ship before the anchor ropes snapped sending the ship headlong into the cliffs[7].

Other artifacts were found in a gully a long way from the wreck which would indicate some survivors made it ashore carrying with

---

[5] Gerritsen,R, *And Their Ghosts May Be Heard,* p53

[6] Photo of the Zuytdorp Cliffs from the Department of the Environment and Conservation

[7] Zuytdorp Cliffs, Department of Environment and Conservation

them bottles[8], goblets, timber, keys, chests and barrels. Remains of all of the above were found indicating the remains of a large encampment. It must have been quite a task to haul these heavy stores 50 m up the cliffs and some distance to the gully. They even brought with them the breech blocks (heavy brass blocks that were part of the cannon). The breech blocks were brought back because they could be fired without the rest of the cannon. Thus it could be used either for protection or to signal any passing ship. But to bring so much back, especially the very heavy objects, must have needed a large number of people[9].

In 1954, a young geologist, Playford, was completing geological survey work south of Shark Bay. He bumped into Pepper who told Playford that years ago he'd found silver coins and other artifacts at an old camp site at the top of the cliffs. On seeing the coins, Playford noted that they were not only Dutch coins, but they were almost all minted in 1711. The date proved to be the key to finding out the name of the ship that must have been wrecked on the cliffs. 1711 was the only mint of that year that went out on two ships. The *Zuytdorp* was the only one that never made it to Batavia.

Playford enlisted Geraldton's Tom Brady and the Cramer brothers to dive at what he believed to be the most likely site: the foot of the cliff upon which Pepper had first found the coins. Max Cramer had already successfully dived on the *Batavia* wreck site in 1963. Searching for the *Zuytdorp* wreck was a much riskier and more difficult operation as it was an enormous task just to get to the most 'probable' wreck site. Once there Max, his brother Graham and Brady had to risk being smashed to pieces against the rocks. They entered the water with great trepidation. *... on my first attempt I jumped into a wave and was washed back onto the reef again, which gave us a bit of a fright. We then tried new tactics and successfully entered the water to view for the first time, the Zuytdorp underwater*[10]. Huge anchors[11] were found which seems to suggest that the captain did try and forestall the inevitable by dropping their anchors hoping to grip onto something solid. Although the waters were murky, several large brass cannons came into view that left them with no doubt: they had found the the grave of the *Zuytdorp*. Although tired and exhausted, Max managed to raise three small brass cannons and somehow brought them ashore but not without an enormous effort.

---

[8] Bottle and coins from the *Zuytdorp*. Photograph from the Shark Bay Heritage Centre

[9] Fragments from the *Zuytdorp*.bell recovered by Geoff Kimpton and Dominic Lamara. Photograph from the Shark Bay Heritage Centre

[10] Cramer, Max*Treasures, Tragedies and Triumphs of the Batavia Coast*, p146

[11] The *Zuytdorp* anchor displayed at the Western Australian Maritime Museum

Disappointed that they could not find any silver coins, Max tried a new strategy. He employed some Geraldton fishermen and their boats to motor directly to the wreck site. This time a large bronze cannon was raised with its barrel full of coins. If you were the captain and you knew the ship was going to sink, then plugging the cannon full of coin was a way of ensuring the location and safety of the coins. The cannon, unlike a chest, was unlikely to break up and because of its weight, unlikely to move about. Should any salvage attempt be made by a passing rescue ship, then a large cannon was much more easily located than a smashed up chest of coins. But where was the rest of the silver?

Brady and his friends Neil McLaughlin and Gordon Hancock made several more dives until they finally sighted the 'carpet of silver'. Although they recovered a few coins, the rest were cemented together into a solid mass resembling a carpet of silver covering several square metres. They kept quiet about the find not wanting irresponsible treasure hunters using explosives to break up the mass of silver. Alan Robinson had done this on the *Vergulde Draeck* wreck and somehow he got wind of the find discovering the 'carpet of silver' at the *Zuytdorp* site. Fortunately the WA Maritime Museum[12] had become officially involved and were able to push ahead with legislation to protect shipwrecks. Robinson would not keep the site a secret which created mayhem for the Museum. The site had to be guarded day and night. They did so until the night watchman's caravan was burnt.

For five years there was very little diving conducted by the museum. It was during this time that the 'carpet of silver' appears to have mysteriously disappeared. Was it the arsonist who firebombed the caravan? Everybody it seemed was a suspect. The Kalbarri fishermen didn't take it too kindly when they had their homes searched. But the treasure has never been found. Max Cramer believes that someone did try and dynamite the silver but the result may have been fruitless for it was possible that the mass of silver could have been swept away into underwater caverns and caves too dangerous and too difficult to explore.

But what happened to the survivors? There is some evidence that they travelled inland perhaps even as far as Mount Augustus. Playford examined historical accounts of Aboriginal people living in the vicinity of Shark Bay from early settlers, the early explorer AC Gregory and Daisy Bates, who all wrote of Aboriginal people of this area having relatively light-coloured skin and 'European' features. Sandra Bowdler, from the University of Western Australia, wrote a report, *In search of the Zuytdorp survivors: report on an archaeological reconnaissance of a site in the Shark Bay area, 1990*. She wrote that 'there is some evidence, to be investigated separately, that a genetically-linked disease, porphyria variegate, could have been introduced to Aborigines of Shark Bay by a survivor of the *Zuytdorp* who had joined the

[12] *Zuytdorp* cannon, Photo West Australian Maritime Museum

ship at the Cape of Good Hope. In addition, in 1834, Aborigines in Perth related a story of Waylmen in the Shark Bay region who had knowledge of a wreck strewn with coins. About 50 km north of the wreck site is a well on Tamala Station called 'Wale Well', which was said to have been a major Aboriginal encampment in the early historical period. This place constitutes an extensive Aboriginal site, being strewn with marine shells and stone artifacts, including grindstones made of rocks that were carried there from sources 100–170 km away[13].

In April 1990, Playford organised a visit to Wale Well with McCarthy and two others, and reconnoitred the site. Within two hours, a find was located. About 10 cm below the surface, a beautifully preserved brass tobacco box was found, inscribed with the name Leyden (the present city of Leiden), and closely matching one from the 1727 wreck of the *Zeewijk*. This object is indubitably of 18th century Dutch origin, and there can be little doubt that it is derived from the *Zuytdorp*, and was carried to the site by either a survivor of the wreck or an Aborigine.'

Nearby, Playford and his associates came across 'an ancient grave ... which had a rectangular border of large stones ... form of burial had not been recorded elsewhere among Aborigines suggested European influence[14].

The grave could have been Aboriginal and the brass box could have been brought there by Aboriginals but there seemed to be a greater probability that the survivors had eventually walked inland probably following the course of the Murchison River.

The mystery of the *Zuytdorp* survivors becomes even more fascinating if we take into account two separate sources: the mysterious painting at Walga Rock.

Whoever painted the ship knew what the underside of a ship looked like. However, the centre of the ship is puzzling. Some interpret it as a funnel which would make the ship much more recent than the *Zuytdorp*. The writing beneath the ship unfortunately is indecipherable.

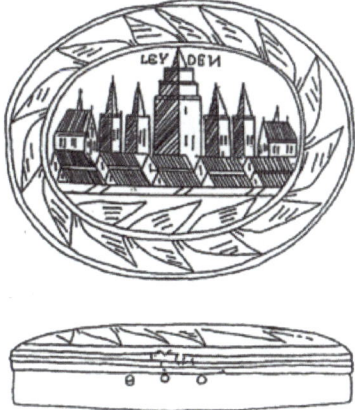

Brass tobacco box with the city of Leiden on lid.,

---

[13] Sandra Bowdler, *In search of the Zuytdorp survivors: report on an archaeological reconnaissance of a site in the Shark Bay area, 1990*. Department of Archaeology, University of W.A. Preliminary Report September, 1990

[14] West Australian, 27 August, 1897, p3

Above: Entrance to Walga Rock and the famous Walga Rock painting[15]

---

[15] Photos by Susi Schoensleben-Vogt/Ruedi Schoensleben

Shark Bay Sightings

Photographer Tony Bell claimed, in 1971, that he had 'traced the course of the [*Zuytdorp*] survivors north for more than 60 miles [97 km] to a remote beach near False Entrance[16] Point on Shark Bay[17].'

Bell uncovered distinct signs left by *Zuytdorp* survivors including a two metre stone cross on the ground perhaps as indicator to where they were headed and for others to follow. He also came across the graves of survivors who had died on their trek north. Realising that they were walking into a dead end, they were forced to change direction and go inland. Physical evidence was left behind at a camp site about 12 km from Tamala Station consisting of a 'trail of camp-fire ashes, metal items and fragments of green bottles.'

Tamala Station[18]

Bell believed that there had been a mutiny amongst the survivors based upon the organisation and arrangement of campfires he associated with the exiles from the *Zuytdorp*. Nevertheless, Bell was able to establish that at least some of the *Zuytdorp* survivors were attempting to travel north. If they did survive, continuing their trek north to the Wooramel River was their only hope. There is some evidence that at least some of the *Zuytdorp* survivors did make it.

---

[16] Photo of False Entrance at Shark Bay. Department of Environment and Conservation Western Australian Government. Dirk Hartog Island can be seen in the background.

[17] Edwards H, Chapter 15, cited Gerritsen, p56

[18] Photo of Tamala Station by Susi Schoensleben-Vogt/Ruedi Schoensleben

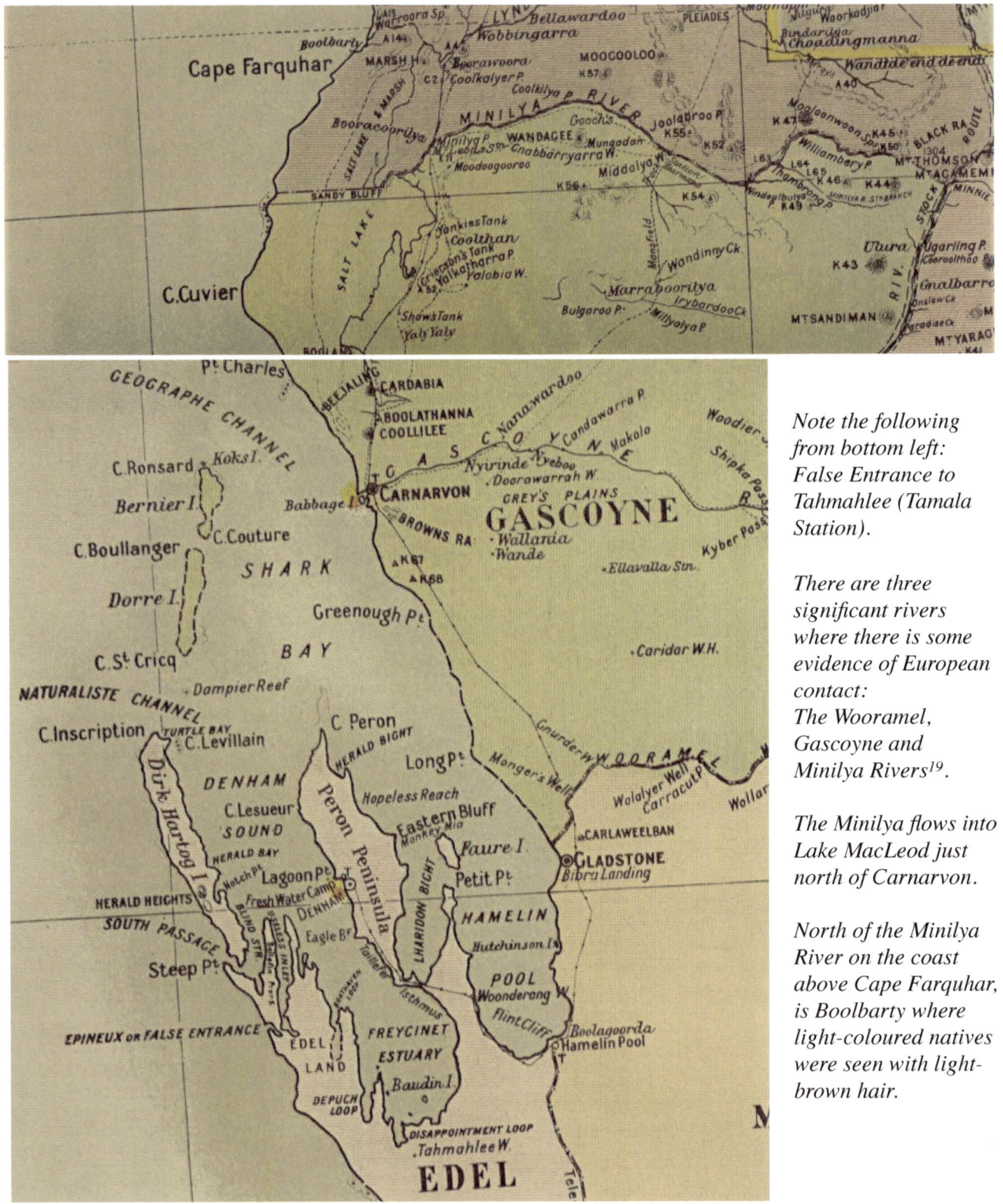

Note the following from bottom left: False Entrance to Tahmahlee (Tamala Station).

There are three significant rivers where there is some evidence of European contact: The Wooramel, Gascoyne and Minilya Rivers[19].

The Minilya flows into Lake MacLeod just north of Carnarvon.

North of the Minilya River on the coast above Cape Farquhar, is Boolbarty where light-coloured natives were seen with light-brown hair.

Manilya, Gascoyne and Wooramel Rivers

---

[19] Map of Minilya, Gascoyne and Wooramel Rivers from the Daisy Bates Map Collection 86, WA Department of Lands and Surveys, National Library of Australia

Circumcision, tallness and baldness

The unlikely evidence is circumcision and a marked language difference noted by a pioneer to the area, RE Bush who wrote the following description in his journal. Keep in mind terms that we consider impolite today were not regarded as bad taste in the 19th century.

*These niggers talk quite a different language to the ones we left on the other side of the [Wooramel?] River 3 days ago, perfectly different. We noticed that all the niggers on this side were **not** circumcised, whereas all the ones we left on the other side **were*** [his emphasis][20].

His companion, Tom Carter, named the tribe Inggarda[21] and noted its proximity to the Minilya River which flows into Australia's westernmost lake, Lake MacLeod. The lake lies north of the coastal city of Carnarvon. Note that the previous map contains three crucial rivers where evidence of possible European influence was found: the Minilya, Gascoyne and Wooramel Rivers.

The natives of the Gascoyne Lower River were of the Inggarda tribe and spoke a quite different language from the By-oong tribe of the Minilya River, only eight miles distant[22]. [13 km]

*Eight miles distan*t would place the two tribes just north of Carnarvon where the Minilya River flows into Lake MacLeod.

Bates noted that there were *peculiar dialects in the Illimbirrie country* [lower Sandford River, near Twin Peaks Station and the junction of the Murchison River], *and amongst some of the isolated northern tribes*[23].

The Sandford River cited by Bates, can be seen running off the Murchison. The Twin Peaks are located at the same location as Illimbirrie close to the river. However, it was the Kennedy Ranges that drew most of my attention with references of a 'white people' living there made by the Gascoyne natives. *The Gascoyne district natives living west and south of the Kennedy Range believed that the Range was full of moondung, **'like white people'**, and that these spirits had strange animals with them*[24]. [Author's emphasis]

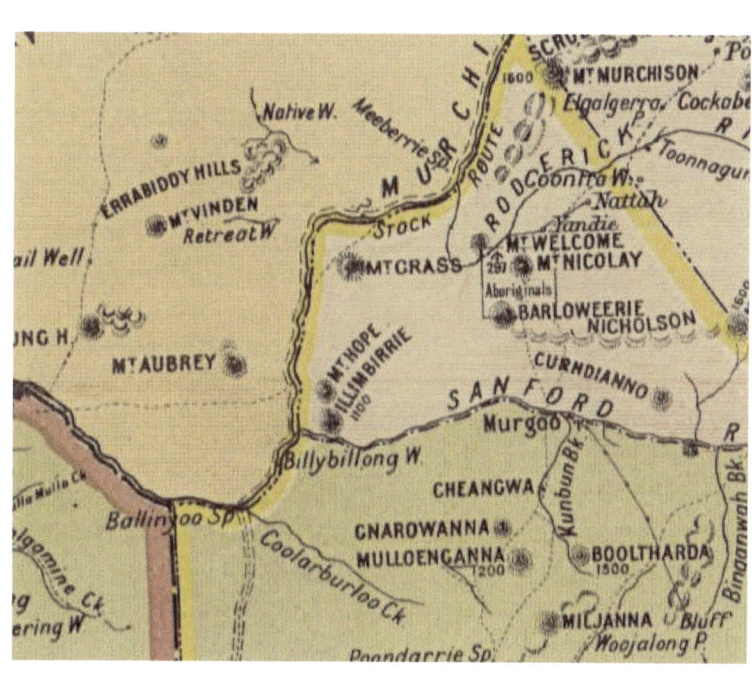

---

[20] Extracts from the *Journal of RE Bush* (BL:COMAP 134, Extract no. 3) 2 November 1879. Cited Gerritsen p110

[21] Tindale, Dr Norman ,'Coast at northern end of Shark Bay between Gascoyne and Wooramel rivers; inland to near Red Hill and Gascoyne Junction.' Collection AA338, SA Museum Archives

[22] Carter, V. *No Sundays in the Bush: An English Jackaroo in Western Australia 1887-1889: from the Diaries of Tom Carter* p30. Cited in Gerritsen p110

[23] Bates, Daisy. Section II Pt 2a: Geographical Description of the Northern and Southern groups of Western Australia' pp. 34-35, cited in Gerritsen p110 Map from the Daisy Bates Collection

[24] Cornally, Edward, Bates Archives, Section XII Pt 1, p24

The Gascoyne natives believed that the Kennedy Ranges is full of ghosts of a superior kind, **who have flocks and herds and houses, the same as white people, an aristocratic tribe**[25]*!*

The Moondung corroborees [were] *somewhat symbolical of the crucifixion. An effigy is made resembling a being and they finish up by spearing it and knocking it to pieces. The women are present but with their heads bowed. Should a woman look up they believe she will go blind*[26].

Anthropologist and linguist Geoffrey O'Grady in his analysis of the circumcision boundary in Western Australia, made the following conclusion:

'One distinction marked by the circumcision boundary in Western Australia appears to be the comparative significance attached to the existence of a supreme being by the non-circumcising tribes, at least north of the Gascoyne River[27].'

The Kennedy Ranges belongs in that non-circumcising area north of the Gascoyne River. The very strong biblical references point to the Kennedy Ranges as a settlement of a Lost White Tribe. The moondung references may have also referred to the geographical area of the Kennedy Ranges. When Cornally remembered the first half-caste child he had seen in Champion Bay, the child said that they had *come from the moon* [Kennedy Ranges][28] *and when asked why the child was a different colour they stated that this was not uncommon amongst them*[29].

---

[25] Moore, GF

[26] Foley, RJ, *Vocabulary of the Champion Bay Tribe* cited in Gerritsen p160

[27] O'Grady, GN, *The Significance of the Circumcision Boundary in Western Australia* p168 Also cited in Gerritsen p164

[28] The Eastern Escarpment of the Kennedy Range, photo by Brian GC Bonzle Showcase

[29] Bates Archives, Section VI Pt 3a: *Legends: Champion Bay East - Native beliefs*, p65

Cornally also related a story of an old Aboriginal who had claimed that they had been saved by 'an old man like a white fellow.' His son later came by to make them a fire. When asked where he had lived, *he told them he lived in the moon.*

The traditional Aboriginal owners of the land surrounding and including the Kennedy Ranges were known as the Maia and the Malgaru tribes. The Maia tribe claimed land as far north as Carnarvon to the western slopes of the Kennedy Range. Fortunately abundant freshwater springs and the equally abundant wildlife, enabled the Maia to survive what appears to be a harsh environment. The Malgaru's tribal borders extended from the eastern escarpment of the Kennedy Ranges, across the Lyons River and almost as far as the Gascoyne River. It wasn't until 1858 when the first European explorer, Francis Gregory, had discovered the region. It was still another 20 years before the first pastoralists arrived. Thus the recollection of Cornally of the Kennedy Ranges[30] Aboriginals in the latter half of the 19th century, occurred when there was little or no European contact.

However, it is not clear as to how long they remained in the Kennedy Ranges. There is certainly evidence that the Lost White Tribe fragmented into smaller groups with some remaining in the Murchison and Gascoyne area while others moved north at least as far as the Ashburton River.

During the latter part of the 19th century, Cornally, a station hand who worked in the Hutt, Irwin and Gascoyne areas, told Bates the following in 1909:

Fair-haired and very fair-complexioned natives are met with on the Gascoyne, Murchison and Ashburton (Rivers). He had *seen men and women amongst the natives bearing **strong facial resemblance to white people** in feature and form*[31]. [Author's emphasis]

Cornally's assertion that 'fair-haired' natives lived as far as the Ashburton River is confirmed by Alec Cameron who wrote: *Hair: Generally strong black hair, but some have fine light-brown or golden hair, inclined to curl, but never woolly*[32].

---

[30] Eastern Escarpment Kennedy Ranges near the Lyons River Crossing, photo by Brian GC Bonzle Showcase

[31] Bates Archives, Notebook 3b, p34 Cited Gerritsen, p72

[32] Cameron, Alec. *The Aborigines of North West Australia*, JW Bernard Perth, 1899, p2 Cited Gerritsen, p73

Bates had no doubts about the origin of these fair-haired and fair-complexioned natives in the Gascoyne and Murchison area when she asserted that: *There was no mistaking the heavy Dutch face, curly fair-hair and heavy stocky build*[33].

In a different publication, Bates repeated the interview she had with Cornally but in more detail.

*Cornally has seen men, women and children with **light-coloured hair**. The women have often had very light-brown hair. He very rarely saw them with jet black hair. He has seen children with **white hair**. They are as a rule straight haired people although some have curly and others have wavy hair*[34]. [Author's emphasis]

Shark Bay – three distinct 'races' of Aboriginals

Written at a time when there was no European penetration, AC Gregory wrote the following remark in 1848 about **a strange new race** that he noted was the least numerous of the **three distinct 'races' of Aboriginals** he had discovered while exploring the Shark Bay area.

*The third and least numerous race ... were fairly proportioned with rather small heads covered with **light-flaxen hair,** the eyes approaching the colour of the same, the features flat and wanting in character*[35]. [Author's emphasis]

Louis Freycinet, the French explorer who mapped the Shark Bay area in his 1801–3 expedition, observed of the Aboriginals that there were *two or three racial hybrids*[36] around Shark Bay.

Tom Carter, Jackeroo from the Gascoyne area confirmed Bates' observation of a light-coloured, fair- haired tribe. *Some of the natives at Boolbarty, especially three of the young women, were quite **light-coloured** with regular features and **light-brown hair**, and doubtless had a **strain of white blood** in them derived from Europeans shipwrecked at some time*[37]. [Author's emphasis]

Although at a much later date, a person using the pseudonym EH wrote a letter to the West Australian newspaper: *A year or so ago ... I encountered an extraordinary human specimen in one Pieter – I spell it that way advisedly – the last of the Ingarra tribe. With a great blond beard, not white but bright golden ...*[38]

Tom Pepper also claimed that Pieter had blue eyes: *a very big man ... he had **blue eyes** and a blond beard,* while Carter wrote in the 1880s that, Pieter was *the last of the Ingarra tribe*, [called the Inggarda by Carter], and was located on the Lower Gascoyne River. Other sightings were made from north of Minilya to Shark Bay of Aboriginals with blue eyes, lighter skin and brown hair.

---

[33] Bates, Daisy, *The Passing of the Aborigines*, p126 Cited Gerritsen, p73

[34] Bates Archives, Notebook 3b, p63 Cited Gerritsen, p73

[35] Gregory, AC, MSS held by Dr J Park Thompson, quoted in Bates Archives, *Origin of the Australian Race*. Additional article, p21 Gerritsen, p74

[36] Zaborowski, M, *Bulletin and Memoriale Societe d'Anthropologique de Paris Vol 8 (1907)*, pp384-93 Gerritsen, p81

[37] Carter, V *No Sundays in the Bush An English Jackeroo in Western Australia 1887-1889: from the diaries of Tom Carter*, p123

[38] Letter to the editor by 'EH' West Australian, 3 February, 1934

EH also stated that *formerly in the sandhills around Shark Bay, where half-castes with **blue-eyes** and **flaxen hair** – a rarity in the first generation – are to be found*[39].

Writer, AW Charnley, made the following remark about European looking Aboriginals. *Around the vicinity of Shark Bay,*[40] *and inland, these [early]* **cattlemen came upon tribes ... members of which deviated markedly from the pure Aboriginal type**. *Hair tending to be **flaxen**, particularly among the children; eyes almost **blue** from which the yellow of the 'white' has disappeared*[41].

Charnley, however, believed that the incidences of *natives with fair hair and blue eyes* was simply the result of the two men marooned from the *Batavia* Mutiny in 1629.

The first white men to settle did so reluctantly as they were the two sailors of the 'Batavia' marooned for their part in a mutiny in 1629, which would account for the natives with fair hair and blue eyes reported by our pioneers[42].

Tallness

According to Professor Elkin the average height of Aboriginals was 'about five feet five or six inches [165 – 168 cm][43]. Other writers such as AA Abbie gave heights according to specific areas such as the Eastern Goldfields where males were 170 cm and females 165 cm. In Guildford, near Perth, while the males were also 170 cm, females were 158 cm[44].

However, GH Withers had estimated the average height of males in the Upper Murchison and Gascoyne, *from about 5.6 to 5.9* [feet] *though occasionally one meets a 6 footer*.[45] [183 cm] Gerritsen concluded that, 'There is some evidence to suggest that the people from the upper Murchison were taller than those on the coast and to the south. The trend towards tallness does continue northwards with the average height reaching 172 cm at Nickol Bay (near Roebourne and Dampier on the north-west

---

[39] Ibid. EH

[40] Satellite photo of Shark Bay by NASA

[41] Charnley, AW, *The Coast of the Lost Treasure*, p116

[42] Henvile, AC [ed], The Shire Northampton, p1

[43] Elkin, AP, *The Australian Aborigines (How to Understand Them)*, p4

[44] Abbie, AA. *The Original Australians*, published by Reed, Sydney, 1967 p36

[45] Withers, GH, *The Native Tribes of the Upper Murchison and Upper Gascoyne*, p1, Gerritsen p77

coast) with some individuals reaching 190 cm[46].'

Salvado reported that Augustus Oldfield had told him that, *Out of the 13 Shark Bay natives who visited the Murchison in 1859, twelve were above five feet ten inches in height*[47]. [178 cm]

Tom Carter informed Daisy Bates that he had three Aboriginal men from North-West Cape *who stood from 6ft 3" to 6ft 4"* [190–193 cm] and that *the Coast natives near Point Cloates* [at the base of North West Cape] *were much more powerfully built and muscular than those from inland*[48].

Bates had also interviewed Cornally who reported similar sightings as Carter. *The average height of the male is about 5ft 7" half;* [172 cm] *the women 5ft 2"* [157 cm] *although Cornally has seen men of 6ft* [182 cm] *and women 5ft 7 or 8 inches in height very frequently*[49]. [170 cm to 172 cm]

Gerritsen, in his research had found that, 'There are numerous other instances of tall individuals (often 190 cm) encountered from Champion Bay, eastern Murchison, Gascoyne and Pilbara[50].

Baldness

Baldness, although a common European genetic trait, was extremely rare amongst Aboriginals. Therefore any area that contained bald Aboriginals could be regarded as a region where possible European castaways had settled. All the sources I checked regarding baldness amongst Aboriginals all agreed on the one statement: baldness was extremely rare amongst Aboriginals.

'Baldness is uncommon in Aborigines ... and I have never seen it carried to completion.' Only the Aboriginal people of the Lower Murray River Valley in Eastern Australia, the Murrayians, 'were given to baldness[51].'

'Baldness is comparatively rare among the aborigines; only a limited number of cases have come before the writer's personal notice[52].'

'Baldness is uncommon in aborigines: in females it is very rare; in males, when it occurs, it does not start before middle age and we have never seen the process carried to completion[53].'
'Partial baldness is common; complete baldness unknown[54].'

---

[46] Gerritsen, R, p77 Bates Archives, Section XII Pt 2D, 11, *Native Vocabulary Compiled from Vocabularies supplied by Yabaroo, Timms, Durlacher, Nyarda.* Answer to question 33 JS Durlacher pp30-31

[47] Salvado, p117

[48] Bates Archives, Notebook 24, p32

[49] Bates Archives, Notebook 3 b, p24

[50] Gerritsen, R, p294

[51] Birdsell, JB, *Human Evolution: An Introduction to the New Physical Anthropology*, p506

[52] Basedow, Herbert, Preece, FW, *The Australian Aboriginal*, 1925

[53] Aboriginal man in south and central Australia: Vol 1 Bernard C.Cotton, British Science Guild. South Australian Branch – 1966

[54] The Journal of the Anthropological Institute of Great Britain and Ireland Vol 65, 1935

Phillip Chauncy, the Assistant Surveyor from 1841 to 1853, stated, *The only bald natives I ever saw are the warran diggers, who are said to wear the hair off the head by pressing it so frequently against the sides of these* [warran] *holes*[55].

Oldfield had heard of bald Aboriginals through Cornally. *Cornally knew an old man named Milleebarra, who was bald – he was a Champion Bay native – walla-pirt-killy was the name given to a bald head at Champion Bay and mugga-been – bald head, is the Gascoyne and eastern Gascoyne name*[56]. Cornally also saw one bald woman.

Gerritsen also points out how the Dutch and Nanda language had become integrated into a new language. He gives the example of *walla.pit.killy* (bald in Amangoo). By breaking up the word into three parts, he compares it to the Dutch. *Walla* (head) *portee* (tending in Dutch) and *kaaltje* (bald) or *kaalheid* (baldness in Dutch). Thus we can translate the Aboriginal word, *walla.pit.killy*, to literally mean 'head tending to bald(ness).'

Natives 'approaching the European type' with distinctly European features were observed by AC Gregory in 1848 countering the variables of British settlement. Gregory had encountered fair people with fair skin, fair hair and light eye colour before any colonists had entered the area. He also said that the *old* natives at Champion Bay had features *approaching the European type*. Therefore they had to have been born between 1800 and 1820.

Gerritsen summed up the three rare features attributed to Aboriginals along the mid-west coast in the following way: '... the appearance of so many atypical features within one region is a remarkable coincidence. At least three distinct mutations are identifiable – pigmentation, baldness and tallness – and the odds against them occurring together in one subgroup are astronomical[57].'

---

[55] Chauncy, Phillip, *Notes and Anecdotes of the Aboriginals of Australia*, Gerritsen p75

[56] Bates Archives, Section XVIII Pt 3, *Native Traits, Characteristics*, Cornally p37ff

[57] Gerritsen, R, *And Their Ghosts May Be Heard*, p78

Zuytdorp site map Map by Henry Van Zanden

Chapter 17
A New Dutch-Aboriginal Language

State Library of Western Australia

An early photo of a blond Aboriginal girl similar perhaps to the Aboriginals the first European explorers had come across in the Victoria district, Irwin River and Champion Bay.

Almost every early explorer and even later commentators, remarked upon the uniqueness of an Aboriginal dialect in the Champion Bay and Hutt River District.

In early 1840, George Fletcher Moore, who was then Advocate-General, embarked upon a northern expedition in the Champion Bay area. Moore, who was an accomplished speaker of the Swan River dialect, ventured south to the Hutt River where he came across a tribe whose language was almost unintelligible. From the discussion that took place between them, it would also seem that Moore possibly misinterpreted an attempt by the Hutt River Aborigines to show Moore the location of a Lost White Tribe that may have lived in the valley.

At last by watching their mode of intonation, and accommodating myself to their dialect I managed to succeed a little better ... their answer at last was precisely in Swan River language 'Gaipbi jera' (water to the north') ... they pulled their beards, and said 'Nanya patta' by which name I have heard it called at Swan River also ... I said they were 'golam biddy' ('boys') which they seemed to understand ... I saw them eating mesembryanthemum (the Hottentot fig)[1]*, but they did not understand the names used at Swan River – 'golboys' or 'mejaruk'. They called it by a different name. One repeatedly asked me 'were we dead?' [a reference to the Djanga Myth, that the white men were the spirits of the dead returned] ... the natives seemed dissatisfied about our going to the hills, and offended, and were very importunate with us to go down to the low grounds in the valley 'Koa yeka' (come this way' as I understood it) ... they became very urgent that we should 'sit down in the shade' – 'Maloka ninenka' (a Swan man would say 'malok nginnow') ...*[2]

Perhaps they were so urgent because they wished to show Moore the remnants of the Lost White Tribe that lived in the valley below. That they were eating the 'Hottentot fig' gives further weight to the Lost White Tribe living in the area.

The brothers Frank and Augustus Gregory also noted the significant difference in dialect when they approached Champion Bay.

... we could not obtain any other useful information as their dialect differs considerably from that spoken in the settled districts though some few words are the same[3]*.*

Even neighbouring Aboriginal tribes could not understand this puzzling dialect. The following was noted in the early 1850s after white settlement had begun in the Champion Bay area:

.... while the two [Aborigines] *taken by Mr Fowler, and said to be brothers of Kardakai* [from Victorian Plains, 110 km north-east of Perth] *cannot make themselves comprehended by any of the tribe near Champion Bay*[4]*.*

Augustus Oldfield was perhaps best able to make a judgement on the dialects of the Aborigines of the Champion Bay area as he had lived in the Lower Murchison River area in the 1850s and early 1860s.

---

[1] Hottentot was the name of a South African tribe and possible the origin of the figs or yams

[2] Moore, GF, cited in Rupert Gerritsen, *And Their Ghosts May Be Heard*, p105

[3] 'The Settler Expedition to the Northward from Perth under the Assistant Surveyor AC Gregory, 1848 in Expedition Diaries, Vol. 4 19 October 1848*.* Cited in Gerritsen, p106

[4] Inquirer 9, January, 1850, *Editorial* p2

Perhaps in no part of the world is there so great a number of dialects, distinct in everything except grammatical construction, spoken by tribes all sprung from the same stock ... In fact so great is the difference between the dialects even of contiguous tribes that I have found my knowledge of the Watch-an-die dialect totally useless, as a means of communicating with a tribe inhabiting a locality only fifty miles [80 km] *from the country of the Watch-an-dies*[5].

Gregory had his own theories as to how these strange dialects came about and he based his theory upon the distinct physical differences that one particular tribe had over the others:

In 1848 I explored the country where the Dutchmen had landed [Batavia *mutineers 1629*], *and found a tribe whose characters differed considerably from the average Australian. Their colour was neither black nor copper, but that peculiar colour which prevails with a mixture of European blood: their stature was good, with strong limbs, and remarkably heavy and solid around the lower jaw. Their dialect was scarcely intelligible to the other tribes further south*[6].

Daisy Bates also made an association with the distinct dialect of some tribes and the colour of their hair. However, by the 20th century, there was a gradual shift of Aboriginal tribes to the east, away from the British settlements.

The prevalence of fair-headed natives far eastward of Dongara, etc. where the changes of dialect are so noticeable, may be due to the same cause. Light, curly, wavy and straight haired natives have been met with as far eastward as Meekatharra ...[7]

She later wrote that she believed that, *the dialects of Dongara, Geraldton and the Northhampton show such marked differences towards their eastern and southern neighbours, that it can only be conjectured that the original people who introduced the dialect variations came by sea, or were wrecked on that party of the coast*[8].

An attempt to pinpoint the exact location of where a portion of the composite Dutch-Aboriginal tribe may have ended up can be gleaned from a later remark where she sums up the language variations:

Along the coastal roads, a person travelling from, say, the Ngurdeemaia country [immediately south of the Irwin River] *to the Ngallooma district* [Nickol Bay area], *would find very little difficulty, after a short interval, in making himself understood, as all along the coast and for some little distance inland, with the exception of the peculiar dialects in the Illimbirrie country* [lower Sandford River, near Twin Peaks Station and the junction of the Murchison River], *and amongst some of the isolated tribes ...*[9]

Gerritsen was able to isolate the language to that of the Nanda people. 'Running from just south of Shark Bay to the Irwin River along a coastal strip perhaps 50 km wide at the most. Nanda was spoken on the Lower Murchison River, Hutt River, Northampton, Champion Bay (Geraldton),

---

[5] Oldfield, A, *The Aborigines of Australia*, p231 cited from Gerritsen, R, p106

[6] Gregory, AC, '*Inaugural Address*', p32 Cited in Gerritsen, p107

[7] Bates, D. *The Native Tribes of Western Australia*, p231

[8] Bates Archives, Section XII Pt 1: *Outline of Grammar*. Gerritsen, p109

[9] Bates Archives, Section II Pt 2a: Geographical Distribution of the Northern and Southern Groups of Western Australia pp34-35 Cited in Gerritsen p110

Greenough River and Irwin River (Dongara). It was the language that Oldfield (his Watch-an-dies), Bates, Moore and the Gregory's referred to ...' [10] 'Watch-an-di(es) or Watjandi was a term used to describe the Nanda and means 'westerners.' Oldfield referred to Watch-an-dies as the natives around Geraldton[11].

Pastoralist JE Hammond, who had a good working knowledge of the south-western Aboriginal language also came unstuck when he reached the Champion Bay area.

I had a similar experience when travelling from Albany to the Gascoyne. I could get on fairly well with any blacks until we got eastward of Geraldton (i.e. Champion Bay). There I found everything quite different. I could not use the south-west language with the natives of those parts, and if our south-west natives tried to talk to them they would simply laugh at each other ... When we got to the Gascoyne our natives could not understand anything that the Gascoyne natives said[12].

It was quite remarkable that tribes so close together could be so different in their language or dialect that they could scarcely understand one another. Bates claimed that a person would have little difficulty making himself understood if they had travelled south of the Irwin River as far north to Nickol Bay which is not too distant from Broome. However, she makes the notable following exceptions: *the peculiar dialects in the Illimbirrie country* [lower Sandford River, near Twin Peaks Station and the junction of the Murchison River], *and amongst some of the isolated northern tribes*[13].

This is the same area that Bates claimed to have found tribes that looked like they were Dutch. While speaking about the Aggardee tribes or circumcised tribes, Bates remarked:

I also found traces of types distinctly Dutch. When Pelsaert marooned two white criminals on the mainland of Australia in 1627, these Dutchmen had probably been allowed to live with the natives, and it may, be that they and their progeny journeyed far along the river-highways, for I found these types as far out as the head-waters of the Gascoyne and the Murchison. There was no mistaking the flat heavy Dutch face, curly fair hair, and heavy stocky build[14].

Dutch influence in Aboriginal language

At Oakabella [31 km south of Geraldton], *Illimbirrie, and a few other places in the Northampton district the most extraordinary dialect changes occur. There is a pause or stoppage in the accentuation of a middle or final syllable or letter, the pause not consisting of an aspirate (unless it is a 'silent aspirate').*[15] *The Illimbirrie dialect,* wrote Bates, *is the same area where the 'white tribe' had reputedly been encountered in 1861*[16].

---

[10] Gerritsen, Rupert, *And Their Ghosts May Be Heard*, p111

[11] t Tindale, Dr Norman Barnet, Collection AA338 South Australian Museum Archives

[12] Hammond, JE, *Winjan's People* p16. Cited in Gerritsen, p109

[13] Bates, D, Section II Pt 2a: Geographical Description of the Northern and Southern groups of Western Australia' pp34-35, cited in Gerritsen, p110

[14] Bates, D, *The Passing of the Aborigines*, Chapter 10 First published in 1938, eBooks@Adelaide 2012

[15] Daisy Bates Archives, Section XII Pt 1, p24

[16] Ibid. p113

The Nanda language was the main language group that differed the most. It was, in turn, divided up into three other main groups based on their geographical regions. They were:
- Watch-an-die in the north (south of Shark Bay to just north of the Hutt River)
- Nandakorla in the centre (south of Watch-an-die to just north of Geraldton)
- Amangoo (south of Nandakorla to the Irwin River).

Gerritsen carried out a study of a Nanda 937 word/6990-item vocabulary based exclusively on historical sources: Moore (1840), Dr Foley (1850s), Oldfield (later 1850s and early 1860s, RT Goldsworthy (1874) and Bates (c1908). Later sources were not used to avoid modern influences to the language.

Gerritsen concluded that the Nanda actually contained three separate languages rather than dialects with the 'Nandakorla and Amangoo so different that they almost belong in different subgroups[17].'

Comparing the Nanda language to the Illimbirrie and the Aggardee or circumcised tribes, Gerritsen showed that they were two separate languages despite their close proximity 'supporting the claims made by early visitors that there was enormous variation in the languages in the region.'

Nandakorla stood out the most because it bore the least resemblance to both common Australian Aboriginal language and to the Nanda languages. In comparing the different Aboriginal languages, Gerritsen used a list of the most common words not only with the Nanda languages, but with a total of 55 different Aboriginal languages. What Gerritsen discovered was that 'the Nanda and Kanyaric languages represent a significant discontinuity. In a number of cases the difference is so marked, given the enormous 'stability' of many of the terms, that there is indeed greater variability over short distances than there is over hundreds of kilometres elsewhere ... Allied with the historical and lexicostatistical evidence of linguistic disturbance the conclusion that there was such a disturbance is inescapable[18].'

In particular he noted words such as 'I' - *kni* and *g'ni*; fire - *karla* or *waru*; to burn – *ow'wa* or *aowwa*. These word structures represented major inconsistencies only to be found in the Nanda languages.

'The KN sound at the beginning of words is a distinctive feature of Nanda and does not normally appear to be found elsewhere in Australia.' Other words 'such as *taarfda* (knee), *mesja* (here) and *wezueda* (possum) are also highly unusual in that they contain the letter F, S and Z sounds ... Generally speaking, Aboriginal languages do not have sounds which equate to the F, S, V, and Z sounds found in English ...

'H also 'is missing' from Aboriginal languages. It does appear infrequently in all the formation of sounds such as CH, TH, DH, WH (all these are found in word beginnings in Nanda) ... Yet Nanda, or at least Amangoo and Nandakorla sections of it, has seven words beginning with H. Words such as *hewerloo* (light), *hot.ther* (dog – wild or tame), *howa* (water) and *hurder* (today).

'Reviewing these phonemic irregularities leads to the conclusion that Nanda is ... the most unusual language in Australia, exhibiting four or five anomalies ... In order to explain the unusual character of Nanda ... the hypothesis that Nanda is a language influenced by the Dutch of the shipwrecked sailors seems a reasonable one.'

---

[17] Gerritsen, R. *And Their Ghosts May Be Heard*, p116

[18] Ibid. p123

Gerritsen explains that Dutch has F, H, S and Z in the language all of which appear in Nanda. However, the greatest significance is the 'presence of the sound KN sound in Dutch, in words such as *kneval* (moustache), *knip* (cut) and *Knauw* (bite / gnaw)... That the full KN sound should also be found in Nanda is either an amazing coincidence or an indication that there is some substance to the hypothesis.'

How letters are pronounced in Dutch can change how we view the word relationship between the Dutch and the Nanda. For instance the Dutch G is sometimes pronounced as a J (as in jump). Compare the Nanda word *wajjeeno* meaning lean or thin to the Dutch word *vergaan*, 'to waste away.' If we replace the G with a J and the V with a W, the words look remarkably similar. *Vergaan* becomes *werjaan*.

Sometimes the language integration worked by combining both the Aboriginal and Dutch words together. The Nandakorla term for native cat was *thin.tha.goo*. However, it was pronounced *tin.ta.kat* in Amangoo. Cat in Dutch is Kat[19].

Gerritsen next decided to test his hypothesis directly with both the Dutch and English languages.

Table One

Dialect: W = Watchandie   N = Nandakorla   A = Amangoo

English	Nanda	Dialect	Dutch	Comments
Aged	Oop'baija	A	Oop bejaard	Dutch J = Y
Bad	Gooraa'ee	N	Goor	Dutch, nasty/dingy
Wooden bowl	Bat.tje	W	Batje	Dutch J = Y
Clod of earth	Turpa	W	Turfje, turf	Dutch, small mound Dutch, lump of peat
Cold	Koon'dhertha	A	Koudachtig Koudete	Dutch, coldish Dutch, coldness
Coughing	Oondoonda mok	A	Aandoen ademtocht	Dutch, affected by gasping
Digging stick	Wippa, Whippa	AW	Wipje	Dutch J = Y Dutch, small plank
Exchange/ Barter	Kooyeroo	N	Koopjeruillen	Dutch J = Y
Hawk	Kir.ken.jo	W	Kiekendief	Dutch, Kite, a hawk like bird
Jaw	Caard.do	W	Kaak	
Many/Plenty	Bool.la	W	Boel	Dutch, a lot / a whole lot

---

[19] Ibid, p125-130

English	Nanda	Dialect	Dutch	Comments
Wind	Windhoo	A	Wind	

In the Nandakorla the word bald is *moggabeen*. In old Dutch *mugge* means 'hair'. If we add other Dutch words to *mugge* such as *been* (bone) *beetje* (very little), or *boven* (thin on top), we get a similar meaning.

Gerritsen points out that some letters or sounds from the Dutch language are difficult for not only Aboriginals but also English speakers to pronounce. The letter J in Dutch is pronounced Y or IY in English. Other substitutions occurred such as the letter W for the Dutch V. Looking at the following table and replacing the letter W with V, we soon get a closer approximation to the Dutch word.

Sometimes letters are dropped altogether after the language integration occurs as shown in Table 2.

Table 2

Dialect: W = Watchandie N = Nandakorla A = Amangoo

English	Nanda	Dialect	Dutch	Comments
By-and-by (eventually)	Walloo Warlow	A N	Verloop = Werloo	In the course of expiration of time. The V is substituted by W and the P dropped.
Brains	Waar.da	W	Vaardig = Waardi	Skilled, clever, capable V substituted for W and G is dropped
Afternoon/ Evening	Warnda Wornda	A A	Avond = Wond	Evening – V to W with A dropped
I am glad	Wee.ka quarlo Wee.ka qwola	W	1. Verheugen 2. Gevallig	Pleasing, agreeable. 1. V to W and the N is dropped. 2. V to W and G is dropped
Good (thing)	Cwar Gwa.lo Kwar	A W A	Gevallig = Gewalli	Pleasing, agreeable. V to W and G is dropped
Half-caste'	Wee.lurdee	A	Vaal gekleurd = Waal leurd	Sallow complexion. V to W with G, E, and K dropped.
To cry	Woolanee	N	Vol Tranen = Wol.anne	Tearful. V to W and T, R, and N are dropped.

The Dutch language connection is not always immediately apparent unless we realise how another language adapts the borrowed words of another. For example the Dutch term for *on fire* is *aanvuur*. The Aboriginal word for fire is *karla* but the Nanda word is markedly different: *ow'wa*. If the V is substituted for W and the N is dropped, the result is *aawuur* remarkably close to *ow'wa*.

Expressions too can be borrowed that have similar meanings in both cultures. For example, Oldfield was puzzled by the term *plokeman* equating it with the term 'blood brother'. He gave an example of its usage in its social context the following passage.

There is a curious custom relative to eating prevalent ... among the Western Australian natives ... Should a person drop a morsel of food, any other striding by immediately picks it up, and merely saying 'Plokeman' proceeds to eat it[20].

Gerritsen explains the similarity in Dutch and the Dutch meaning for the word. The Dutch word *pluk* means gathering/picking, *plok*, handful and *plokkeman* meaning scrounger. 'The contextual meaning that can be inferred from Oldfield's account, implying scrounging rights accorded to those bearing a close relationship (blood brothers).

Sometimes a word can have several meanings depending upon the circumstances. The more powerful and dramatic the circumstances the greater any new word might have upon the receiver. The Dutch word for 'waste away' has already been noted as *vergaan* with the V more easily pronounced as a W and the G sounding like a J producing *werjaan*. *Vegaan* has also another more significant meaning: 'to be shipwrecked.'

Gerritsen noted the connections in the following Nanda words:

Wajjanoo (Amangoo, Nanakorla) **Fire**
Wa.jan (Amangoo) **Fire**
Wad.jan.o (Watch-an-die) **Fire**
Wajjeeno (Amangoo) **Lean/thin**
Wajjeeloo (Nandakorla) **Thirsty**
Woojanoo (Amangoo) **Stranger/Traveller**[21]

Closely corresponding to the same idea, the Nanda tribe Watch-an-die is remarkably similar to the Dutch word *wachhtaandezee* meaning 'the sea watch'. Aborigines could not pronounce the Z and so it was dropped. The *Zuytdorp* coincidentally was wrecked along the Watch-an-die coast. Logically the survivors would have maintained a sea watch for a considerable time hoping for a passing ship to sail by where they would send a signal fire which was perhaps kept at the ready permanently for such an occasion.

Gerritsen provides numerous examples like the above and finishes by concluding *that at least 16% of the Nanda languages are actually derived from Dutch*[22]*... Dutch influence was principally centred upon the area from the Murchison to Irwin Rivers radiating outwards from there*[23]*.*

---

[20] Oldfield p285, cited Gerritsen, p131

[21] Ibid. p131

[22] Ibid. p130

[23] Ibid. p133

However, Gerritsen did not know of the existence of the Karakin Lakes settlement and its forced migration after 1833 most likely into the Irwin River valley. The *Zuytdorp* survivors gradually found their way along the Murchison as well as north of the Murchison River.

Interestingly Gerritsen identified another small subgroup that may have also been influenced by Dutch sailors stranded ashore: the small Kanyaric subgroup whose influence extended into the northern Gascoyne and the southern Ngayarda subgroup (Ashburton district). The origin of these sailors are uncertain. They may have been some of the *Zuytdorp* survivors or descendants moving north or, as suggested by Gerritsen, an unknown wreck in the North West Cape. There is also one other possibility: the *Zeewijk* twelve who set out in their long boat from the Abrolhos Islands and were never seen again. Sailing north, they may have encountered difficult weather conditions and their boat inevitably was forced towards the Western Australian coastline until they became shipwrecked again somewhere around the North West Cape region in 1727.

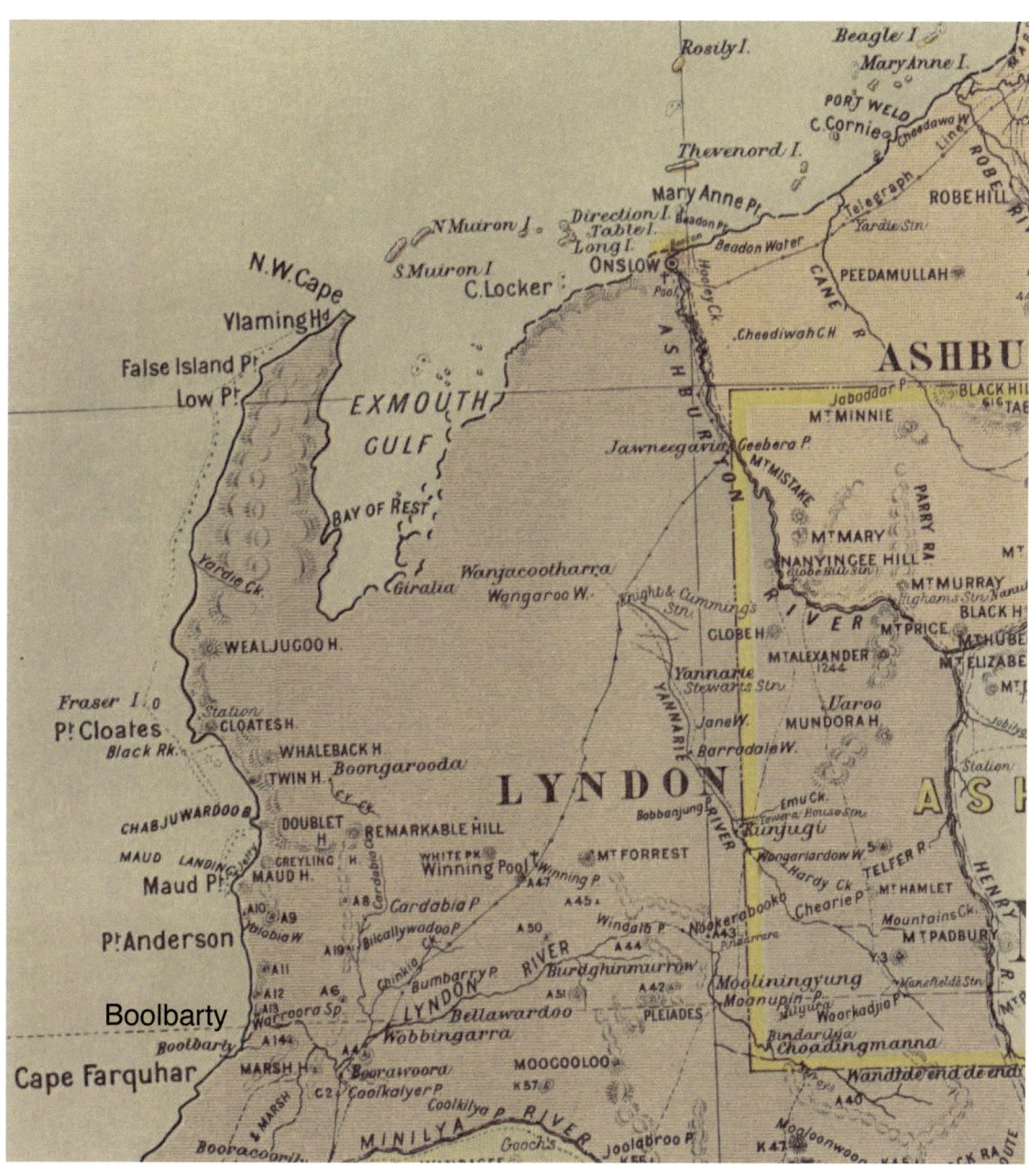

Map of the North West Cape / Ashburton River region. Positive sightings of fair-skinned / fair-headed Aboriginals have been noted from the Minilya River in the south, Boolbarty and the Ashburton River. Map from the Daisy Bates Collection held in the National Library of Australia.

Jun-Gun
The Argus, Melbourne, reported the following on 4 February, 1890

What is it? With a curious and pathetic interest one asks that question when looking at "Jun-Gun," the Australian albino … this thing brought in from the wilderness … this queer white flower from the black garden? Crowds come to look at it, to wonder, to gloat, to go away … satisfied jibbering monstrosities which figured in the same place a few months back. But this creature is not monstrous in any sense and does not seem burdened with the incapacity which characterises most of the freaks of nature. His colour did not save him from the disciplines of savagedom; he survived it and held his own.

Jun-Gun's Discovery

Jun-Gun was discovered by a Western Australian pastoralist, Alexander McPhee, who had been visited by an isolated group of Aboriginals who had only ever seen one other white person before. They spoke of a white Aboriginal who had visited them at a corroboree. McPhee believed that he may have been the descendant of a white man and decided to find out the truth for himself.

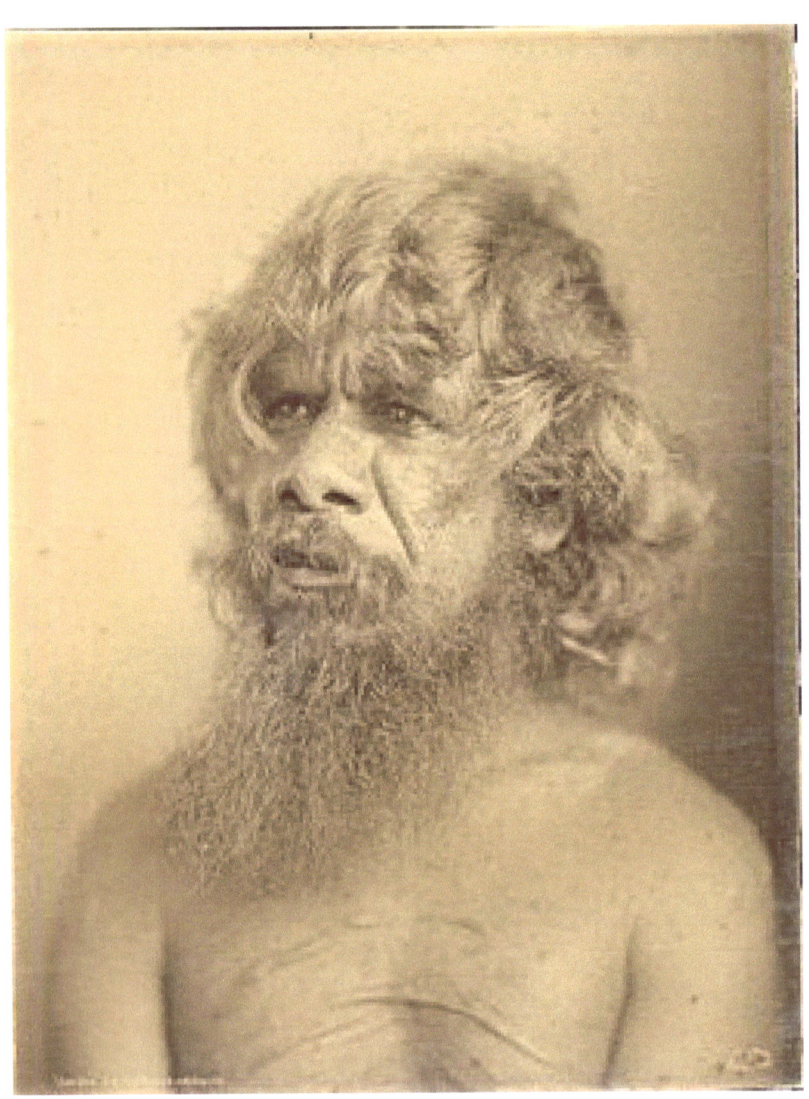

Jun-Gun, the blonde Aboriginal

Taking six horses, and escorted by two Aboriginal scouts, he set out a 480 km expedition. He finally came across the tribe and found the the golden-haired Jun-Gun. McPhee, who could speak the Aboriginal language fluently, asked the tribal group whether they had ever seen a white person such as himself. Emphatically they all answered, 'No! Never!' Jun-Gun's parents were charcoal black as was all of his relatives.

"You are like me," said McPhee to him in his Nagamont tongue. "You are not black like your people, you are white like me; you had better come and see my people."

Jun-Gun replied, "Jun-Gun will come!" The West Australian, 18 January, 1893

Chapter 18
Lost White Tribe Descendants

Len Ogilvie, an elder of the Nanda people from the Murchison River area, said that his relatives had long suspected they might have Dutch ancestry.[1]

---
[1] Jessica Strutt, *The West Australian*, 17 April, 2010

The Nanda People

Possibly more than any other Aboriginal tribe, the Nanda stand out the most as the one that seems to have the closest links and received the greatest influence of the Lost White Tribe.

The relationship the Nanda people had with the land was probably the most important of these influences converting the Nanda people into an agricultural or semi-agricultural society.

*They had their **landed estates,** the boundaries of which were better defined than many of the squatters leases now are. The **daughters inherited landed estates as well as the sons**. I have heard an Aboriginal lady say, 'What are you? Why, before I married you your land only comprised the miserable range of hills which are not fit to feed an emu. It was my dower which brought you that fine valley, with its yams and springs of water' & etc.*[2] [Author's emphasis]

Men and women both engaged in the farming of yams. In 1851 William Burges, the Government Resident of the newly formed Champion Bay settlement wrote:

They seem very little addicted to hunting and very few of them are even expert at tracking a Kangaroo. This may result from the great variety of edible roots, particularly the A-jack-0 or warang [warran] *which grows here in great abundance and to a very large size.*
William Burges to Acting Colonial Secretary, 9 June, 1851

AC Gregory commenting upon the social organisation of the Nanda people:

The women were far better treated or, rather, they have emancipated themselves from the extreme condition of social slavery which generally prevails. I have, for instance, known the queen of the district give her consort king a sound thrashing with a yam-stick and escape being speared for such an assertion of co-ordinate authority.[3]

I have seen both men and women sinking in loose sandy soil for an edible root called warran, one of the dioscorea ...[4]

Many examples have been written regarding the superior habitations of the Nanda, especially in the Champion Bay area. The differences were noted in the newspaper, *The Inquirer*, 1850, commenting on the tribes of Champion Bay and the Victoria District:

---

[2] Gregory, AC, Gerritsen, R, p138

[3] Gregory, AC, 'Inaugural Address', p23 Gerritsen, R, and p139

[4] Chauncy, P, *Notes and Anecdotes of the Aborigines of Australia* Appendix A in R Brough Smyth, *The Aborigines of Victoria, Vol. 2* p246

There is every reason to believe that the Aborigines in the neighbourhood of Champion Bay are susceptible of the softening influences of civilisation than the unmitigated barbarians by whom we are surrounded. Their weapons are in greater variety, and exhibit more polish and finish than do their southern neighbours; their huts are more substantial and more worthy for the dwellings of humanity than are the worse than dog-kennels that are erected by the natives in the settled portions of the province.[5]

Much had already been written regarding the European-looking appearance of some of the Nanda tribe and there had been some debate as to the origin of the Aborigines. Bates disagreed that the first arrivals had landed in the north-east and crossed Australia obliquely by way of Cooper's Creek. The natives themselves, she argued, pointed to the north-west as their place of origin.

Bates recognised the impossibility of proving each other's arguments. However, *she had sent some samples of Aboriginal hair to Professor Cleland, the Government pathologist, for analysis. His report that the hair was elliptical meant that **the western Aborigines**, like the Europeans, **were Caucasian** and not negroid, by origin.* [Author's emphasis]

The report had confirmed her view that there was an obvious European influence. Bates had little doubt as to the origin of the fair-haired Nanda she had come across: *The prevalence of fair-haired natives far eastward of Dongara,*[6] *etc., where the changes in dialect are so noticeable, may be due to the same cause Light, curly, wavy and straight-haired natives have been met with as far eastward as Meekatharra ...*[7] *The dialects of Dongara, Geraldton and the Northampton district show such marked differences towards their eastern and southern neighbours, that it can only be conjectured that the original people who*

Aboriginals seek Dutch DNA link

Stolen Generation Aboriginal Len Ogilvie[8] is one of a number of West Australians who has undergone DNA testing as part of a research project that has the potential to re-write Australian History.

Theories have abounded for years as to whether Dutch crew, whose ships came to grief on the treacherous reefs off WA, married or fraternised with West Australian Aboriginals, producing children of mixed ancestry.

Perth-based amateur historian Thomas Vanderveldt, president of the VOC Historical Society, has teamed up with Dutch scientist Dr Pieter Bol to test the genetic links between the ancestors of those sailed on the United East Indies Company's ships and WA Aboriginals. The DNA of 80 West Australian Aboriginals has already been sent to a medical laboratory in the Netherlands for testing.

Mr Ogilvie, an elder of the Nanda people from the Murchison River area, said yesterday that his relatives had long suspected they might have Dutch ancestry.

"My mother she was as white as you and she had red hair ... you don't see many red-headed Aboriginals around here," he said. The project hopes to settle speculation on whether Europeans were living in Australia long before the arrival of the British First Fleet in Sydney Cove in 1788 ...

Mr Ogilvie, 81, of Innaloo, said he would "feel good" if the research revealed he had Dutch ancestry.

Mr Vanderveldt said the biggest group of shipwreck survivors most likely to have made it ashore were the crew and soldiers aboard the *Zuytdorp*, which was lost without trace in 1712 and discovered more than 80 years later wrecked off Shark Bay.

He said early test results had confirmed there was Western European, not English, DNA in some WA Aboriginals. The next tests are critical as they should allow the researchers to pinpoint the date when that genetic link came about and whether it predated British settlement.

Jessica Strutt, The West Australian, 17 April, 2010

---

[5] Inquirer 9 January, 1850 Editorial, p2

[6] Map from the Daisy Bates Collection, National Library of Australia

[7] Bates, Daisy, Section VII Pt One: *Outline of Grammar,* cited also in Gerritsen p107

introduced the dialect variations came by sea, or were wrecked on that part of the coast[8].

Gene Tests Seek Dutch Links to WA Aboriginals

It is interesting that some West Australian Aboriginals are now cliaming or believe they have direct links to Dutch shipwrecked sailors that arrived on West Australian shore in the 17th and 18th centuries.

Reporter Beatrice Thomas in 2008 wrote:

Helping with the research is society vice-president John Alexander, a Noongar elder, who said the historical ties between WA Aboriginal communities and the Dutch were commonly discussed among Aboriginal groups. He said while he was "50-50" on what the tests may uncover he believed much of the link was acknowledged through oral stories passed down through generations.

When I meet some of the elders from the Tuart mob they tell me openly that they've got Dutch ancestry and it's something that academic Australia has overlooked, he said. *On the South Coast with our mob we have clear examples of two dark-coloured people with white children with blonde hair and blue eyes.*

Mr Alexander, who is married to a Dutch woman, said while the testing would not be welcome by all sections of the indigenous community he believed it was important. *It's only the tip of the iceberg for all parties, I think there's something very special in the whole thing*, he said[9].

Piece by piece, whether by DNA, artifacts or the discovery of a new wreck, the puzzle of the Lost White Tribe will be finally revealed. An archaeological dig will be necessary to confirm the location of the settlement at the Karakin Lakes.

The VOC Historical Society was able to enlist the services and valuable research of a Dutch historian and scientist, Dr Pieter Bol who was interviewed by Ross Coulthart, a reporter on Channel 7's *Sunday* program. Dr Bol told Coulthart that there were *at least 11 Dutch vessels wrecked on or near the Australian coast. Several of these ships had say 65 or 100 or even 150 who survived and invariably smaller boats were sent to the capital of Indonesia to come to the rescue of marooned sailors and they found nobody; they had disappeared.*

When asked what had happened to them, Bol replied:

It must have been that they were helped and there is much evidence that there was a Dutch mixture in the genome of Aboriginals. In specific reference to the *Zuytdorp* wreck, Bol added:

In some days, some must have died from the cold, from thirst, from hunger but we think that a vast majority has been rescued by the Aboriginals and has been mixing with them.

DNA Testing

In 2012, the DNA testing and analysis was assigned to Professor doctor Peter de Knijff (human geneticist) of Leiden University Medical Centre (LUMC). 43 samples of DNA were collected by the VOC Historical Society between 2009 and March 2010 but only from male Aboriginals. The reason why only male samples were collected was because the Y-chromosome passed nearly unchanged from father to son.

---

[8] Ibid, p109

[9] Beatrice Thomas, Gene Tests Seek Dutch Links to WA Aboriginals, *The West Australian*, (Perth), December 18, 2008

There are only about 25 Y chromosomes worldwide that show a strong regional link. By examining the Y-chromosome, the geneticist can determine the continent from which the male ancestor's originally came from.

I was quite surprised to discover that more than half of those Aboriginals have a Western Y-chromosome.[10]

However, neither the exact area of Europe or the number of generations the Y–chromosome refers to is still unknown. It could be as little as two generations or as high as ten. According to Professor de Knijff, a clearer profile can be obtained by extending the research into not only the chromosomes but the mitochondrial DNA that mothers pass to their children. Unfortunately, this will take a further year to complete and the results won't be available until 2013 at the earliest.

Dutch Aboriginals

The 2010 Chairman of the VOC Historical Society, Tom Vanderveldt, collected the DNA from Aboriginals such as Paul Clayton and the Drages family. The samples were then sent to Leiden. In March 2010, a Dutch film company, VPRO, with the assistance of the VOC Historical Society, a short film titled, *Dutch Aboriginals*. Excerpts of the film are detailed below.

The Nanda's brief was very simple: they wanted to know if they have Dutch genes. If DNA testing helps us to prove they have Dutch genes they were probably introduced by the Dutch shipwrecked sailors aboard East India Company ships, that between about 1620–1720 sank off the Western Australian coast. There are many different Aboriginals in Australia. The Aboriginals in the north and the north-east are very different from the Aboriginals we've tested in the far south-west and west of Australia. No one has ever done a genetic study in these areas before. It is a blank area on the genetic map, so anything is possible.

In Leiden, Peter de Knijff has the first preliminary results.

Of the 45 men we examined, we see that only three of them have the standard Y chromosome found in Australian Aboriginals. All the other men have a type of Y chromosome that either comes from north-west Europe or a Mediterranean country. And we hadn't expected that.

Tom Vanderveldt felt certain that some of the 286 people aboard the *Zuytdorp* survived the wreck and came ashore to become one of the Lost White Tribes of Australia. [Author's summary]

There is little doubt that some of the survivors explored the river inland for 2 silver coins were found 22 km inland at the junction of the Gascoyne River; equally there was talk of a white tribe in that region in the 1830s. [Vanderveldt]

Vanderveldt asserted that *an aggressive integration took place.* Although they found water fowl, fish, and kangaroos to eat, they were forced to locate into smaller groups due to the scarcity of food.

The film also looked specifically at the Clayton family to explain why proving their Dutch ancestry was important to them.

Clayton and his family take Sarah to Murchison House Station, an old sheep farm where they lived and worked for years. They believe that this is their land, the land of their ancestors but they have no title deeds as they knew nothing about ownership.

---

[10] de Knijff, Peter (Professor Doctor), *To the Roots*, Holland Focus, p24 November -December 2012 Courtesy: *Kennislink 13.09.2010,* Raymond Heemskerk, President VOC Historical Society Inc. vocsoc@iinet.net.au

As soon as they can show, with the help of the professor from Leiden, that they are descendants of the shipwrecked sailors, they have proof their family lived here in the 17th century long before the first English settlers stole their land. And their family told the shipwrecked sailors where to find fresh water. The possibility of having Dutch ancestors has really raised the hopes of the Drages. Everywhere in Australia Aboriginals have been given land.

While in Western Australia during my first expedition to the Murchison River area, I interviewed one of the Nanda Aboriginals, John Mallard, whose family had always believed that they had Dutch ancestry.

John Mallard

John had always believed that he had Dutch heritage and became even more convinced of this after asking his grandfather questions when he was a young boy. I was introduced to John by Tom Vanderveldt, who was then President of the VOC Historical Society, who knew that John was related to Ken Mallard. I had come across Ken's name while investigating the genetical disease *porphyria variegata*. Ken Mallard was John's grandfather's brother's son. This was a peculiar disease that was prevalent only in South Africa. Usually when a ship stopped at Cape Town, it allowed the sick ashore to recover while it picked up those sailors who had recovered from previous ships. Ken had believed that he had suffered the rare disease after a sailor for a Dutch shipwreck had landed on the West Australian coast.

However, researchers from the Department of Genetics University of Stellenbosch investigated 296 cases of *pohyria* in Western Australia which included three Aboriginals and came up with the conclusion that the disease was not inherited from shipwrecked sailors[11].

Although we cannot attribute the disease to the survivors of the *Zuytdorp*, there was another rare genetic disease, Ellis-van Creveld syndrome[12], that was prevalent in the Mallard family. The syndrome is characterised by the growth of extra fingers and toes. Two children and two other family members in the extended Mallard family had variations of the Ellis-van Creveld syndrome. The researcher, Goldblatt[13], *documented the second highest incidence of Ellis-van Creveld to be among the Aboriginal population in the south-west of Western Australia who have a purported carrier prevalence of 1/39 live births.*

Goldblatt, et al implied the syndrome was introduced by Dutch seafarers[14].

Goldblatt et al were able to find the founder or ancestor of these families who introduced the syndrome to a Nanda woman, Alice McMurray. Her first marriage was to Charles Mallard Jnr. She later remarried to John Councillor who lived in the Hutt River area. The family is also related to the Drage family in Carnarvon who are related to the Mallard family. Both the Mallard and Drage families claim to have Dutch ancestry.

---

[11] International Medicine J 2002; pp445–450

[12] Ellis-van Creveld syndrome, also known as 'chondroectodermal dysplasia', is a rare genetic disorder characterised by short-limb dwarfism, polydactyly (additional fingers or toes), malformation of the bones of the wrist, dystrophy of the fingernails, partial hare-lip, cardiac malformation and often prenatal eruption of the teeth [Dr Nonja Peters]

[13] Peters, Dr Nonja, [Research conducted by Goldblatt, JC Minutillo, PJ and J Hurst.1992. Ellis-van Creveld syndrome in a Western Australian Aboriginal community, Postaxial polydactyly as heterogenous manifestation, Medical Journal of Australia, 157: pp271-272.]

[14] Peters, Dr Nonja

I was able to interview John Mallard who was the Coordinator from the Aboriginal Health Unit at Curtin University in Perth. He was also from the Nanda tribe or as he pronounced it, Nunda.

We discussed the boundaries of his tribe where he gave the southern most boundary as the Bowes River and the northern most border as the Wooramel River. The tribe used the Murchison River as well as other rivers to travel inland until they reached the Mt Hope and Twin Peaks area where the two rivers joined.

John spoke of the stories he had heard from both his father and grandfather of contact with marooned Dutch sailors. His grandfather covered a large area as a stockman riding from Northampton to as far as Carnarvon. However, he usually only spoke of it in a general sense.

When asked where he believed the Lost White Tribe might have ended up he replied:

The key to where I would look would be water and there some soaks just in this area here. [Points to areas close to the shoreline near the Murchison River] *It's a bit of a hollow area along the coast. It ranges from cliffs really which ranged in height to this building* [at Curtin University – multi-storey building] *and we could go down and get crayfish and abalone.*

There's another settlement too ... at the mouth of the Bowes River. There were apparently huts built there. Like the Aboriginal people don't build huts. They build smaller shelters but this one was fairly big. It was apparently thatched roof. They don't have that in Australia with Aboriginal people. You know this is where the Dutch influence could have come particularly from South Africa.

William (Bill) Mallard

And there's probably the Zuytdorp. My uncle, Bill Mallard, he's been there and apparently there are artifacts still there.

Mallard was subsequently interviewed by Historian Dr Nonja Peters[15] where he produced a Western Australian newspaper clipping from 1941. There was a photograph of his grandfather with the *Zuytdorp* figurehead, which had become an important part of his family's history – a lieu de mémoire of cohabitation. The existence of many light-skinned, with blue eyes and fair hair, Aborigines in Nanda folklore and the belief that there is some truth to the legends is the basis upon which the National Library conducted interviews with Nanda for their collection[16].

'*I also descend from the European side. Not just the British. I descend before the British are come. I descend from a far greater race of people. who are explorers, who had culture, who had life, and in today's society, they are looked upon as leaders for human rights. And that's what I look to. And that's what I aim to.*'

William Mallard[17]

John also spoke of stories from his mother's side where they travelled up the Greenough and Chapman Rivers.

My mother actually has heard of stories of people walking up this river. I think that it would be the Greenough or the Chapman River ... From her oral history, they have had stories of people

---

[15] Presentation by Dr Nonja Peters at the Maritime Archaeological Association of Western Australia, 18 October, 2011

[16] Ibid. Nanda, Oral Tradition and Archives – *Lieu de Mémoire*

[17] Scott, Anne M, *European Perceptions of Terra Australis,* published by Ashgate Publishing Limited, Farnham, Surrey, England, 2011. Interview with Wiliam Mallard from episode 29 of the television program *Beagle, in het kielzog van Darwin*, entitled 'Hollandse Aboriginals' [Dutch Aboriginals]. First broadcast on 18 April 2010.

following inland as well. Now that could have been from the Dutch shipwreck or it could have been from the Abrolhos Islands ... [Two marooned sailors from the *Batavia*]

Mallard, in the 2011 interview with Peters, added the following in regards to '*white people*':

She tells a story about white fellas, going way back, that was walking up one of the rivers through where Mullewa is now[18].

However, what interested me the most was John's answer to the question of Christianity's influence on the dreamtime and Aboriginal traditions.

Our dreamtime stories are very similar to Christianity. The Ten Commandments for example. The Bible. They are just fundamental values of the Aboriginal Community. Aboriginal values you know relating to each other.

We don't believe we come from monkeys rather that there was some interference from a higher being. We call it various names rainbow serpent. We all had our origins somewhere in the Kimberleys ... the rainbow serpent. It's something that has always been there.

After I pressed Mallard further on the Ten Commandments, I was stunned at the reply:

The Ten Commandments are very close, very close.

I went through the ten commandments with Mallard but they were exactly the same. If there was one thing that a small group of 17th century Dutch castaways would try and pass down from generation to generation, it would be the Ten Commandments. It was their moral compass; a glue to bind their community and a basic set of common sense laws. We get a sense that the descendants of the Lost White Tribe did try and maintain some basic Christian values from the Leeds Mercury article.

They are nominal Christians ... they retain a certain observance of the Sabbath by refraining from their daily labours, and perform a short superstitious ceremony on that day all together.[19]

After the Lost White Tribe was migrated north, they were forced to assimilate into the northern tribes. However, they did try to hold onto some traditional values. Circumcision was perhaps one of these traditions. When asked about the practice of circumcision amongst the Nanda Tribe, Mallard was quite definite in his response emphasising that the area of circumcision was inland from the Irwin to the Murchison Rivers.

Yeah that's certainly from my mother's area. It is definitely from my mother's area. I don't think that circumcision was practised on the coast. It was more inland yeah – the Irwin, the Murchison.

In regards to the differences between the Nanda and other Aboriginal tribes, Mallard replied:

I think one would be the semi-permanent nature of the camp. So there is evidence that the huts over Bowes River were of a permanent type. When I grew up we used to go camping at the river mouth at Galena and Kalbarri, Lynton Station, I think that's where there are salt flats. That salt would have been an important trade for trading inland. As a kid we stayed at those places except for the Bowes River Mouth.

---

[18] Ibid.

[19] Leeds Mercury Newspaper, *Discovery of a White Colony on the Northern Shore of New Holland*, 25 January, 1834

I'm not sure why there are some areas we don't go to because of cultural significance like there might be an area where they practise law and you only go there for certain purposes but certainly that's where there were semi-permanent dwellings.

Mallard had high hopes that proof of their unique Dutch ancestry would provide them assistance in: *getting evidence to support the western law about land ownership over native titles. That type of information would be good for us. I suppose in terms of heritage it's important for us what Dutch influences we've had. It's important to know who we are today.*

We have always said that we have had influence from the Dutch before Cook ever sailed over here you know.

Mallard explained that the Nanda people were hoping to run accommodation and tours out of the areas to Aboriginal sites and where there were Dutch shipwrecks such as Kalbarri.

Yeah the uncle knows all about that area and his father's and brothers pretty well worked on this area. Even their forefathers before them so there is a long history of knowledge of this area where waterholes are. Actually some waterholes are right on the beach.

When asked about other places where there may be evidence of Dutch Aboriginal contact, Mallard immediately replied:

Shark Bay. You need to see the Holts. That's a Dutch name is it? What happened a lot of our people moved up there from this area. [Kalbarri – Murchison River] *These people generally regard themselves as been from this area.* [Murchison River]

What Mallard had confirmed was the northerly migration of an Aboriginal tribe or families from Kalbarri to Shark Bay yet they still identified themselves as being from the Murchison River region.

When questioned further, Mallard stated that it was due to *intermarriage with this mob* [Shark Bay].

I was surprised to learn that his family was related to Tom Pepper, the stockman who located the shipwreck and gold coins.

Actually up here you can talk to another uncle [Shark Bay] *my grandfather's brother's son's called Tom Pepper. The sailors came ashore and took stuff with them. Locating that stuff is still a mystery. One of my uncles actually chiselled a bit off it. He was working as a stockman and he followed some sheep down the cliffs to something and he found these chests ...*

My grandfather Jack Mallard, chiselled something off it and brought it back. He was a bit wary of it because he thought it was a mine – a shipping mine. But when he got back the prevailing winds covered it all up. Every seven or so years there's quite a shift in the sand. So when he went back there it was all covered up. I'm not too sure about the timing of it so it could be still out there somewhere. It could be a chest of silver. It's still there don't worry about that. Black fellas can't keep things like that quiet but apparently you can still find gold coins on the beach. My grandfather has been back there several times to have a look.

When asked if there were any important areas or significant Aboriginal sites nearby the *Zuytdorp* shipwreck, Mallard spoke of a campsite at Galena *as a fairly important area*. However, he signalled out a place called Woola Gully for special mention.

It makes your hair stand up but those areas we avoid. [Woola Gully] Mallard added:

When you see something in the bush that's not a part of the bush I suppose. I remember seeing a pole on a mound sticking out of the ground. We quickly walked away from it.

I showed John a copy of the Leeds Mercury article and asked him for his reaction.

He made comment that his mother's group had fair hair, his father had blue eyes and his grandmother was very fair. But his mother's mob had less exposure to Europeans than the coast yet they were more fairer. They were from around the Mullewa district.

He remarked that north of Geraldton on the Bowes River there appeared to be something like the wall of a dam. At the mouth of the river, huts were built that held 13 adults. Mallard described it as having a pole in the middle and thatched roof. He added that there are also a lot of waterholes in the area.

Mallard noted that the physical features of the people were much more European than other areas and the way of life was also more European. For instance, over 100 years ago, they were more inclined to start a business.

The Aborigines in that area belong to the Yamatji Nation which cover quite a large area from the coast down to Bowes River, the Shark Bay area and as far inland as Meekathara, Wiluna, Mt Magnet and Mt Newman. Within this nation there are three tribal areas. Aborigines could travel through their Nation. Marriages were arranged between the different tribes. On his mother's side, John recalls hearing of some of the tribe walking inland.

Meanwhile other sites, such as the Irwin River Valley and the Champion Bay area may reveal further evidence. However, the length of time and European occupation will mitigate against that. Perhaps new cave drawings such as those on Bigge Island and Wandijana will be discovered.

More likely further written evidence will be revealed as other historians and researchers trawl through the volumes of diaries, newspapers and letters. Stories told from generation to generation may arouse the curiosity of the descendants of the Lost White Tribes such as John Mallard. Stories of light-skinned, blue-eyed Aborigines with fair hair were part of a lifetime of stories handed down from his grandfather, mother and father.

Perhaps the final word should be left to arguably Australia's most respected Historian, Geoffrey Blainey:

The Dutch were great explorers. Cook was a great mapper and a wonderful navigator. A wonderful man. But what the Dutch discovered along the coast of Australia and NZ in terms of first there, was better than anything Cook did in that era.

At least a few hundred Dutch people, having been shipwrecked, spent a long time on the Australian coast. Some of them were abandoned here. They lived with aborigines and gave birth to children of mixed ancestry. I don't think there could be much doubt about that ... **The evidence suggests that the first Europeans who lived on Australian soil were the Dutch. The first who lived in any number were the Dutch**[20]. [Author's emphasis]

---

[20] Blainey, Geoffrey, taken from an interview with Ross Coulthart from Channel 7's Sunday program, 2012

Timeline

1606 – Captain Willem Janszoon
The first authenticated discovery of Australia was made by Captain Willem Janszoon in his ship the *Duyfken* in either late January or early February 1606.

After sighting the west coast of Cape York Peninsula at Pennefather River (north of Weipa), he explored southwards to Cape Keerweer (Cape Turnaround). The *Duyfken* continued sailing the length of the peninsula until it reached Torres Strait. Although, they thought that an opening might exist, it was too risky to attempt further eastward exploration. Janszoon had already lost eight of his crewman, and so decided to sail back to the East Indies. For further detail of the life and career of Willem Janszoon, read *Captain Willem Janszoon and the Discoveries of Australia*, Henry Van Zanden [Part 1 and Part 2] (Publication date, 2013)

1616 – Dirk Hartog
Captain Hartog was the first European to land on the Western Australian coast.

1618 – Willem Janszoon and Captain Jacobszoon
Second discovery by Janszoon on board the ship *Mauritius*

1619 – Frederick de Houtman
Mapped the Western Australian coast south of Perth. Discovered and named the Houtman Abrolhos.

1622 – The ship *Leeuwin*
Mapped the south-west corner of Western Australia. (Captain unknown)

1623 – Voyage of the Pera and Arnhem
Mapped the west coast of Cape York Peninsula to Arnhem's Land (Northern Territory)

1627 – Pieter Nuyts and Francois Thyseen
Discovery of the south-west coast of Australia by the ship *Gulden Zeepaard* (Golden Seahorse) commanded by Pieter Nuyts and by the skipper Francois Thyssen.

1628 – De Witt
Discovery of the North-West coast of Australia by Gerrit Frederikszoon De Witt in his ship the Vianen. Named the land, De Witt's Land.

1629 – Commander Pelsaert, wreck of the *Batavia*, Abrolhos Islands
The book, *Mutiny on the Batavia*, by Henry Van Zanden, will be released 2013/14.

1642 – Abel Tasman
Discovered Tasmania, New Zealand and Fiji.
The book, *Abel Tasman*, by Henry Van Zanden, will be released 2013/14

1644 – Tasman's second voyage
Mapped the north-western part of Western Australia to Cape York Peninsula.

1656 – The wreck of the *Vergulde Draeck*
The beginning of Australia's first white settlement.

1712 – The wreck of the *Zuytdorp*
Survivors assimilate into Aboriginal tribes.

1770 – Captain Cook
Discovery and mapping of the east coast of Australia.

Early 1780's – Dutch galliot wrecked at Port Fairy, Victoria
Survivors assimilate into Aboriginal tribes. Second ship drops a cannon at Apollo Bay after either running aground or threatening to run aground.

Early 1780's – Possible landing of a Dutch ship at Balmoral Beach
A comprehensive account will be released in Part 2 of *The Lost White Tribes of Australia*.

1788 – Britain establishes a Penal Colony at Port Jackson, NSW
Claims the eastern half of Australia as a British possession.

1829 – Swan River Colony founded
New Holland annexed from the Netherlands.

1832 – Lost White Tribe rediscovered by Lieutenant Dale

1839 – Lieutenant George Grey discovers *individuals of an alien white race*
Grey came across a *race, to appearance, totally different, almost white, who seemed to exercise no small influence over the rest ... when we were attacked, the hostile party was led by one of these light-coloured men.* [Part 2 *The Lost White Tribes of Australia*]

1840 – Captain Usberne, of the *Beagle*
Usberne made the following observation: the native, *appeared of an entirely different race: his skin was a copper colour, whilst the others were black; his head was not so large, and more rounded; the overhanging brow was lost; the shoulders more of a European turn.*
[Part 2 *The Lost White Tribes of Australia*]

1848 – AC Gregory
Reported sightings of *light-coloured Aboriginals*.

1840's to the early 20th century
Frequent sightings and stories of *fair-headed, blue-eyed, or European looking* Aboriginals by the first explorers into the region or by the first settlers.

Please note that future publication titles are subject to change. Please check website for further details: www.australiadiscovered.com.au

www.ingramcontent.com/pod-product-compliance
Lightning Source LLC
Chambersburg PA
CBHW040533020526
44117CB00028B/11